DISCARD

BETWEEN TWO WORLDS

BETWEEN TWO WORLDS

ESCAPE FROM TYRANNY: GROWING UP IN THE SHADOW OF SADDAM

ZAINAB SALBI

AND LAURIE BECKLUND

GOTHAM BOOKS

GOTHAM BOOKS
Published by Penguin Group (USA) Inc.
375 Hudson Street, New York, New York 10014, U.S.A.

Penguin Group (Canada), 90 Eglinton Avenue East, Suite 700, Toronto, ON, Canada M4P 2Y3
(a division of Pearson Penguin Canada Inc.); Penguin Books Ltd, 80 Strand, London WC2R 0RL,
England; Penguin Ireland, 25 St Stephen's Green, Dublin 2, Ireland (a division of Penguin Books
Ltd); Penguin Group (Australia), 250 Camberwell Road, Camberwell, Victoria 3124, Australia
(a division of Pearson Australia Group Pty Ltd); Penguin Books India Pvt Ltd, 11 Community
Centre, Panchsheel Park, New Delhi - 110 017, India; Penguin Group (NZ), cnr Airborne and
Rosedale Roads, Albany, Auckland 1310, New Zealand (a division of Pearson New Zealand Ltd);
Penguin Books (South Africa) (Pty) Ltd, 24 Sturdee Avenue, Rosebank, Johannesburg 2196,
South Africa

Penguin Books Ltd, Registered Offices: 80 Strand, London WC2R 0RL, England

Published by Gotham Books, a division of Penguin Group (USA) Inc.

First printing, October 2005
10 9 8 7 6 5 4 3 2 1

Gotham Books and the skyscraper logo are trademarks of Penguin Group (USA) Inc.

LIBRARY OF CONGRESS CATALOGING-IN-PUBLICATION DATA
has been applied for.

ISBN 1-592-40156-2

Printed in the United States of America
Set in Legacy Serif ITC Book
Designed by Lynn Newmark

PUBLISHER'S NOTE
In many cases, names and identifying characteristics have been changed to protect the privacy
of the individuals involved.

To My Mother

Contents

1

⬧

THE ABBASID COIN

MY MOTHER GREW up in a grand house, with a courtyard and sixteen rooms, on the Tigris River. The house belonged to my grandfather, who died before I was born. Mama inherited from him a modest fortune—a share of the house and his factories, a quantity of gold, and a family name that means something still. But the one physical object of his that I ever really cared about was a gold coin forged a thousand years ago by Abbasid caliphs who moved the political and cultural center of the Islamic empire from Damascus eastward to Baghdad. Baghdad yields its secrets reluctantly, to those who dig, and a friend of my grandfather's discovered a bag of the coins in the course of demolishing an old building. He gave three to my grandfather, who gave one to each of his three young daughters. Mama, the youngest, designed a frame for it in the shape of a small chain and wore it around her neck always. It had a dent on one edge I can still visualize because I so often wondered what sort of blow might have caused it.

She was a teacher when I was little and when she came home from school she would take a nap on the sofa. She had the gift of being able to fall asleep almost instantly, and she radiated utter peace as she slept. I would squeeze in next to her, take in the slightly sweaty smell of the classroom she brought home with her, and try to make my breaths match hers exactly. Between her full breasts lay the Abbasid coin. I remember breathing to the rise and fall of that ancient coin against her skin, its worn symbols gleaming softly in the afternoon light. I assumed I would wear it when I grew up and became, hopefully, as smart and beautiful as she was. Of course, I also assumed back then that Iraq would always be my home.

Though it is hard to imagine, given all that has happened since, growing up in Baghdad was for me probably not unlike growing up in an American suburb in the 1970s. I spent many hours driving around with my mother, running errands and shopping, driving to and from school, going to piano lessons, ballet lessons, swimming lessons, and just tagging along. She kept a busy social calendar then, and in the car was the place I got to spend time with her. She loved Baghdad—she was *of* Baghdad—and as we drove back and forth along the boulevards lined with palm trees heavy with dates, she would tell me a little about each neighborhood as we passed through it. I took in my city through the passenger-side window—old Baghdad with its dark arcaded souk where men hammered out copper and politics, and the new Baghdad with its cafes and Al-Mansour boutiques. What I learned of my heritage, as was true for almost everything else in the first nine years of my life, I learned through her.

We happened to be driving down the Fourteenth of Ramadan Street one day with Aunt Layla in July 1979 when an announcement came on the car radio saying that Ahmad Hassan Al-Bakr, the gray-haired man whose portrait had hung in all of my elementary school classrooms, was stepping down from the presidency in favor of his cousin, Vice President Saddam Hussein. Aunt Layla and my mother were in the front seat talking about the news, which seemed to make them ecstatically happy. I think they were giggling.

"That's the last we'll ever see of *him*!" Aunt Layla said.

"No . . . more . . . Aaaahmmo!" Mama whooped.

This puzzled me. Did they know the man who was going to be the new president? Was he an uncle—an *amo*? Was I related to him?

If our uncle was the president, why would they be happy about not seeing him anymore? I didn't understand. I asked about this puzzling new development and got a clear directive from my mother.

"Some things aren't meant for little ears, honey," she said over her shoulder. "Some things that enter one ear need to fly straight out the other. They need to be erased from your memory."

I learned the concept of guided imagery at age nine and a half.

Mama's elliptical answer only made me more curious, of course, but I had a lot of time to myself in the backseat with two women as chatty as my mom and Aunt Layla in the front. So, as we drove, I practiced. I pictured this thought that they had just shot into my right ear as an arrow and tried to make it shoot straight out my left ear without leaving anything behind in my head. But each time I asked myself if the thought was still in my brain, it would pop right up again. I obviously didn't master this skill because I remember the whole scene quite clearly today, down to the route we were taking through the Khadhimiya district past the old shops selling twenty-four-karat gold that led to the mosque with the turquoise and gold dome. But, I wondered even then, if I managed to erase that thought from my brain, how could I tell?

Every instinct in me—survival, loyalty, anger, horror, resentment, guilt, and most of all, fear—conspires to prevent me from speaking Saddam Hussein's name out loud. The fact that I use his name now, acknowledge a personal connection to him at all, is for me a watershed no matter how trivial that might seem. He wasn't related to me or my family by blood, but some of my childhood and virtually all of my teenage weekends were merged with his nonetheless. I was taught to call him *Amo* and he treated me like a niece. Though it disturbs me, I can still reach back and conjure up a few fond memories of him. I would convict him of crimes against humanity without a second thought, but not because he singled me out for unkindness.

Technically, he was just my father's employer. My father was his pilot, a commercial airlines captain Saddam drafted to serve as his personal pilot in the early 1980s. When I was growing up in Iraq, people used to refer to me as the "pilot's daughter." I hated that term. I still do. It stole from me my very identity, everything I wanted to be. It defined me in terms of my father and defined him, in turn, by his most infamous passenger: a despot millions of Iraqis feared. Had I stayed in Iraq, there are people who no doubt would be calling me that still, though my father stopped being his pilot many years ago and no longer flies. Instead, because of a chain of events Saddam Hussein set in motion, though I did not know it then, I found myself stranded in America by the Gulf War. That was the most painful time of my life. For very good reasons, I had come to trust no one, not even my mother. I had just turned twenty-one, and I found myself all alone for the first time as fresh new fears were heaped on all the old ones. I did what I needed to do in order to survive, though it was not nearly as simple as I make it sound: I erased the pilot's daughter and started over. I creased my life down the middle like the spine of a book when you bend the pages back very hard. You could read the first half of the book of my life, then read the second half, and not know they were lived by the same person. I wanted it that way. I needed it that way.

I created a whole new identity for myself as the founder and president of a nonprofit women's organization called Women for Women International, which supports women survivors of war. For over a decade now, I have gone around the world, meeting with victims of war and the awful mass rape the world seems to accept as an inevitable consequence of war. Seeing the criminal patterns behind such violence, I began encouraging women to break their silence and speak out so their oppressors could be punished. Yet, I have been unable to break my own. It's remarkable, really. I appear on television and give speeches around the world, but I still can't say the words Saddam Hussein on my front porch. The many reporters who have interviewed me never asked if I knew Saddam Hussein personally—why would they? So, I was permitted to remain silent, telling other people's stories and never my own, hiding in plain sight, ever fearful someone would recognize me someday and say hey, there she is, the pilot's daughter, the friend of Saddam.

When Saddam Hussein was finally captured in 2003 in that hole he had dug in the dirt, I found myself fighting tears. I didn't want to enjoy another person's humiliation, even if it was my enemy's. I think my tears were more for me than for him, to protect my own humanity against feelings of vengeance and hatred. I happened to be at a conference in Jordan that day, and everyone erupted in cheers. One of my friends cheered in the name of her father, an official who had been publicly executed by Saddam. Another vowed to charge him with genocide to avenge Kurdish relatives who were among thousands he had gassed. I yearned to seek redress on behalf of my mother. But who would charge Saddam with crushing human souls? I thought of all my beloved aunts, the spunky ones, the stylish and determined ones the West still gives him credit for liberating, and I wondered, who would remember, given the countless people he killed, the seemingly trivial wounds of those he allowed to live? Would women once again fall beneath the radar screen of history, which preferred to measure war in terms of incident reports and expenditures and kilotons and battles and casualties? How long would women continue to be complicit in their suffering by remaining silent?

For the first time in years, I could feel the girl that I had been nagging at me, bringing back memories I had struggled, at great personal cost, to suppress. I wanted to make myself whole again. I wanted to come clean. I wanted to do my job without feeling like a hypocrite. But I had been afraid for so long I didn't know how to get rid of the layers of fear inside me. Because I had survived by hiding my past, even from myself, I had never really pieced together the story of my own life. Which of the things that had happened to me were causes and which were effects? Which were common to all Iraqis, and which were unique to my family? Certainly, I had never come to terms with the big questions, like how Saddam Hussein had managed to stay in power for a quarter century when most Iraqis hated him and there were ongoing plots to kill him. Certainly there were guns. Certainly there was funding early on from the U.S., European, and Soviet governments, each pushing its own geopolitical agenda. But not even he had enough bullets to kill twenty-five million people. How did he manage to dictate the way virtually every Iraqi spoke, loved, married, prayed, played, smiled, learned, dressed, ate, deceived, despaired, celebrated, and died? Make decent people like my parents complicit in their own oppression? Turn my mother from a free spirit into a premature matron who managed to fit in at palace parties? Keep me scared to death of him long after he had no power to hurt me?

When did it all start? I suspect the answer to that question is this: the moment a mother is afraid to answer a young child's question honestly. By the time I left for America at age twenty, so many silences and half-answered questions had accumulated between Mama and me that I blamed her for certain ugly turns my life had taken. Only when she was dying, and I had learned how to listen to women who had survived other despots, did she tell me secrets she had kept from me for most of my life. I still cry when I think how young she was, just fifty-two. She was unable to speak, and the only means she had of communicating was by writing. I asked her then about what her life was like during the two decades she and my father lived under his thumb and she wrote her thoughts to me in a drugstore notebook. Writing was very difficult for her, and her observations were often short and dispassionate. I include some entries here to give a sense of how much she spared her children. I keep her notebook in a white carry-on bag I used to sit on in airports. I open it rarely because it is the only thing I have that brings back the smell of her.

Iraqis have a saying about Saddam Hussein. They say he wooed us in the 1970s, we endured the 1980s, and we paid the price in the 1990s and beyond. I have always thought of myself as the lucky one, and one of the many reasons is that I grew up in modern Iraq's most promising decade. While the West struggled with the oil embargo of the early 1970s, petrodollars poured into our nationalized oil monopoly. The Iraqi dinar soared, electricity lit up mud villages, modern schools and hospitals mushroomed, Japanese cars sped across new highways, and whole office buildings rose up while we were away on summer vacation. Iraqi students went abroad then on government scholarships and Saddam's socialist-based Baath Party instigated a massive compulsory campaign to combat illiteracy (and spread his ideology) that taught so many people to read so fast that Iraq became a model for the developing world and won a UNESCO prize. I try not to dwell on how Iraqi faith was squandered or how my parents' generation deluded itself into assuming it came with no price tag.

My parents were married on the cusp of all this progress in 1968, shortly after my mother graduated from college and my father graduated from a pilot's academy after studying in Scotland. My favorite picture of the two together is a black-and-white snapshot taken at their engagement party that shows them standing against a garden trellis with white wrought iron furniture in the foreground, my father trim and debonair in a suit and my mother a dark-haired beauty wearing Piccadilly makeup and a 60s miniskirt. An English term springs to mind for which I can think of no adequate Arabic equivalent, and it almost breaks my heart when I think of it. They were *happy-go-lucky*.

I was born the year after they were married, the same month my father was promoted to captain by Iraqi Airways. New subdivisions were being laid out in Baghdad at the time, with names like the Professors Neighborhood and the Engineers Neighborhood (as well as neighborhoods with smaller lots for blue-collar workers) and government incentives were offered to people in those fields to move there. My parents took advantage of his promotion to build a home in the Airlines Neighborhood and were proud that they were able to do so without help from their families. Because my birth coincided with my father's promotion, my parents referred to me as "the child who brought blessings," *baraka,* to our family, and that small superstition would follow me as I grew. Whenever there was a new moon, Mama would ask me to smile at her, saying my smile would bless the upcoming month as my birth had blessed their first year. Five years later, they would have a son, Haider, and five years after that another, Hassan. With each birth, my father would plant a palm tree in our backyard, and they would name the palm tree after the child. My father was the gardener in our family. Our backyard was filled with his gardenias and narange, limes and sweet lemon—native citruses I often crave and rarely find outside Baghdad.

Mama started a scrapbook for me when I was a baby, a white quilted volume I still have, with a glittery stork and a lavender puppy on the cover. Inside are pictures of our family, my childhood birthday parties, and casual snapshots of friends like the Christian neighbor who used to ask my mother for advice on her daughter's Muslim boyfriends—all defined for whatever reasons by their inclusion in this album as relevant to my birth. I noticed after she died that there is not one picture of Amo in this book, though many were taken, and I wonder if she took them out or never included them in the first place. She was always selective in her choice of memories to preserve for me.

I sometimes forget how close my father and I were then and how easily he made me laugh. In one photo of us together we are modeling twin *dishdashas,* long cotton tunics that are worn by both sexes. How many fathers have matching outfits made for them and their two-year-old daughters? I called him *Baba,* the word for "Daddy" in Arabic, but his name is Basil. Most of his pictures show him on vacation, mugging for the camera with a child's plastic swim tube around his waist at a tropical beach, perched atop a statue in Thailand, chatting like an old friend with the statue of a bearded miner at Knott's Berry Farm. To cool off on scorching late summer afternoons we used to go swimming at the Hunting Club or go with my cousins on my uncle's boat to Pig's Island, a large sandbar in the Tigris that must have been named for wild boar. My father had spent time there as a boy and our outings seemed to bring out the little boy in him. Some of my fondest memories are of calm summer nights in that place filled with the peaceful sound of the Muezzin calling evening prayers, and laughter; my mother's strong and engaging, my father's mischievous as he dropped ice down my mother's bathing suit, and the normal shouts of a gaggle of children. After sunset, the lights from the riverside cafes on the Corniche would come on and reflect in lazy lines of blue, green, white, and red on the river. The colors would sparkle if the breeze picked up and I imagined fairies were dipping their wings into the water.

I was loved, educated, and spoiled. Thanks to airline perquisites and the fact that my parents were descended from the same line of prosperous merchants, we traveled the globe—Brazil, Greece, Japan, and a dozen other countries. Culturally I was probably as much Western as Middle Eastern. Harrod's was purportedly the source of my first solid food when I was a baby. I knew the theme song to *Happy Days* and informed my father that Wonder Woman could beat the Six-Million-Dollar Man because, well, she was a woman. When my father returned to Baghdad from flying passengers to foreign capitals, he brought me back the latest toys, clothes from foreign boutiques, chocolate you could never get in Iraq, and Big Macs he kept fresh in the galley refrigerator. Because he was away from home so much, he came to take on, in my mind, qualities of the mythic Santa Claus, another romantic figure in a uniform who flew through the skies bearing gifts.

But it was Mama and her friends who showed me what life meant and how it should be lived. There was a network of women in Baghdad who, in the Iraqi tradition of respect for all elders, I grew up calling aunts or *khala*. There were many dozens of them over the years, friends and extended relatives, mothers of my friends, artists and teachers, wives of other pilots, women from the Hunting Club and overlapping social circles. While post–World War II socioeconomic forces pressured American women to retreat into their homes, inverse pressures created by Iraq's socialist industrial models gave my mother's generation the opportunity to leave them, breaking molds that were centuries old. Rooted in ritual Islam, my mother and most of her friends were nonetheless culturally secular. Photographs I have of these women, hands encircling each others' waists, remind me how invincible they seemed, allies out to define womanhood, stylish and independent, who spoke two or three languages and saw no reason they couldn't have it all: advanced degrees, fulfilling jobs, children, travel, a good time, and husbands who loved them.

No law spelled it out but Saddam's Baath Party discouraged women from wearing the traditional *abaya,* the long black robe worn by my grandmother and more traditional women in rural areas. Many of my "aunts" pushed the envelope and wore miniskirts. My mother and her friends preferred London to Paris and either to the new Baghdad boutiques that were stocked with the identical red-haired, industrial-strength Russian mannequins that seemed designed to inspire the "glory of Iraqi womanhood." Amo loved that phrase. Iraqi women were all the more glorious, of course, because they continued to run their households while they manned his factories and ministries, and organized political meetings.

Our home was the site of frequent potluck dinners, where fifteen or twenty women would gather at any given time, filling the air with laughter and chatter, steaming casseroles, and foreign perfume. Ripping tiny cellophane strips off their packs of Kents or Virginia Slims, they would light up and a blue-gray haze, which seemed romantic to me then, would hover just below the ceiling. I wandered among them, listening to their laughter and stories, knowing I was welcome unless they adjourned to our aromatic garden, where they gathered in a tight circle and passed on in whispers whatever new gossip or secrets seemed to bind them. Irreverent, spontaneous, sometimes a little profane, Mama was inevitably the one to break things up so the dancing could begin if the talking went on too long. "Life is like a cucumber," she might say. "One day it's in your hand, the next day it's in your ass." Everyone would laugh and the tension would ease. Mama always laughed louder than what was considered polite for women in Iraqi society. Her laughter was like a geyser that started deep down and fairly erupted.

In Iraq, as in much of the Arab world, men and women socialize separately. Women dance together throughout their lives, a joy most Western women miss out on. One of the most enchanting images in all my memory, the one that symbolizes for me carefree moments now lost, is of my mother handing out dozens of exuberantly colored scarves to her friends. Then, with Arab music turned all the way up on the stereo, these professional women would belly dance in their ridiculously heavy platform shoes and *Vogue* outfits, pull bright strips of chiffon against their hips and shoulders, and ululate at the top of their lungs. Aunt Samer, my mother's tall and graceful older sister, moved her hips in slow classic patterns of seduction. Mama was the most raucous and fun to watch. Her body shimmied faster than a tambourine in tight little waves no one else could match, her long dark hair shining as it whipped around her head like a halo playing catch-up.

My father was a fabulous dancer as well, and particularly adept at bop and rock. Popular and outgoing, he and Mama were famous for hosting "couple parties" that were considered Bohemian in conservative social circles. Observant Muslims refuse alcohol, as it is forbidden by the Quran. At our house, drinks were passed to men and women who mingled easily over the sounds of Western and Arabic music and plates of fresh pistachios, almonds, and pomegranate seeds. Baghdad's famous masgoof fish from the Tigris would cook slowly on tall sticks over open fires and the carved rosewood table we brought back from Thailand would fill up with great quantities of rice, lima beans and dill, lamb stuffed with almonds, and fruits and chestnuts. Watching these parties from our roof in the arms of my grandmother, my only fear was that I would never live up to the standards my mother had set, never emerge from my shyness to learn to dance like her or laugh with such unadulterated joy.

Iraqi heat is so intense that much of Baghdad slept on the roof during the summer. The sound of heavy mattresses being brought upstairs and thumped out onto specially made metal bed frames each night is one of my clearest memories of childhood. Because the main meal of the day is served midday in Iraq, we always ate lightly at night. On summer nights, you could look across the Airlines Neighborhood and see families with children eating watermelon or cheese and bread before bedtime on their rooftops.

We stopped sleeping outside when Abu Traib, the "Machete Murderer," began terrorizing Baghdad for a time in the 1970s in a crime wave that seemed to foreshadow some of the violence that was to come. A serial killer, he invaded wealthy Baghdad homes, reportedly along with his own wife and children, hacking families to death and stealing their belongings before disappearing into the night. Many of these homes had walls and guards, yet Abu Traib somehow outsmarted security measures. Rumor spread that he must have entered through the rooftops so we sealed the doors to our roofs and let fear drive us into our sweltering homes. Because I couldn't imagine anyone in our social network doing such horrible things, I imagined Abu Traib as a peasant with scary, focused black eyes and a white head piece held in place by a black rope. In my mind's eye, his wife wore a black headscarf and a peasant dress. Their sons dressed like him and their daughters dressed like their mother. While he and his wife murdered the adults, I imagined their children murdering other children—all as their victims slept peacefully in their beds.

When Abu Traib was finally caught, he turned out to be a high-ranking member of the security forces, giving rise to plausible speculation later that the whole bloody rampage was a government experiment to instill fear and gauge its travel through the city. Except for his thick black hair and scary eyes, he looked little like what I had imagined. He was clean shaven with a huge black mustache, and appeared on television in a white shirt and sports jacket. He was later executed, yet he lived on in urban legend. It was Abu Traib who taught me that fear outlives its origins.

"Abu Traib has chocolate-colored skin and coarse black hair," our servant Radya told me authoritatively at least three or four years after he was dead. "He has very deep-set eyes—cat's eyes—so he can see at night. And all his family has coarse black hair and deep-set eyes too. Even his children can see at night like little cats."

Radya was the daughter of a security guard who watched our house sometimes when we were away. She came to live with us when she was just fourteen, a common way of providing income and improving living conditions for poor girls. I wasn't used to having a servant so near my age and one afternoon shortly after she arrived, I ordered her to bring me lunch. She snapped at me and we started arguing. "You're the servant," I told her. "That means you have to do what I tell you." "No I don't!" she screamed and ran out of the house crying. When my mother came home, she scolded me in front of Radya, made me apologize, and gave me my own household duties.

Radya always wore long clothing that covered her arms, even in summer when I wore sleeveless blouses and shorts. One day I finally asked her why and she shyly showed me her arm. "I help my mother bake bread," she explained, revealing a scar from wrist to shoulder. I felt bad for her that she felt so ugly she had to hide her body. She had very dark skin and I later told her that women in America who looked like her were beauty queens. Mama told me I was to treat Radya as a sister and we eventually became good friends, but I knew we would never be sisters. We went everywhere; she went nowhere. I played basketball in our cul-de-sac with my cousins; she worked in the kitchen. I went to school during the day; she went to school at night.

Our family helped enable Radya to graduate from high school, but it wasn't until I went with my mother to drop her off for a weekend that I saw how her family lived: eight people in a two-room house of yellow sun-baked mud on government land near the airport. There was no privacy. I wondered where she did her homework and where her parents had sex, which I had some knowledge of because I had peeked through my parents' bedroom keyhole. Radya's mother wore a black *abaya* and a small tattoo on her chin and spent her days baking bread in a mud oven to bring in a few extra coins. Radya's salary was their family's only steady income. It would take years of working with women in other countries for me to question what I had accepted as a given in my own home: that girls like Radya could be sent away to help pay for the education of a brother selected for his potential to help raise the family out of poverty. There were thousands of poor families like Radya's living on government tracts. Abu Traib was famous for targeting wealthy areas of Baghdad, yet fear of him seemed to persist in her neighborhood. When she returned from her weekends at home, she often brought back ghoulish new stories about his exploits.

"Do you know how smart Abu Traib is?" she whispered to me one afternoon when we were sitting together on the blue sofa in our living room. "He is so smart he can hear through walls. He can probably hear what we're saying at this very moment."

My parents gave their largest party of the year on my birthday when the worst heat of summer was past. Before the adults took over with their live bands, they would bring in a puppeteer with stringed marionettes for all my cousins and friends. One of the photos in my scrapbook is of my sixth birthday party. It shows the backs of little girls sitting on the grass with their heads tilted up toward a puppet stage: me in short, curly dark pigtails on the left, and a taller girl with a long, chestnut-colored braid reaching to her waist on my right. Basma, my best friend. I had dark skin and hair like my mother. Basma had the hazel eyes and fair complexion so prized by Iraqi society. She was shy like me, and when we found each other we became inseparable, often playing without even the need to talk. She lived in the prestigious Al-Mansour neighborhood, and her house was enormous, far more extravagant than our three-bedroom home with ranch-style kitchen and family room. Her father was a government minister, and armed guards had to open the gates for me before I could run up the stairs to her pink bedroom, which was filled with even more toys than my own. That year Basma gave me my favorite birthday present, a large doll I named after her that had the perfect combination of beauty: dark skin like my mother's and hazel eyes like hers.

We attended Al-Ta'aseeseya School, a modern school run by the

British when they ruled—or tried to rule—Iraq in the early 1900s. The school, with its vast grounds and elite student body, was considered the best grade school in Baghdad. Basma sat in the front row where teachers tended to seat kids with prominent parents. I used to tease her about the way teachers sweetened their voices with honey when they spoke to her, "Oh Basma, dear, just bring your homework in tomorrow." I never got such treatment. My family was well-to-do, but we weren't famous or important; I would get yelled at if I forgot my homework.

There was a great religious diversity among Iraqis then, and our schools, which had been nationalized in the mid-seventies to ensure we all followed the same government curriculum, were secular. Islam was one of the subjects we studied, but students who weren't Muslim could leave class during those periods if they chose. One day when I was in fourth grade, shortly before Saddam Hussein became president, our religion teacher told us we were going to learn Islamic prayers. She told us to bring a white dishdasha to school and to ask each of our parents how they preferred to pray because different families prayed in different ways. On the day we were to learn our prayers, I happened to arrive early—the lights weren't even on yet in the classroom. There was only one other person in the room, and my heart sped up when I saw him. Mohammed, the smartest boy in class, was standing on the other side of the room by the windows. I can still see him, bathed in sunlight in his white dishdasha with very black hair that contrasted with his snow white skin and hazel eyes. I had a crush on Mohammed, but had never been bold enough to talk to him. As I nervously put my books on my desk, we talked about our homework and I showed him how we prayed, holding my hands to my side as my mother had taught me the night before. He screwed up his face and stared at me as if he had just seen something repulsive. "Oooh," he said. "You're *Shia*."

I wanted the ground to swallow me up. I felt humiliated and I didn't even know why.

When the other students arrived, the girls with white head

cloths and the boys with white *alakcheen,* or woven hats, the teacher took us outside and we lined up on the grass in front of the garden faucet to learn the ablution, the ritual cleansing required before prayer in Islam. We lined up before the faucet as each one of us practiced. It was a beautiful day. The school yard was full of flowers, and I loved watching the water from the faucet as it reflected the sunlight. When it was my turn to practice ablution, I took my time as I rinsed each hand, my face, the top of my hair, each ear, and each foot as the teacher taught us. It was a hot day, and the water felt not only cooling, but spiritual. I was enjoying that moment until Mohammed belittled me again, this time in front of everyone.

"This isn't bathing, Zainab," he said. "This is ablution! Don't you know the difference?"

Afterward, when we went into the gymnasium where we were going to practice praying, I looked around and saw that some kids were holding their hands at their sides like me and others were holding their hands over their stomachs like Mohammed, and I remember feeling newly drawn to those who prayed like me, if only because I had been judged inferior by someone who prayed like Mohammed.

I asked my mother about this when I got home, and she gave me the standard schoolteacher answer: "In Iraq, we have people who are Shia and people who are Sunni, but we're all the same, we're all Muslims." That was the first time I can remember thinking my mother wasn't exactly telling me the truth. I knew there was a difference. I had seen it in the sneer on Mohammed's face. I thought about Mohammed's behavior before I went to sleep that night and came to the conclusion he had been rude to me, a major transgression in Arab culture, and I privately decided to penalize him by not liking him anymore. It would be years before I dared to let myself have a crush on another boy. Only later when I was living in America did I come across an expression that described exactly how he made me feel. He made me feel like I had *cooties*. If I had to come up with a way to describe a child's first premonition of danger, that would be it: she would feel as if she had cooties, and she would fight the instinct to hide.

On July 22, 1979—Saddam Hussein made sure his cameramen were there to record the date—my mother was sitting at the kitchen table staring at the screen of our little black-and-white TV. I stood at her side and watched over her shoulder. A tall man in a suit with a large black mustache, our new President Saddam Hussein was standing on the stage of a large auditorium filled with men I would later understand were ruling Baath Party members and government officials. Looking very stern and sad, as if one of his children had disappointed him by doing something very bad, he announced that he had come upon "disloyal" people in the government. He brought out onstage a stiff-looking official who confessed to taking part in a plot to overthrow him. He began announcing his "co-conspirators," and as he called out their names, armed guards went into the audience, found them, grabbed them by the elbows, and walked them out the door. I remember the faces of only two men of the hundreds who were present in that hall. Once was a man who was screaming his innocence as he struggled with guards as they took him away. The other was the man I later came to know as Amo, who watched it all onstage with a paternal expression on his face. He was smoking a cigar.

After the president had the last of these "traitors" taken into custody (effectively eliminating his principal political opponents) he praised everyone left in the hall for their loyalty. The men shifted uncomfortably in their seats. I could see how scared many of them looked. Then, group by small group, they stood to applaud him. Whether they approved of his actions or were just terrified of being next, they gave a standing ovation to the man who was about to execute friends and colleagues who had been sitting next to them just minutes before.

The event was broadcast and rebroadcast around the world. Saddam Hussein never tried to hide what he did that day. He wanted those men and others like them to be afraid. I have seen the tape since then, so it is hard for me to distinguish what I saw then from what I have factored in as an adult. I know I didn't fully grasp as a nine-year-old that those men were about to face a firing squad—or understand that the man who was ordering their execution was the "Amo" my mother and Aunt Layla had been talking about a week before. But I felt fear stream out of that small television screen and chill our kitchen, where until that moment I had always felt safe. I remember exactly the look on my mother's face. I remember her eyes growing very round and fixing hard on the screen. I had never seen that look on her face ever before, but I recognized it anyway: it was horror.

When the session ended, Mama sat there, still, before turning off the television. I could see her trying to gather her thoughts before she looked across into my eyes and spoke to me. I was small enough then that when she was seated and I was standing, our eyes were at the same level.

"Honey, things are going to be different with Basma's family from now on," she said. "You can still be friends. You can see her at school, but I'm afraid you can't go to her house to play anymore and she probably won't be able to come here."

"Why not, Mama?"

She took both my hands in hers and leaned close.

"Zainab, her father was one of those men who was grabbed and taken away," she said.

I wonder if I cried for Basma—or for myself at the restriction on our friendship. I don't remember. We flew to Seattle, as we often did in the summer, for my father's two-month pilot's training at Boeing. The next time I remember seeing Basma was when school started in September. She was sitting at the back of the classroom. Teachers avoided calling on her. Other kids avoided her altogether. We spent recess walking around the playground holding hands and looking down at the ground. A terrible thing had happened, but I don't think either of us named it. One day Basma didn't come to school, and I never saw her again. By the time I met the man who had ordered her father's execution three years later, I had taught myself to forget her last name.

From Alia's Notebook

We weren't excited about this friendship. We did not accept his invitations many times and managed to be away from him for two years while he befriended other families we knew, but we couldn't avoid him forever.

We stopped by a friend's house after leaving a party around 11 P.M. and Saddam was in his living room. We spent three hours that evening listening to what he was saying. I will always remember his eyes. They focused on each one of us, examining each person very closely. We talked about many things, including different hobbies and particularly hunting, as it was one of his favorite. When we arrived home that night, we were surprised to find a hunting rifle that was sent by him as a gift. This was his invitation to friendship.

In the days before he was president, he would visit us alone or with the company of only one guard. He often spent the nights roaming in the streets of Baghdad visiting one family after the other. It wasn't unusual to get a call from him in the middle of the night to say that he is coming in a few moments and to ask us to invite so many friends to join us. One had no choice but to invite him and manage to entertain him even if one was in the middle of sleep.

He was a heavy drinker. Chivas Regal Scotch Whiskey was his favorite. He always made sure to bring boxes of it to all the parties he attended. He loved dancing, particularly to Western music. He never got tired of dancing despite the fact that he was not a particularly good dancer nor drinker. He was a strong man with energy equal to ten men. I don't deny his strong personality. While we liked him for his charming personality, we were also afraid of him for we couldn't say no to any of his requests.

He often told us his youth stories during these nights. He talked about his childhood and how he escaped his stepfather's torture one night in his uncle's house: how the dogs followed him, how the darkness of night did not manage to scare him as a ten-year-old child. He was determined to go to school and he knew only his uncle could help him accomplish that. He started first grade when he was ten years old. He often talked about how excited he was wearing underwear for the first time in his life. That day in school, he kept on lifting his dishdasha to show his schoolmates his underwear. He thought that it was the best thing anybody had and he wanted to brag about it. He also talked about his days of political activism and these stories took hours of narration as we sat around and listened to him carefully.

We were not sure how things would change when he became president. He surprised us with a visit to our home at 8 P.M. one night in July 1979. I remember he told us, "I got rid of the old man" (referring to the president at the time, Ahmed Hassan Al-Bakr). He was very happy and merry that night. Saddam despised the fact that Al-Bakr used to consult with his fortune-teller before he held his meetings. He hated the fact that this blind fortune-teller, who lived in an area known as Al-Doubjee, had so much influence on political decisions. He told us that he had sent for her at the palace and killed her himself. "She knew too many secrets and I had to get rid of her," he told us.

He talked about friendship that night and how death would be the punishment for any friend who betrays a friend. We were silent and focused on what he was telling us. It was both a threat to us as well as a reference to his killing of one of his best friends, Mahmoud Al-Hamdanee, who was the Minister of Education at the time. Saddam had had dinner with Mahmoud the night before he killed him.

2

❖

STRINGS

WHEN MAMA BEGAN WRITING to me in her notebook in 1999, there was so little affect in her entries that they felt more like footnotes in a history book than the story behind my parents' relationship. However, I understood the missing emotional context because for years that was all I had; it was facts I was missing. I was twenty-nine years old then, and that was the first time we were able to discuss Amo more or less openly. Iraqi parents never had the luxury many parents do of telling their children, don't worry, honey, there's nothing to be afraid of. My mother was perpetually caught between telling me the truth, which was her natural inclination, and holding back because simply knowing the truth was dangerous.

There are probably four recurring themes in my life—women, war, family, and religion. I learned about them first through stories and overheard conversations, then wove in my own observations. I grew up with two great storytellers, my grandmother, Bibi, and her youngest daughter, my mother. Mama, a Pisces, spun utopian fantasies that wandered off into green fields and rainbows. Bibi, a traditional Muslim mother, favored fables from *1001 Arabian Nights* that were studded with princesses and swashbucklers who galloped in on white horses to save them. It was from these stories that I drew my earliest lessons about women and men, about being Muslim and being secular, and about war and whatever you call life between wars, which I never knew to be peace.

Mama's utopia was the Women's Village, a place she and my aunts—particularly Aunt Samer when she was arguing with her husband—would slip into conversations over the years. I heard about the Women's Village for the first time when I was still little enough to sit on Mama's lap on field trips with her students to the Hanging Gardens of Babylon and ancient Hatra. She and her fellow teachers would find a shady spot for a picnic, open Tupperware full of grape leaves, burak, and tabouleh, and wind up sharing complaints about their husbands the way wives often do. How moody men could be, how demanding! How carefree life would be without them! How much better the world would be if women ran it! And so they conjured up an idyllic village filled with cottages and farmhouses that were close together so their children could grow up like cousins. The skies were always bright over the Women's Village and the river that ran through it glinted with sunbeams. There were birds and flowers everywhere, and women spent their time singing and dancing with lovely children. There was no poverty and no war, for in this lovely meeting place between real life and fantasy, women were smart enough to talk with each other and find answers to those problems. Men were admitted to this paradise only for weekly visiting hours which, I innocently assumed at the time, were for fathers to visit their children the way Baba visited us when he was home. Like all utopias, the Women's Village probably revealed as much about the teller's reasons for escaping the present as of any idyllic view of future, but I didn't grasp that then.

Bibi had hazel eyes and long, ever-so-thin wispy white braids that she wore under an *abaya* when she went out and under a loose white kerchief when she was indoors. She had pale, moist skin that always felt cool to me, even in summer. She would gather her grandchildren around her in her parlor with rich rugs of burgundy and gold and red—wool on the floor, silk on the walls—and we would recline on cushions embroidered with poetry and scenes from the same age-old fables she recounted. Toothless in her old age, she would transport us into ancient worlds of shipwrecks and battles and magical happenings. When I was older and decided to read the stories myself, I was appalled by the violence and misogyny I found there. But Bibi's sibilant tellings were always captivating and romantic. My favorite was the tale of the king with three daughters who asked each daughter whether his wealth belonged to him or to God. "Your wealth belongs to you, of course," the two eldest daughters told him, and he rewarded each with a bag of jewels. But the youngest daughter told him that his wealth belonged to God, and her father expelled her from his palace. She was taken in by a poor servant whose son was so crippled and dependent he needed someone to help him to the toilet. The princess nursed him and taught him to be independent. They fell in love and married, and together they forged a new kingdom based on faith and true love and business acumen that prospered as her father's old, corrupt one crumbled. Bibi always ended her stories with simple teachings. Everything we have belongs to God; be grateful. Take care of the weak; we are all the same under heaven. Believe in true love; you will be rewarded.

From these two very different storytellers, my liberated mother and her traditional mother, I learned that men were born with power and women obtained it through sharpness of intellect and good hearts. If you were kind, wise, and did good works, you could wind up being the princess who had it all.

Karbala' is one of two holy cities in the south of Iraq. About fifty miles south of Baghdad, Karbala' was the site of the watershed battle in which both of the prophet Mohammed's grandsons were massacred in 680. That battle caused the great schism in Islam. Those who believed that Mohammed's legitimate heir and caliph was the slain father of the massacred brothers, Mohammed's favored son-in-law, Ali, became known as Shia. Those who favored a caliphate established by the opposing Umayyad family after Ali's murder became known as Sunnis. Over many generations, those political positions evolved into doctrines, as well as sectarian differences that are often stereotyped. Shia came to harbor suspicion of authority, believing that true justice on earth would be established only by the return of the Mahdi, a figure like the Messiah. Sunnis, in turn, developed a more accommodating attitude toward the ruling elite. In Iraq, Shia came to outnumber the Sunnis, yet the government was run predominantly by Sunnis. Today, the principal theological difference between the two sects is that Shia theologians tend to accept the necessity of continuously applying independent reasoning to contemporary life while Sunni theologians are more comfortable relying on doctrines established centuries ago by religious scholars who established four different schools of Sunni thought.

For me, going to Bibi's house in Karbalā' was an adventure into an exotic past, a premedieval city that was also a commercial center. The streets were narrow, some disappearing into walkways lined with small shops selling prayer beads and sizzling kababs and pickles and window after window of gleaming gold jewelry. Outside our car window, vying for space with cars in the congested streets, were bicyclists and donkeys carrying people and supplies. Women bustled purposefully through the streets in black *abayas,* and many men wore traditional long dishdashas. The whole city seemed to glow golden from the surrounding sand, the gold jewelry in the shop windows, and the sun glinting off the gold-leafed domes of the two mosques that dominated the city. When we stepped inside Bibi's house, we were met with the rich, steamy air of roses distilling and stove pots bubbling with the tang of soursweet Iraqi stews. Bibi had set up her own rosewater still in her kitchen, and I remember armloads of roses lying out on the counter, waiting to be fed into this laboratory of plastic tubes and glass flasks that would magically turn them into rosewater for cooking and religious devotions.

In Baghdad, my mother was a whirlwind of appointments and social obligations; we were always hurrying somewhere. But in Karbalā' with Bibi, Mama calmed from the moment we walked in the door and Bibi greeted her a full embrace. The love between them was obvious, the differences in lifestyles and dress irrelevant. I couldn't imagine living like Bibi any more than a city child could imagine making a living behind an ox and a plow, yet when she hugged me, I felt myself collapse into a rustle of unquestioning love. She was the symbol of premodern women my generation revered even if we didn't choose to follow in their footsteps, the only human being in my life who never changed. Gentle, soft, and strong in the way people of unveering faith are strong, she seemed the same from the time I was born until she died.

Oddly, the first time I heard about her childhood, I thought of Cinderella. Her parents and siblings had died, one at a time, when she was very little, until finally she was an orphan. An uncle was assigned to be her guardian and manage her inheritance for her until she grew up, but the guardian handled that responsibility badly and lost most of her fortune—a grave misdeed under Islamic law. So, when she was just thirteen, he arranged for her to be married to a wealthy businessman in Baghdad and reportedly emigrated to Iran. Bibi was not old enough for the marriage to be consummated, so she was commended into the care of her future mother-in-law, my mother's paternal grandmother. That grandmother was a storied matriarch in our family, a woman who established her own sewing factory at the dawn of the twentieth century and died decades before I was born. For some reason, the one detail I remember hearing about her was that she ordered her own factory supplies from London, which was apparently remarkable at the time. This matriarch was determined never to lose control of her household, so she raised her young daughter-in-law to be subservient to her and her daughters, who in my mind played the role of Cinderella's evil stepsisters. Bibi thus grew up passive and sub-servient, remaining at the beck and call of her mother-in-law, sisters-in-law, and husband, until she outlived them all. She sought her solace in religion and later her children. When her husband died a few years before I was born, she moved out of their sixteen-room mansion on the Tigris in Baghdad, where they had lived with a staff of Farsi-speaking servants, and into a small house in Karbalā', where she found a spiritual adviser named Ruholla Khomeini, a new circle of friends, and a courtyard she planted with rosebushes.

Bibi lived within walking distance of the two mosques that were built on the site where the prophet's two grandsons had been massacred in the seventh century. The mosques, with towering golden domes and minarets, were always full of people, including pilgrims from all over the Muslim world. Because women and girls wore *abayas* at the mosque, Bibi would lend me one of hers, and as a child, I remember hiking up the long folds of black cloth around me so they wouldn't drag on the ground. Then one day she made me my own little *abaya*. We were invited to a picnic with Bibi's friends at the Al-Hussein mosque that day, and when I walked into the enormous courtyard surrounding the turquoise-and-blue tiled mosque, I felt I was being ushered into a world of women who knew the secrets of spirituality and dolma—grape leaves stuffed the Iraqi way, with onion peels and minced meat and rice and lots of sour lemon. Around us, flocks of pigeons cooed and poor pilgrims who could not afford hotels rested in the shade.

When we went inside, I held my new little *abaya* under my chin so my hair wouldn't show as I took in the huge crystal chandeliers hanging from the towering ceilings and the prone bodies of men and women scattered praying on an expanse of enormous red and burgundy Persian rugs. At one end of the mosque, surrounded by enormous silver bars, was the place where Ali's martyred son was buried, and everyone gathered around it, tying green threads or pieces of fabric in the grillwork, each representing a wish they asked to be granted. I remembered the basic line I was taught to say when called to prayer, "I believe that there is no God but one God, and Mohammed is his Messenger, and Ali is his Friend." But that was about all. I watched Bibi and my mother and emulated them as best I could. When Bibi bowed, I bowed. When she prayed, I prayed. *Bsm Allah Al Rahman Al Raheem*. By the name of God, the most merciful, the most gracious.

After we came out of the mosque that day, we went into a candy shop that sold imported Soviet chocolates.

"What a pretty little girl you are!" the shopkeeper told me. "You have an Iranian beauty."

"I'm not Iranian," I said. "I'm Iraqi."

"You're from Baghdad, aren't you?" he said.

"How did you know that?" I asked.

"Because you're holding your *abaya* so tight, you look like you're afraid it's going to fall off."

I didn't think it was funny, but Bibi laughed, a warm laugh that was somehow devoid of all pretense and judgment.

I remember her laughing like that when Mama and Aunt Samer teased her about the cleric she sometimes consulted named Khomeini, a fiery, Iranian-born religious scholar they thought was just plain weird because he seemed on a mission to send women back centuries. Khomeini had settled in Karbalā' after being deported by the Shah of Iran for fomenting revolution in the 1960s. In 1978, at the request of the Shah Reza Pahlavi of Iran, Iraq deported him too because he was deemed a destabilizing influence in the region. My father happened to be the pilot who flew him westward that day, toward Paris, but Khomeini didn't stay put. A year later, in early 1979, he was swept into power in a popular uprising in Iran that shook the Muslim and Western worlds. Shah Reza Pahlavi had ruled Iran for nearly four decades. His openness to Western business, culture, and military interests had netted him the support of the West. But, in a classic and profound backlash, millions of Iranians who had been marginalized by the corrupt and brutal dictatorship behind the Western façade rose up and demanded change. The revolution was the work of nationalists, communists, student unions, women's groups, and others, but it was hijacked by religious extremists who put Khomeini in power and named him the Grand Ayatollah. Arab leaders, especially Saddam Hussein right next door, began to fear this revolution would spread.

I was at an amusement park for an end-of-summer outing with my cousins the day we went to war with Iran. I always counted myself fortunate to have lots of cousins my age, and there were seven of us that day between the ages of ten and thirteen, most of them boys. Several of my parents' siblings had children about the same time as my parents, and because my own brothers were five and ten years younger than I was, these cousins were like siblings and friends combined.

Naim was the son of my father's brother, and he lived in our neighborhood. A straight-A student a year older than I, he was thin and interesting, the sort of friend you could talk to and play with at the same time. I remember filling a plastic bag with race cars my father had brought back for me, picking dozens of limes from our garden, and heading over to his house, where we would stick holes in the fruits, fill them with salt, and suck on them all day as we raced toy cars and argued and shared confidences.

"Can I tell you a big secret?" I asked him when he was over at our house for a barbecue. It was Friday, the Islamic weekly holiday.

"Sure," he said.

"I think about God in the bathroom," I said.

"Me too!" he whispered. "I can't help it. Every time I go to the bathroom, I think about the fact that I'm not supposed to think about God in the toilet, so I think about God."

"But, it is *haram*!"

Haram was an all-purpose word that applied to anything that was forbidden by religion. It was *haram* to think of God in the toilet because cleanliness is so much a part of Islam. It was also *haram* to think of God as an image. God was everywhere. He was on earth, on the sky, behind us, everywhere. Yet I sometimes committed the sin of trying to imagine God too.

"Is there such a thing as double-*haram*?" I asked.

"I don't know," he said.

Dawood, the oldest son of Uncle Adel, my mother's brother, was the eldest of the cousins, the one the adults always put in charge of minding the rest of us. I spent so many hours hanging out at his house on the Tigris that he and his brother treated me like a little sister. He had the large round eyes like my mother's side of the family, and slightly pudgy cheeks that gave him a friendly look. He was always cool and fashionable—for some reason I remember him in a sweater with stripes of gray, green, and burgundy. He was studying the oud, a ten-stringed Arab instrument, and I was taking piano lessons, so we occasionally played together. He was always kind and gentle toward me, even when we were in elementary school and I would run over to him on the playground and ask him to tie my shoelace when it came loose. Then one day he taught me to do it for myself.

Dawood was the leader of our pack the day war broke out with Iran. That day was special because it marked the first time we cousins were deemed old enough to roam the park more or less on our own, with just one adult chaperone in tow. I remember bright lights and laughter, cotton candy and ride after ride on the Tilt-O-Whirl before we left the park to cap the day off with a stop at a famous ice cream shop in Al-Mansour, the Beverly Hills of Baghdad. When we headed home, it was almost dark, and there seemed to be a power outage. I was the first to be dropped off, and all the lights were out when our noisy carload drove into the Airlines Neighborhood and pulled up in front of my house. My mother was waiting at the front door.

"Where have you been?" she asked. "Haven't you heard there's a war going on?"

War? What war?

She hurried me inside and ran to call the other parents to tell them their children were safe. No one, possibly least of all Saddam Hussein, imagined then that the war would last so long that all my cousins in the car that day would find themselves of draft age before it ended, at risk of being sent to the front, where hundreds of thousands of young men would lose their lives for nothing.

I turned eleven a few days after the war started, too young to understand what lay in store for our family, let alone to comprehend what impact that war would have on the Middle East and global politics. When the opening of school was delayed, my first thought was more cartoons, more summer. The first time I saw antiaircraft fire in the night sky, I ran out into our garden, jumping up and down, thinking it was like the Fourth of July in Seattle. My father was stuck outside the country when the fighting started and wasn't able to get back until a few weeks later, so it fell to Mama— as so many things would—to help her three children cope with war. There were frequent air raids at the outset, and many of my friends spent nights huddled together with their parents under stairwells when the sirens went off. My mother didn't want us to live that way, so if the electricity went out for a blackout, she closed the curtains, lit candles, and made puppet shows with her hands for us on the walls. Then she would kiss us good night and put us to sleep in our own beds.

"Life moves on," she declared. "You can't just freeze it—not even for war."

My brothers were so little, I knew she was talking to me.

After school started, an Iranian missile landed on the house where a friend of my brother's lived. Half the family died that night and the other half lived. I remember watching my seven-year-old brother sitting on his bed, looking through his stuff for pictures of his friend because his mother had come to school to say she had lost not only her son, but every single likeness of him. Later I heard about another house being hit by an Iranian bomber, and the entire family died. I had never seen their house, but I imagined it was on a corner, like ours. And I imagined the children's bedrooms were upstairs, like ours.

Life got scarier after that. When Baba left on his trips, I remember him kissing and hugging Mama as if he were afraid he would never see her again. Bibi would come stay with us, and so would Radya's whole family, though I never understood how Radya's father's rifle could protect us from Iranian bombers. I would lie in bed at night and wonder if the Iranian pilots who were bombing us knew they were killing children they couldn't see. Sometimes a missile would cross the night sky outside my bedroom window. I would pray it wouldn't land on our house, and feel guilty when it landed, in a half circle of intense light, on someone else's house. I could feel the ground shake if the missile landed close, and there would be a sliver of perfect stillness before the shattering of glass reached my ears and the haunting wail of ambulances began. It never occurred to me to wonder whether children in Iran were wondering the same thing about Iraqi bombers. Iran was our enemy.

One day early in the war something happened that was in equal parts terrifying and amazing. Mama and I were driving home from the grocery store one day when an Iranian jet suddenly zoomed down so low over the street we were on that we could see the pilot. Iraqi television had broadcast footage of some captured Iranian soldiers a few days earlier, and my mother and a friend of hers had whispered about how beautiful their Iranian faces were. Time froze. I remember looking through the windshield at the pilot to see if they were right. As he zoomed over us, I saw his face, and I know he saw ours. He had a mustache. He was just an ordinary man. What was he thinking as he looked at Mama and me? Was he going to kill us? Did he hate us? Had he meant to come to this part of Baghdad, or was he lost? They said on television that the Iranian mullahs were so ignorant that they sent their pilots to Iraq without any maps. Was he going to bomb a house like ours? Was I going to lose friends because of his bomb?

Logic tells me there was no time for all those thoughts to pass through my brain in that second or two, and yet I remember those and more.

Mama did an extraordinary thing as the young pilot zoomed past us that afternoon. She raised her hand and waved at him. Then, after he was safely back up in the sky where he belonged, she looked over at me and took my stricken face in both her hands.

"How cool was that?" she asked.

When the war started, the atmosphere in Baghdad changed almost immediately. You could feel it in the air. Iraqi flags—red, white, and black with green stars—were everywhere and somehow intimidating, rather than reassuring to me as a child. Streets filled with Baathist marchers chanting anti-Iranian slogans. Anti-Iranian graffiti proliferated on public walls. Almost overnight, there were soldiers with guns and pictures of Saddam Hussein everywhere. Our state newspaper portrayed Iraqi military leaders as uniformed generals sitting politely in a round table taking instructions from the president; Iranians were shown as crazy mullahs in dirty beards who stood on chairs arguing and yelling at each other. These crazed zealots had attacked us because they wanted to spread their revolution throughout the Arab world, Saddam Hussein had told us, vowing to defend us. He titled this war the Second Qadissiya, after the First Qadissiya, which was fought in the seventh century to advance the progress of Islam into Persia, and compared himself to the great Muslim warrior of that war, Saad Ben Abi Waqaas. He didn't call our enemies Iranians, but *al furs Al Majoos,* "fire-worshiping Persians," a term I later realized must have been designed to revive ethnic hatred that had lain dormant since Persians, mostly Zoroastrians who worshiped fire, had converted to Islam many centuries earlier. By reviving ancient animosities and claiming that he was protecting Iraq from the spread of the Iranian revolution, he was able to portray this as a defensive war, not a war of aggression, which is forbidden by the

Quran. Our media was so controlled that I didn't find out until I left Iraq that Iran wasn't the one that even started the war.

At school, we learned to defend our country and our lives. We practiced hiding under our desks for air raid drills, took instruction in first aid, and found out that our enemies weren't just Iranians, but unseen Iraqi collaborators who secretly supported Iranians. To combat these insidious traitors in our midst, we learned there existed a secret government agency called the Mukhabarat, which was described to us as men in civilian clothes who were working quietly to protect us from the danger these Iranian sympathizers posed to our safety. Mukhabarat means "informers" in Arabic.

"I know who they are—the men with the big black mustaches!" Mohammed said, as always ready to show off his superior knowledge.

Funny how you forget so many things teachers try to teach you, but you remember the looks on their faces when they're caught off guard. My teacher looked nervous when Mohammed said that. I remember. After a moment, she corrected him.

"No one knows what they look like because they are *secret*," she said. "That is the point."

But Mohammed was right. Even I knew what they looked like. Mama had just complained about them hanging around outside the ice cream shop the week before, a bunch of men with big black mustaches who looked as if they were entitled to just stand there and look us over from head to toe as we came out licking our pistachio ice cream cones.

My parents had zero interest in politics. My father, the son of a prominent Ministry of Education official who had suffered censure for being frank about his political views, actively shunned politics. So, as I understand it, did many other educated Iraqis as Saddam Hussein brutally solidified his control of Iraq through his nationalistic pan-Arab Baath Party. Because both schools and airlines were nationalized, however, my parents had to join the Baath Party like most Iraqis just to hold a job. There were several levels of membership, however, and everyone came to know the difference between getting along and being a true believer. The entry level, *moua'ayed,* or *endorser,* was the least you could get away with. If you wanted a little more protection in your job then you could attend meetings for a few years and rise to *naseer,* or *follower.* Later, of course, it became clear to us all that to rise in the ranks of the Baath Party, you had to write reports on other people, in other words, become a spy.

My mother resented the notion of anyone trying to tell her how to act or dress, let alone how to think. When she got her recruitment notice to attend a Baath Party meeting, she showed up in heels and her Nina Ricci mink—a combination (from what I could ascertain later) of the bold and the oblivious. When the leader said, "One Arab United Nation with a United Glorious Message," she knew enough to stand in unison with her fellow teachers and respond, "Unity, Freedom, and Socialism." But, in the process of delivering her one required line, she fainted dead away on the floor. She had a tendency to faint, which I saw as romantic, one of her many skills I never quite mastered. I remember when a group of aunts brought her home that night, and how they were teasing her.

"Can't stand the heat, can you?" teased her sister, my aunt Samer. Aunt Samer was a onetime political activist who felt her Baath revolution had been stolen by Saddam Hussein just as the Iranian revolution had been stolen by the Ayatollah Khomeini.

"It's not that," insisted Mama, fanning herself. "It's my allergies. I'm allergic to the Baath Party!"

With the help of hindsight, I realize that sexism gave women a slight advantage over men when it came to political dissent. Slips of the tongue could be written off to ditziness. Once, when Aunt Samer answered her phone, a friendly voice greeted her with, "Hi, Samer, how's the Baath Party?" and she quipped, "Oh God, *what* Baath Party?" Then she recognized the chuckle on the other end of the line: it was Saddam Hussein. No man could have gotten away with that. Early on in Saddam Hussein's reign, a woman could occasionally express a contrary opinion as long as she joked, cried, or sounded like a bit of an airhead. My mother, I suspect, understood that game and played it occasionally, with utmost discretion, when it suited her needs. She was excused from future meetings on a technicality—my baby brother had just been born and was ill at the time—but she quit teaching not long afterward because, I suspect, of her allergies.

As war revived up, anti-Iranian sentiment grew. In the name of patriotism, people even stopped listening to Iranian music and buying Iranian pistachios. Our family didn't vilify Iran as many people did, but we stopped dying eggs for Norouz, or Persian New Year, on March 21. We had always decorated dyed eggs with faces of a mama, baba, and children, glued cotton on top for hair, and displayed our egg family on our dining room table along with yogurt, cardamom and other foods to bring *baraka* for the new year ahead. I didn't understand. Norouz wasn't just a Persian holiday. It was an ancient holiday marking the coming of spring. Kurds, a separate ethnic group in the north with their own language and culture, celebrated Norouz too. Why couldn't we? "Things are different now," Mama told me with an unsatisfying vagueness. "We can't do that anymore."

Because our enemy's government was run by Shia clerics, all things Shia began to feel suspect. Karbalā' itself seemed to fall under suspicion, so my mother and her siblings moved Bibi to Baghdad and instructed me to erase from my mind the fact that Bibi had once known Khomeini. It was as if that look of disgust I had seen on Mohammed's face in fourth grade was spreading nationwide, as if all Shia had cooties. I could feel the difference in school. Zainab is a common name across the Middle East, but Iraqis consider it classically Shia because it is the name of the daughter of the slain caliph Ali. Every time the teacher called on me, I felt she was labeling me. Zainab = Shia.

"I want to change my name," I told Mama one day when she picked me up from school.

"Why, honey? Zainab is a beautiful name," she said. "Zainab

was one of the most courageous women in Islam. I thought you liked your name."

I had always admired that historical Zainab. It was because of her that we celebrated Ashura, the night Shia commemorate the massacre of Ali's sons with public acts of charity and mournful ceremonies retelling the massacre. In some areas Shia men flog themselves in symbolic penance for their ancestors who failed to prevent the murder of the prophet's heirs that night. Even the public displays of charity for Ashura ended when we went to war. I'm not sure to this day if they were formally banned, or if we just thought they were; either way, they were forbidden. That year, instead of going to Uncle Adel's house for a ritual that ended with sharing pots of steaming food with hundreds of people, we stayed home. That day, Mama listened to a voice on a distant radio station wailing the traditional stories of mourning as she prepared a single special dish, rice pudding with saffron and cinnamon.

Then, like generations of women before her, she recounted for her children how Ali's sons and cousins were massacred on the Night of Ashura. She talked in particular that night about Zainab, who had witnessed a bloody battle in which her brothers and cousins were all beheaded. Zainab had already lost her mother, Fatima, the daughter of Mohammed and Islam's earliest heroine, as well as her father, Ali. After the massacre, she and the other women and children were taken prisoner by the man who had led the uneven battle, and she dared to speak out against him to his face. So eloquent and powerful was she that he became afraid and sent her into exile. She spent the rest of her life spreading word about the atrocity and urging others to repeat the story so no oppressor could ever commit such an injustice again.

I loved that story of Zainab. But I was a preteen. I didn't want to stand out. I wanted to fit in. It had nothing to do with religion, I told myself. Zainab was an old lady's name, and I just wanted to be called something cool, like Jasmine.

Mama was right, you can't freeze life, not even for war. In that first year after war broke out, my baby brother began to walk, I got my period, and I found out that my mother was keeping secrets that could take her away from me.

I was the very last one of my friends to get my period. Every other girl I knew got hers before I got mine. This is an important rite of passage everywhere, but particularly in Islam, where a girl is treated as an adult and starts fasting at Ramadan. In some societies, she takes a veil. In our more liberal circle in Baghdad in the early 1980s, it meant that I was supposed to stop swimming with the boys and girls at the Hunting Club and start swimming with my aunts on days set aside for women, which as far as I could see was the only downside of being an adult. I learned about reproductive health, as we later called it in school, when Mama and I went to pick up my friend Wasen to spend the night with me. Her mother was in London at the time, and when I went inside her house to get her, she said something was wrong with her, that she was bleeding "down there." Her grandmother was home, but she was uncomfortable talking to her about it.

"Don't worry," I told her confidently. "My mother's a teacher. You can ask her. Mama knows about *everything*."

When we went outside, I got into my normal seat in the front of the car next to Mama, and Wasen climbed in back. I started tuning in the radio, and when Wasen didn't say anything, I finally turned to Mama and told her that Wasen had a secret question to ask her.

Wasen leaned over, put her arms on the top of the front seat, and told her what had happened.

"I don't know what to do, Aunt Amel!" she said. "What's wrong with me?"

"Oh, honey, don't worry!" she said. "You're fine. You're perfectly normal."

And, when we got home, Mama and Wasen and I sat down at the kitchen table, and Mama talked to her in such a gentle way, her eyes searching Wasen's eyes, being a mother to her at that moment.

She explained that what had happened was a wonderful thing, the thing that makes a girl a woman and allows us to have babies. As I listened, I felt proud that I had a mother who was so knowledge-able and gentle. Yet I felt left out. Wasen was an adult now, and I was still a child.

Later, my friends teased me that I just a little girl playing with Barbies. I went into my room, packed up all my dolls except for Basma, and gave them to Radya to take home to her little sisters. Then I took the Quran down from the highest shelf in our house, where the holy book is supposed to be kept, and put it in my lap. I didn't exactly pray to get my period, I just recited some phrases I re-membered from Bibi and wished. Not long afterward, I got my wish.

I was the only girl I knew who was excited about getting her pe-riod, and certainly the only one who ran out of the bathroom upon discovering it and told her father. This sort of openness was unique to my family. A woman's body is considered very private in Arab cultures and not to be discussed with men, even fathers.

"Congratulations, you are a woman now, *habibiti*!" he said, us-ing the arabic term for "my beloved" or "honey."

Mama was a biology teacher; she had an embryo in a jar in her high school classroom of a baby that had died in utero. She was also a natural artist. After I got my period that day, she took me into the kitchen and took out the pencil and white notebook she kept by the telephone. Mama always sketched when she was on the phone. She sketched on the margins of books as she read. Her hands were always drawing, always in motion. She drew graceful, lifelike nudes on the walls of her bathroom, then periodically painted over them over and drew more and painted over those. Curious, Haider left his Legos and followed us into the kitchen. She didn't send him away. She began drawing sketches of men's bodies and women's bodies and explained how each worked. Art and science came together in her graceful diagrams with all the curving lines. There was an elegance inside me, inside all women, I never could have imagined. She drew a circle that was a woman's egg and a small creature that was a man's sperm, and said that when the sperm met the egg, a cell was formed. She drew pictures of cells dividing and of those cells dividing until finally a baby was created.

"But how does the sperm find the egg?" I asked.

"When a man and a woman love each other the way Baba and I do, they get married, and they start having sex, and the man puts the sperm into his wife," she said, and she drew a diagram of this.

I started giggling. My parents didn't exactly talk about sex in front of us, but I somehow knew it was something secret that they did in private that made them feel good, a forbidden thrill that I would understand one day when I got married.

"There's no need to giggle about this word, Zainab," Mama said. "Sex isn't silly. It is a beautiful thing. It is a time when a man and a woman come very close to each other and produce beautiful children like you and Haider and your baby brother."

I remember Haider staring at her drawings through his long dark bangs. Haider was very smart for a second-grader. He was smart in the way my father was smart, in math and science. He didn't say much unless he was arguing with me, but he didn't just memorize new information, he processed it inside his brain until it made sense. I learned by observing and asking whatever questions popped into my mind until I was satisfied I had figured things out.

Before we finished talking that afternoon, Mama put her physiology lesson into a spiritual context. God had arranged men's and women's bodies to complement each other perfectly, she said. The pleasure that came with sex was one of God's gifts to each of us, like the gift of being able to have a baby. Men and women were equal in marriage and equally entitled to the gift of that pleasure, she said, but they had to wait until after they were married. So that was why only married women had babies, I thought to myself. It was *haram* to have sex before you were married.

Three years later, when I was in ninth grade, they taught us these things in school. I was the only one who raised my hand to answer questions without shyness, the only one who didn't giggle.

"It should not be *ayeb* to talk about sex," I said. "Sex is a natural thing. It is one of God's gifts to us."

Like all Iraqi children, I was raised to obey my parents, tell the truth, respect my teachers and other adults, and do nothing to dishonor my family. These are complex concepts, but to break any of those rules was essentially *ayeb,* which means "rude" or "discourteous." To whisper in front of anyone or to interrupt an adult or question their judgment was *ayeb*. To enter a room of adults without being invited was *ayeb* in a culture where adults and children usually socialized separately. Women in particular had to be careful not to do anything *ayeb,* because any behavior that was less than modest and courteous could draw shame or *aar* not only upon themselves, but on their whole family. Even in our home, the most liberal I knew, curiosity was encouraged, but questioning the judgment of adults was not. My parents were as secular as any I knew, but it was still *haram* to cause them even to sigh with concern, because that was written in the Quran. So I asked many questions, sometimes to the point of impertinence, but when I felt my world begin to turn upside down, I couldn't ask what was wrong.

Uncle Adel began spending the night at our home, and I assumed at first that he had had an argument with his wife. Then Aunt Samer, Uncle Adel, and my parents began gathering in our living room and closing the door nervously behind them so we wouldn't hear what they were saying. I looked to Mama for an explanation, but the expression on her face told me I was not to ask. Something was clearly worrying them, yet every time I tried to approach anyone I would be asked if I had finished my homework, or told to please watch my baby brother. I spent so much time with Hassan during that time that when he began to speak, he sometimes called me "Mama." My initial reaction to their rebuff was hurt. I was supposed to be an adult, and they were still treating me like a child, or maybe a ghost that everybody just looked straight through. One day, I lay down on the sofa and covered my head with a sofa pillow in hopes I could make myself faint so someone would pay attention to me the way they did to Mama when she fainted. But nobody noticed. I fell asleep and woke up an hour later, tired and sweaty. Didn't adults realize a child doesn't stop observing what's going on around her? Didn't my parents understand how lonely it was being inside my own brain with all these questions it was *ayeb* to ask?

One night when I heard my parents talking in their bedroom downstairs, I tiptoed out of my room and sat down on the terrazzo tile staircase to listen to what they were saying. I had never eavesdropped on anyone before, and it was a sign of how scared and left out I felt that I would even consider it. But I learned something important that night as I stared down at my bare feet on the step: my mother's cousin, Aunt Ishraq, and her family were no longer living in Iraq. Aunt Ishraq had an enormous house in Al-Mansour with girl cousins my age and older boy cousins I had kind of practiced flirting on.

"Mama, why didn't Aunt Ishraq and my cousins say good-bye to me before they moved away?" I asked Mama later. My feelings were hurt.

"How did you know about this?" she demanded.

"I just figured it out from what everybody was saying," I said.

"You must erase this from your memory, Zainab," she instructed. Her voice was firm and clear. There was no room to play around here.

"But, I can't, Mama," I confessed.

"Well, don't mention this subject again, not even to your cousins," she said. "We'll talk about it later. Not now. You must *not* say anything about this to anyone. Do you understand?"

I knew all the looks on my mother's face. When she was angry, her face grew very red, and drops of sweat appeared on her upper lip. When she was serious about something, her skin would pale noticeably, and her face would set, her lips taut. That day, I took her by surprise, and I saw her scared. Something about Aunt

Ishraq's move had scared her. She was more afraid because I knew about it, and that made me feel not only guilty, but sad. I adored my mother, and the last thing on earth I wanted to do was to cause her pain.

It was cold and pouring rain in Baghdad when Baba asked me if I wanted to go with him over to Uncle Adel's. We rarely spent time alone together, so I jumped at the chance. It had rained so long that our cul-de-sac had filled up with water. Baba always complained when that happened because the government had been promising to fix the drainage, but I loved it. If Baba happened to be home when this lake appeared in our front yard, he would make a fleet of boats out of newspaper and my brothers and I would set them sailing. But that was obviously far from his mind as we got in the car to drive to Uncle Adel's. He put on a tape of the Egyptian singer Abdul Haleem Hafez and tried to chat with me as we drove. I don't remember what he talked about. I just remember feeling that he was trying to make a special effort to reach out to me and that he wasn't comfortable chatting with me the way Mama was. Casual conversation didn't come naturally to him. When he came home from a long trip, we would rush in, open his suitcase to see what he had brought us, jump all over him, get our hugs, and then let him alone. He was a little like a cat when it came to emotions. He needed his space.

The short street leading to Uncle Adel's house was muddy and empty and dreary. I noticed a large stack of crates half-covered with blue plastic tarps in front of the house of one of his neighbors. I was surprised to see them still there. There were only four houses on that street, and I knew the neighbors well enough to know that the crates contained valuable factory equipment.

"Why did they leave the equipment out?" I asked Baba. "It's going to rust in the rain."

He waited to answer until he had parked the car in front of my uncle's house. Then he turned to me, and I realized this drive had been building to something. He was trying to find the right words, and I could see it wasn't easy for him. I remember staring down at the floor and thinking I wasn't actually an adult yet because I couldn't drive. My legs weren't long enough to reach the pedals.

"The neighbors were deported to Iran," he said. "That's what happened to Aunt Ishraq and her family too, Zainab. That's why they didn't say good-bye. They didn't have time."

He explained it to me in the way he said everything—facts only. The government was deporting Iraqis "of Iranian origin." Nobody knew how many people had been deported, or exactly what happened to all those who had gone. Uncle Adel was staying at our house so he wouldn't be taken away too. I listened with growing fear and confusion as I realized that my parents must have planned this conversation together. Why hadn't Mama told me herself? Why was Baba the one to tell me these things, sitting here in the car in the rain outside Uncle Adel's house?

Then he broke the unthinkable news.

"Zainab, it's possible your mother may have to leave the country too," he said. "The government is giving two thousand dinars [six thousand dollars] to Iraqis to divorce their spouses if they're of Iranian origin."

Until now, I had sat still, staring at my feet in petrified silence.

"You're not going to divorce Mama, are you?" I said in a sharp, accusing voice. Of everything he had said, that scared me the most.

"No, no," he said gently. "But you're an adult now, so I thought you should understand what is happening."

Then he opened the car door and got out. When Mama and I talked, I could usually ask questions, even if I didn't always get answers. With Baba that was impossible. I got out and followed him with my head full of questions. Was I going to lose Mama? If Baba wasn't going to divorce Mama, why did he say that? Would he even *think* of divorcing Mama? Didn't he love her anymore? If she left, what would happen to me? Could I go with her? What about my brothers? What would happen to them?

When Aunt Najwa opened the door, I hardly recognized her. A

tall, beautiful woman who ran one of Uncle Adel's factories and always had her hair done at a salon, she looked haggard and thin. There was no makeup, no elegant business suit. The aunt I knew as almost imperious had been replaced by a frightened woman who kept running her hands through her hair. She started talking fast to Baba without even saying hello. I found my cousins in the living room looking as scared and pale and ignored as I had been feeling for weeks. They told me they hadn't seen their father in days.

"Two Mukhabarat agents came an hour ago asking for our citizenship papers to prove we weren't Iranian," Dawood said. "Mama told them Baba had them and he was out of town."

"But how can you be Iranian!" I said. "You've never even been to Iran! You're Iraqi! Your parents are Iraqi!"

"The neighbors are all Iraqi too, and we woke up one day and they were gone," said my littlest cousin, near tears. "And now we're the very last house on our street left with people in it!"

Why was this happening? Why was the Mukhabarat coming to their house and not my house? Why were my mother and their parents in danger, but apparently not my father? What about me and my brothers? Were they trying to deport us too?

"If Mama and you guys get deported, I'm going with you," I declared.

"I don't know if you would be allowed," Dawood told me.

"If anybody tries to pull us apart, I hold on and I just won't let go," I vowed. "They'll have to take me too."

We sat there for a long time, listening to bits and pieces of our parents' conversation in the next room. This apparently wasn't the first time the Mukhabarat had come; it was the second, and Aunt Najwa said they had told her they would be back again. I looked around at the big dining room table, the backgammon board, the wedding pictures, the baby pictures, the pictures of us on the Tigris in their boat last summer. I'm sure we were all thinking the same thing. Were the secret police going to take all this away from them? Would we ever be able to play together in this house again? I felt great, nauseating, roller coaster loops of fear in my stomach.

When Baba came over to tell me it was time to leave, Aunt Najwa was pleading with him, holding his shoulder.

"Please do something, Basil!" she said. "I don't know how much more time I can buy. They will take us if you can't manage to do something!"

My cousins all turned and stared at me.

Baba? What could my father do?

For the life of me I can't remember the next few days. I can't remember running to Mama, though I must have when I got home. All I remember is that a few days, maybe even a few weeks, later, Mama drove me to an old neighborhood in downtown Baghdad. She stopped to buy fresh fish for dinner and chatted with the fishmonger. The worry was gone, she looked herself again, and I sensed the crisis was past. Something had been resolved. The streets were too narrow in that neighborhood for cars, so she suggested we get out, and we walked along the river until we stopped in front of a very old house. I had heard about it, but never seen it: the house where Mama grew up. In the fourteen years since Bibi had moved out, it had been given over to Boy Scouts, health clinics, a watchman's family, and now stood empty. Mama went over and unlocked the old-fashioned door, and we stepped into an airy interior that seemed to have come from another time. There was an inner courtyard lit by shafts of diffuse sunlight from high overhead, which gave the whole place the feeling of an unused sanctuary. High above, wrapped around the inside of the second and third floors, were walkways with wrought iron railings and doorways that led to rooms beyond. We passed an empty, tiled fountain covered now with pigeon droppings and dust. Mama said she and Aunt Samer use to play in it when they were little.

I heard the flapping of wings somewhere above as she led me up one of several staircases. Running her hands along the old walls, she told stories as we entered each room, recalling the Farsi-speaking servants, the strong patriarch who had been her father, a brother who had died, and Uncle Adel, the big brother fifteen years older than she was, who always watched out for her. Finally, we reached the third floor, and she led me into a room that had been hers and Aunt Samer's, overlooking the river. She walked across the dusty floor and opened the high old wood-framed windows, and we stepped out onto a sagging wooden balcony. Laid out in front of us were the Tigris River and a centuries-old skyline of domes and minarets beyond. We stood there for a while, just staring at history and the boatmen ferrying passengers back and forth across the river. I wondered how many generations of Iraqis had stood on the earth right beneath where we stood, how many peoples led by how many different rulers had passed over this precise spot, what they wore, what they believed, how much of their blood I had in me now, how different they looked from me.

"First, *habibiti*, I want to let you know that our family is safe," she said. "No one is going to be deported. I want you to know that."

"So they won't take you away?" I said.

"No, honey, nobody's going to take me away. Or Uncle Adel or your cousins."

I hugged her and almost cried.

"I was so scared, Mama!"

"I know. Baba and I had hoped we would be able to resolve this without worrying you, but at one point . . . Well, we decided that you would rather be prepared in case we couldn't work things out."

"So no one will ever take you away from me?"

"No, honey. No one's taking me anywhere. Everything is going to be all right. It just got very complicated there for a while."

The sun was warm on our faces, but the wind was brisk. Mama kept her hands in her coat pockets as she looked out over the river, then back at me, her long black hair blowing away from her face and the slightly bent Abbasid coin around her neck glinting. Her large brown eyes, rimmed with kohl, filled with nostalgia.

"I remember standing on this balcony waiting for my father to come home for lunch," she said, looking out over the narrow river road where men and women and children went on about daily things. "Every afternoon when he walked up this street for dinner, he'd bring somebody with him. A porter, a driver, somebody he had just met somewhere. How I resented it! Why did he have to bring a total stranger to eat with our family? It was *our* family. But he explained to me that charity was mandatory in Islam."

She talked about how Bibi used to supervise the preparation of enormous tubs of *fesenjoon* and *durshana* for Ramadan, and they would open the house to the poor, who would come from all over the neighborhood with pots to fill and take home to their families.

"I stood right here on this balcony and saw a man stuff rice in his pocket once when I was a little girl and felt so fortunate for the *baraka* that had been bestowed on us, Zainab. Those were good days. It is so sad, *habibiti*. Now we can't even give away food on Ashura without endangering the lives of our children."

Many parents have the freedom of handing down ancestral history without fear, but when my mother began telling me the history of our family that afternoon, I had to stand very close to hear her as she entrusted me with the story of our family.

"Everything started with my grandfather—our fortune and our problems," she said. "He was born in Baghdad in 1865. We even have his birth certificate. He is Iraqi! How could anyone think he was Iranian!"

But her grandfather was born at a time when Iraq was a battleground of two empires, the Safavid Empire of Iran, which was Shia, and the Ottoman Empire, administered in Iraq by Sunnis, that reached all the way to the Mediterranean Sea. This grandfather—my third grandfather, *jeddo* we call it in Arabic—married a wealthy woman and built a successful business fabricating strings—ropes, sausage casings, threads. He plied ancient trade routes while his wife managed the finances and raised their children, including Mama's father, a man fluent in five languages who would expand the business into leather factories. This wife was the matriarch I had heard so much about.

"My grandmother was a strong woman," Mama said. "Your

aunts and I couldn't help but want to be strong like her. So competent. So commanding. Yet how little freedom she allowed Mama! I wonder sometimes if that is why Mama allowed us so much."

At some point, probably in the nineteenth century, Mama explained, our original family surname had been lost. Men marrying into wealthy families often adopted their wife's name, and birth names were sometimes replaced by occupations. By the time Mama was born, the family surname meant "Maker of Strings," which made our family records hard to trace. It was possible, she said, that her grandfather's grandfather was born in Iran. Bibi had a vague memory of visiting Tehran with her guardian when she was very small, and Mama said she thought we had relatives there, somewhere.

"I went to Tehran once when I was your age," Mama told me. "It was a beautiful city. I've been thinking since all this happened that maybe I have cousins there. I always wanted to find them someday. But how is that possible? Now we are shooting each other."

The odd part about it, as Mama explained it to me that day, was that the deportations weren't even based on birth. Iraq, a vast plain with two great rivers and fertile soil between them, had been invaded many times over the centuries—Bibi herself had lived under an Ottoman Empire, a British occupation, an Iraqi kingdom, a Communist government, and several Baathist regimes. At the end of the Ottoman Empire in the early twentieth century, a census was taken in which heads of households were asked whether they were of Ottoman origin or of Iranian origin. This was not as innocuous a question as it seemed. Fearing induction into the Ottoman army and mindful of the importance of maintaining travel documents to conduct business across the border into Iran, my great-grandfather and many other Shia men registered as being "of Iranian origin." All Iraqi citizenship papers still divided us that way, based on those grayed registration papers.

But I still didn't understand why my mother was at risk of being deported and my father was not. They were first cousins, marriage between cousins being permitted in Islam because inheritances are kept in the family and it is believed that a husband is likely to treat a cousin better than a stranger. But national origin apparently was deemed to follow the father's bloodline, and it was their maternal grandfather they had in common. My father's grandfather on his father's side had registered as being of Ottoman origin while my mother's, the one who made strings, had registered as being of Iranian origin. My father was therefore considered to be of Ottoman origin and Uncle Adel of Iranian origin, which is why my brothers and I were safe from deportation, and my cousins weren't.

"They're deporting the wealthiest people first," Mama said. "That is why we think Aunt Ishraq and her family were among the first. I think they just want to steal our homes and businesses. Will this corruption never stop? They have no right! How many people are gone? Thousands, tens of thousands maybe. We are all Iraqi, and yet there are empty houses all over Baghdad!"

So how come we were safe now?

"We talked to the president," she told me. "It just took us a while to reach him. But when we sat down with him, he was very good about it. We showed him my grandfather's birth certificate—not that that means much, but it was something. So he made us a 'special file.'"

A special file. I mulled that phrase. I wasn't sure if it was good or bad.

"Don't worry, honey," Mama said. "Iraq will always be our home."

We had been standing on the balcony for a long time that afternoon. Mama drew me inside her fur coat to warm me, and I saw the bend in the graceful calligraphy of the gold coin where it had been dented. I wondered, as I did every time I looked at that dent, what force had been so strong as to cause it.

Because of our special file, Aunt Ishraq and her family were eventually allowed to come home. Everybody brought food to their house and we had a picnic on the floor. There was no table. Everything in their house—the furniture, their dishes, their toys and school books—was gone. The house was empty. They said almost nothing about what had happened to them while they were gone.

Being a "special file" was a threat that remained with our family all our lives. At any time a government official could request our citizenship papers and, because the papers were signed by a single recognizable officer in the Mukhabarat, anyone checking them knew immediately that my mother's family's "Iraqi" citizenship was in question, subjecting them to fear and intimidation. I happened to be at Uncle Adel's house the night his younger son, Hussam, started a new school, and Hussam looked so dejected that I asked what was wrong. It turned out that Uncle Adel had been so afraid to send Hussam to school with his "special file" papers that he had told Hussam to tell the teacher he had forgotten them. His teacher sent him to the principal and, following Uncle Adel's instructions, he told the principal that his parents were out of town but that he had an adult friend he could call who could come in and vouch for him. Hussam sat in the principal's office for an hour until the friend, a high-ranking Baath official, showed up and registered him. "I felt as if the whole school was looking at me," he told me, his face down. "What did we do wrong? Why do they treat us this way?" To this day, Hussam gets tears in his eyes remembering his fear and humiliation. When he tried to register his own son for school twenty years later, he was told, "Oh, your papers are in not in this office—you have to go the *special* file office," and the nightmare was passed down to the next generation.

There is only one memory I truly wish I could erase. It is of my mother.

I was upstairs in my room doing my homework some months after we had secured our "special file." It was late, and my brothers were already asleep. My father was downstairs watching television, and he called out to ask me to check on my mother. I went to their bedroom door and found it closed. I knocked, then knocked again. She didn't answer. Finally, I went inside and was hit by a blast of very warm air. The heater was on high. All the lights were on. It seemed very bright, almost glaring. Their room was all white then, with white closets and white furniture and white walls. The bed was empty, unmade and messed up, as if she had been sleeping restlessly and gotten up to go into the bathroom. She didn't answer my call. Then I caught sight of her on the floor on the other side of the bed. She was sprawled awkwardly on the Persian rug in her white nightgown, her arms and legs and hair askew. Around her were pills—pink and blue, white, yellow—bright pastel colors on the burgundy pile of the rug, and empty plastic bottles.

I was so scared. I ran to her and pulled her up into my arms. She was breathing, but her body slumped heavily as I tried to hold her up. "Mama, Mama! Wake up, Mama! Can you hear me, Mama?" I could see her eyes trying to open, but there was no focus. The skin on her beautiful face was slack, her face whiter than I had ever seen it. Was she going to die? "Baba!" I cried, but he didn't answer, so I ran to get him. It was dark. The lights were out. All I could see was the shifting bluish light of the television and the sound of the TV coming from the family room. I found Baba sitting on the blue sofa, a glass of whiskey at his side. I ran over to him, but he seemed almost as numb with whiskey as Mama was with pills. Finally he came back with me and looked in a daze at Mama on the floor. I sent him to telephone for help while I stayed with Mama. I sat there with her head in my lap and kept her awake, cooling her face with a wet towel, brushing her long hair with her hairbrush, and telling her not to die, please not to die.

Uncle Adel arrived and he and I managed to get Mama to his car. Baba stayed home. When we got to Uncle Adel's house, I refused to let Mama out of my arms. I would not, would not, would not, let go of her. We took her into the bathroom, and Uncle Adel brought milk to force her to drink so she would vomit the pills. But she couldn't seem to swallow, so Aunt Najwa brought me a funnel from the kitchen, and Uncle Adel held his baby sister, tears streaming down his face, as I poured milk down her throat. I had stopped crying. I was utterly focused on getting that milk down her throat. I was on a mission to save her life. I held the back of her neck as she had held mine when I was sick, and finally she vomited the awful pills.

By the time the doctor arrived, Aunt Najwa and I had washed her and changed her clothing and put her to bed. I put on a clean nightgown Aunt Najwa gave me and crawled into bed with Mama. I put my arms around her and held her all night like a mother holding a sick child, listening to her breathing, afraid I might lose her again if I fell asleep. Mama had tried to kill herself. Why, Mama? Why? Don't you know how much Haider and Hassan and I need you? Don't you know how much I love you? By the time I finally slept, I felt like all the child had been wrung out of me. I had seen a side of adulthood I wasn't ready for, something that reeked of sour milk and whiskey and pain, but I had no answers and no one would ever really explain what had brought it all on.

Mama slept a long time and awoke weak and exhausted from the ordeal. I wanted to ask her what was wrong, but she looked embarrassed and funny.

She just kept saying, "I'm sorry, Zanooba. I'm so sorry, honey. I'm so sorry." She patted my hair. Then she said something I will never forget:

"I feel like a bird in a cage," she said. "Don't ever let yourself be a bird in a cage, Zainab. Promise me, honey. Always be a free spirit."

"I promise, Mama," I said.

But I didn't understand. She was telling me not to be like her, and until that night I had never wanted to be anything else.

From Alia's Notebook

One night, he sent for us and we were partying by the Tigris River. There were only a few of us around him that night, and Saddam was drinking whiskey as if it were water. Every hour one of his bodyguards came to whisper something in his ears. At midnight, after he had drunk about three-quarters of a bottle of whiskey, he responded in a loud voice to a bodyguard, "Hit them and let the game start, may God curse them all!" We didn't know what he was talking about until the next morning when we learned that he had sent his ships sailing in Shat Al-Arab [the waterway dividing Iraq and Iran near the Persian Gulf] thus the beginning of the Iran-Iraq war.

He was very happy the first few months of the war. As a matter of fact, we had never seen him as happy as he was these few months. He was partying almost every night. These nights were filled with village women who would dance and sing for him. A band often showed up in these parties known as Thubab's band. Its lead singer was a woman known as Aneesa who used to sit by his feet as she sang traditional melancholy songs from rural areas that made him emotional as he remembered his past. He used to distribute about 2000 dinar for his friends at the party so they could throw this money to the dancers and the singer. Money was everywhere in these parties, flying around the dancers and filling the floors.

We used to leave these parties with headaches from the Bedouin music and his war talks, but we had no choice but to attend. He wanted everyone around him in those days, so the parties were big and loud. Sometimes he would talk about his military plans at these parties and brag about different battles that he orchestrated. He enjoyed reviewing scenes from these battles, and he ordered the TV station to broadcast them for hours at a time so he could watch them. Your father and I couldn't even look at these scenes, which were filled with images of dead Iranian soldiers. He, on the other hand, would talk about how these scenes would open his appetite for food.

3

❖

AFTER PIG'S ISLAND

I ENTERED JUNIOR HIGH SCHOOL a year after war began. In Iraq, boys and girls attend elementary school together and are separated in junior high and high school. I decided I didn't want to attend the elite girls' school with my friends who were suddenly into gossip and clothes, so I asked to go to Al-Shamella, the Comprehensive Experimental School, a model junior high–high school. My mother had a friend who was a teacher there, and she had gotten me excited about its nontraditional curriculum where homemaking classes included budgeting, electricity, carpentry, and metal work. They also offered extracurricular music, pottery-making, and a variety of other subjects that other schools didn't.

I didn't know anyone at my new school, and the adjustment turned out to be hard. The school wasn't far from our home, but it was located in a marginalized neighborhood that was part of a whole different world than the one I lived in. The first day of school, I felt eyes from all over the schoolyard look at me when my mother dropped me off in our Toyota. It would never have occurred to anyone in our family to send me on the bus because public transportation was used only by people who didn't have cars. Here, everyone walked or took the bus. It turned out I was the only rich kid in a school filled with kids from poor and working-class families.

A fair number of students dropped out at fourteen or fifteen to be married. We all wore the same uniform, but mine was imported from Germany or England while my classmates made their own. I could go home and take a bubble bath and start classes the next day smelling like kiwi or lavender, while some of them went home to abusive parents. I began hearing about domestic violence for the first time and began to understand the price classmates paid for generations of endemic poverty and inadequate education. I remember one girl telling me about how her stepfather had beaten her, thrown her out of the house, and left her to spend the night all alone on the doorstep. I could not find the right words to say to her. There were none. Nothing I could say would matter. Her life was unfair. She had done nothing wrong except be born into the wrong family, and I had been lucky enough to be born into the right family.

I did everything I could at school to prove I wasn't a spoiled rich kid. I joined the Iraqi Girl Scouts. I participated in afterschool activities. If our driver was late coming to pick me up, I would use his tardiness as an excuse to board the bus, oblivious to the fact that I was acting exactly like a spoiled kid by leaving him waiting, fearing something had happened to me. One time he apparently saw me get on the bus and followed it to every stop. When I finally saw him, I had to climb down off the bus and get in the car as everyone I had been trying to impress stared at me out the windows. I wanted to fit in, to make friends, but I had left the largely secular world I was used to and found myself plunged into a world of observant Muslims, both Sunni and Shia. Prayer was a part of daily life for most of my classmates. One day, I found myself standing quietly, somewhat awkwardly, with a group of other girls who were talking about prayer.

I said, "I pray too."

"Oh, sure," one girl said. "I don't believe you. Tell us the order of what you recite in a prayer—if you really know it."

I started with the Shahada, the phrase that makes Muslims Muslims: "I witness that there is no God but one God, and Mohammed is his Prophet." Nervous about the ending, I left off the part about Ali. Then, I said the declaration of the intention of the prayer, and a verse from the Quran.

"Okay, go on," the girl told me.

They let me keep talking, searching my memory, until they finally all started laughing.

"You don't even know how to pray, you rich girl!" one girl said. "You're from the ooh-la-la class!"

I tried to make light of it as the bell rang and we went back inside. But I felt hurt and shunned, back to being judged on the basis of how I prayed—or didn't pray—and I felt angry at my parents for failing to teach me or even to pray themselves. When Bibi came over, I asked her to show me how, and I got out my prayer rug and made a point of praying in front of my family. Aunt Samer was visiting. The television was on. The mothers were laughing and drinking Turkish coffee. My brothers and cousins were playing all around me.

"This is good, Zanooba," Bibi said. "But next time you might try praying with the television off, maybe alone in your room—it feels better if you concentrate." I dutifully prayed at dawn and dusk for a while. I got more religious the night before tests.

One day, fighting my own shyness, I gathered my nerve and joined a basketball game during recess. I had played with my cousins in our cul-de-sac and with Mama during one of our summers in Seattle when she was pregnant with Hassan, laughing as she ran around the court, her belly as big as the ball, calling out coaching instructions in a mix of Baghdad-accented Arabic and the occasional "go, go, GO!" in English. One of the players came over to me after the recess game and complimented me on my playing. We started talking. I liked her, she liked me, and we exchanged telephone numbers.

"I have a new friend!" I announced over lunch that afternoon.

"That's nice, honey," Mama said.

"Where does she live?" Baba asked.

"In the Al Iskaan neighborhood near school," I answered. Al Iskaan was a neighborhood known for its public housing projects.

"What does her father do?" Baba asked.

"I don't know, Baba," I said. "I haven't asked. Why would I?"

"I need to know," he said tersely. "Did you give her your phone number?"

"Yes," I said. "We're friends, Baba."

"You need to get it back," he said.

"Why, Baba?" I protested. I didn't understand this whole conversation. Just when I had found a friend, Baba was trying to take her away from me.

"Because I am telling you to," he said.

"But, Baba, I like her!" I said. "Why are you asking me this? You're putting me in an embarrassing position with a girl I just met. It is *ayeb*."

"Just do it, Zainab. I have my reasons. Just do it, okay? No more arguments."

I looked at Mama for help.

"Your father knows what he's doing, honey," she said. "Do what he says. Trust him. He's your father."

Feeling embarrassed and resentful, the next day I walked up to the girl I wanted to be my friend knowing that I was about to hurt both of us.

"I'm so, so sorry," I told her, "but my father said I cannot share my phone number with you."

She looked me in the eye and brought out her notebook and a pencil. She had written my phone number on the cover of her notebook, and I watched as she scratched out my name hard, over and over again, until all that remained was a swath of shiny black graphite.

"Just to show you that I will never, ever, be able to see your number again," she said.

Then she walked away.

I didn't even have an explanation for her. I had no idea that my father had made me take back her telephone number because of Saddam Hussein. I didn't understand at the time how well my parents knew him. To me, he was a face on television, a man we were taught to sing to and march for and pray for the health of: the President of Iraq.

All children in Iraq were taught to call him "Amo Saddam," which means "Uncle Saddam." (That is the traditional form of address that Iraqi children use to address male adults. My friends didn't call my father Mr. Salbi, for example, they called him Amo Salbi.) Loyalty to Amo Saddam was so instilled in every student in school that it became almost indistinguishable from loyalty to family and to Iraq itself. Boys and girls joined the Vanguards, the *tala'a,* and wore camouflage uniforms of blue and white with matching hats as they practiced marching and singing at school to songs like "Amo Saddam will break the teeth of the coward Khomeini!" Teenagers were taught to address him as adults did— Al Sayed or Al Ra'aees, the sire or the president—and we competed against one another to show our love for him through poetry contests, art contests, and endless marching contests. I was selected to help raise the flag at the ceremony that took place every Thursday, the last day of the working week in the Muslim calendar. That was an honor, and I remember how intent I was standing before the class in my Girl Scout uniform: raising the flag properly, tying the knot, and saluting my flag. After we sang the national anthem— which he changed in favor of a new one that sounded to me like a militaristic march—we had to stand at absolute attention listening to speeches by the principal, poems by students, and songs played by the school band—every one a devotion to president and country.

Everyone was expected to join in an extracurricular activity showing our patriotism. I joined the school's marching band. We practiced hour after hour, in four straight lines, holding flags or pictures of Saddam Hussein, shouting "May God protect the president! and "May God prolong his life!" We were taught not just how to move our feet, but how to look—focused and determined—and how to sound—loud and sharp. "Yes, yum! Yes, yum!" we shouted in response to every command the teacher gave us. The "yes" was presumably left over from our days as part of the British Empire. I don't know what "yum" meant; no one explained. The sheer monotony and repetition took something out of us. Later, I realized it was our own individualism. After a while I could hear no single voice, not even my own. I was part of a united whole, doing what our leader wanted us to do: march and shout. I turned my brain off and shifted to automatic pilot, one of the thousands upon thousands of young Iraqis marching for Saddam Hussein. Sometimes our whole school would empty out and join others for massive demonstrations through the streets of Baghdad, and I would slip away in the confusion. I never felt like jumping up and down as many did, shouting slogans like "With our blood, with our soul, we will protect you, oh, Saddam!" Even if he had helped spare my mother with our "special file," I was old enough to comprehend that he was ultimately in charge of the system that had initiated the deportations in the first place and made my cousins suffer.

On television he came across as a handsome, friendly man who liked to drop in on ordinary citizens for tea. A housewife would open the door, gasp in shock and astonishment at being selected by the president for one of his frequent home visits, and invite him in. He seemed homey and respectful as the camera followed him. "How's your family?" he would ask. "How are your children doing? Are you eating well?" And he would follow the housewife into her kitchen, take a look at whatever she had cooking on the stove, and open her refrigerator. I remember him looking into lots of refrigerators and always commenting at how well stocked they were—I'm sure there were women who kept their refrigerators tidy just in case he dropped in. In all the televised visits, the families were happy and thankful to see him, though through Aunt Samer I later learned that there was one woman who, when he asked if there was anything he could do for her, said, "Yes: I'm so worried about my only son, could you bring him home from the war?" The episode was never televised, and the woman had sought out Aunt Samer in hopes she could somehow convey her apologies so her son would not pay for her mistake.

Saddam Hussein's birthday was a national holiday. Streets were closed, stages were set up, and bands played for him as people danced and marched in the streets. In the evening, everyone would gather around their television sets and watch him walk down past long banquet tables and survey his presents. Each had a card with the name of the giver on it, which the camera showed, and everyone wanted to see who had given what and what Amo's response was. I always had my doubts that the day we celebrated his birthday, April 28, was the real day he was born. Many people his age who grew up in rural areas had parents who were illiterate or did not bother to register their children's birthdates, so they were assigned birthdates of July 1. I remember my father telling us a funny story once about a time he and his crew were laid over in Bangkok on July 1 and a hotel manager was so struck by the fact that so many of them were born that day that he gave them a little birthday party.

Our schools were free—we were given notebooks, books, coloring pens, and anything else we needed for studying—but we were expected to "give back" to patriotic causes, contributing to buy the president a cake for his birthday on April 28. I remember students scrambling to come up with enough coins, but never questioning why. Yet they must have wondered, as I did, why our little brothers and sisters were also donating money for birthday cakes. How many cakes could he eat? How would they be delivered? One day after school, I saw the teachers eating his cake at a meeting, like a Baath Party meeting, and I felt stung by the hypocrisy. My mother and I happened to visit a former teacher friend of hers that night, and as we walked up to her house, we saw a picture of Saddam

Hussein taped to her front window and two candles burning on her front porch. I remember taking in the look that Mama and this teacher gave each other. I don't believe any words passed between them, but this was the conversation I remember they managed to exchange through their eyes and their gestures—it would have been too dangerous to say these things out loud:

Mama: "Gee, you've really gone all out with this Baath Party stuff, Kawbob. Don't you think you're going a little overboard with the candles?"

Aunt Kawbob: "Ah, Alia, it's getting worse every day. It's degrading, but one does what one has to. Baath Party members have been stopping by the house lately. If you're not excited about celebrating Saddam's birthday, they'll think you don't like the president."

Mama: "I'm sorry. I'm lucky I got out of teaching when I did, I guess. But then, none of us can be too careful these days. Do you have any birthday cake?"

And, we went inside to eat cake with her. Mama already knew what I was coming to understand. Lighting those candles, chanting for Amo Saddam, and even eating that cake were shields we used to ward off danger, and those who were the most vulnerable needed them most. Everyone had to prove their loyalty, just in case. When we got home that night, Mama told me, "Zainab honey, go bring some candles. I think we should also put them in front of our house. Aunt Kawbob has a point."

I was just falling asleep one night when I heard the unfamiliar sound of my parents arguing downstairs. I had heard them argue before, mostly when I was little, mostly over small things, and mostly in English because they figured we didn't understand it yet. This was very different. My parents were fighting, and I could hear my father's voice raised. He was very upset. I got out of bed and sat down on the terrazzo tile step. Baba was angry, and Mama was trying to sound reasonable.

"What are you *thinking* of, Alia?"

"You wouldn't be the only one. Lots of men are volunteering; maybe you should do the same."

"Don't you love me anymore? Do you want to get me killed?"

"Of course I love you. Of course I don't want you to get killed."

"I can't believe my own wife is telling me this! Other women are trying to help their husbands escape the draft, and you're telling me I should go to the front lines?"

"You saw him the other night. He was looking straight at you when he said city men were spoiled. All that talk about how you don't know what hardship is, what it means to grow up without shoes, that men from Baghdad need to toughen up and this war will teach them how. You know Amo expects you to go, Basil."

"So what? What if I get shot? Is that how I'm supposed to prove I'm tough? By getting myself killed?"

And I heard Baba get up, open the front door, and stalk out into the night. I just sat there in my pajamas in the silence that followed. I was scared. Was I now at risk of losing Baba? Why would Mama even think of such a thing? Was she trying to be one of those "glorious Iraqi women" they were always talking about on television who sent their husbands and sons off to war? I hesitated for a minute, then went downstairs to find her. There had to be an explanation.

"Did you hear us arguing?" she asked, looking up when she saw me come in. "I'm sorry, honey. I didn't mean to wake you up."

"Mama, does Baba really have to go to the front? What if something happens to him?"

"Nothing will happen to him, honey. They won't send him anywhere dangerous. He'll just go away for a while to fulfill his national duty, then come home. It'll just feel as though he's away on a long trip."

She made it sound almost routine. She seemed to think that my father would go off to a safe area, prove his loyalty, and be back in a matter of months—which is exactly what happened. I later learned that Saddam Hussein was the one who had called him home and that he had complimented Baba in private for his courage. But for the first time I saw a crack in my parents' marriage. Except to say that he thought Iraq would win because our army was stronger than Iran's, I don't remember Baba saying much at all when he came home. I just remember that when he returned, his boots left mud on the terrazzo tile, and he wouldn't look at Mama, though she went out of her way to be nice to him. My father loved my mother. I am certain of that, but I don't think he ever got over her imprecations to risk his life for show.

While men were under pressure to donate their time and even their lives for the war effort, women were asked to donate gold. Baath Party members began going door-to-door in suburban neighborhoods asking women to donate jewelry, and some felt pressured to give away even their wedding rings in the name of supporting our troops. In the Arab world, a woman's wealth is often displayed in public by her gold. Under Sharia, Islamic law, men inherit twice as much from their parents as women, because they are responsible for paying for household expenses. A woman's portion of her inheritance, however, is hers alone. As far as I know, my father never asked my mother about her inheritance; that was hers. Along with properties and other assets, when a woman marries, her women relatives and friends slip twenty-four-karat necklaces over her head and rings onto her fingers until, by the end of the evening, she is often adorned with jewels, and these are hers to keep even if the marriage ends in divorce.

When I was twelve, we got an invitation to donate gold at a televised ceremony as I was finishing seventh grade. Mama didn't like the idea of appearing on television and, in her own way, was shy about such publicity. I suspect the whole concept seemed gauche to her, but participation was not optional, so my parents asked me to go instead. When I arrived, I found women lining up in front of the camera to make their donations. I believe I was the only child. I said my name clearly, as they had, so my family would be given proper credit, and handed over the bag of jewelry my mother had given me so they could weigh it and announce the exact weight on television. I don't remember how much it was, but the point was that everyone in the country knew exactly how much everyone else gave, so that, even as everyone quietly complained, they wound up competing to see who could donate most. A few months later the president held a private ceremony in which he pinned a silver pin on my lapel as a donor. He talked for a long time, praising or criticizing specific families by name. He knew exactly how much each family had donated. One family had been "stingy," he said, naming them and adding that they loved their dogs more than their country. Later, I found out that their assets had been confiscated and the couple, childless, was imprisoned.

The summer before I started eighth grade, a huge convoy of black Mercedes and police vehicles roared into the Airlines Neighborhood and parked under the basketball hoop in our cul-de-sac on an otherwise quiet Friday, the Muslim day of rest.

In Baghdad, people often drop by to visit in late afternoons—not between the hours of one and four, because that is a time for meals and naps—but later on, for tea or coffee. It was apparently in that tradition that the president decided to drop in on us for a surprise visit. My parents were playing backgammon at the time, and they jumped up as soon as they heard all the noise outside. It was Radya's day off, so Mama nervously sent me into the kitchen to make coffee while she and my father answered the door and invited the president into the parlor. I peeked outside as the water was boiling and was overwhelmed at the sheer military power I saw through the grill on the kitchen window. The cul-de-sac was filled with automobiles and men in uniforms and guns and black mustaches.

I got out our special pot for Turkish coffee and set three little gold-embossed cups and saucers on my grandmother's engraved silver tray from Iran—a political faux pas I would have known better than to commit even a year or two later. I prided myself on knowing how to make Turkish coffee even though I was too young to drink it. I carefully measured every ingredient and made certain to take the coffee off the heat at exactly the right moment so there would be froth on top. No froth meant mediocre coffee and a neglectful hostess.

Then I nervously carried my tray into the parlor. My parents were seated together on the small sofa. Saddam Hussein was seated alone on the big sofa, with one arm draped casually over the back and the other resting near the gun at his waist. I immediately knew by the way they spoke that they were more than just acquaintances; they knew one another well. He looked very much at home in our house—more so at the moment than my father did. Baba was smiling and trying to look relaxed, but I could see he was nervous as well. I set the tray down very carefully, focusing on the cups to make sure nothing spilled.

"And here is our Zainab," Baba said, his face lighting up when I walked in. My father's love for me could feel like sunshine. I remember feeling it in particular that day. I could see how proud he was to present his daughter to the president of Iraq.

"Ah, so this is Zanooba!" the president said, as if he'd been hearing about me for years.

I was instructed to call him Amo, just Amo, as my parents did. Later, Mama told me this was a kind of a code name he had asked his friends to call him.

"Good afternoon, Amo," I said politely. I smiled and leaned down to kiss him three times, as Iraqis do in greeting, once on one cheek, then on the other, then back to the first cheek again. He had surprisingly soft cheeks, as if he had recently shaved, and he smelled of cologne. He gave me a beautiful smile, a wide smile with very white, even teeth. When he picked up the cup, I noticed a small tribal tattoo on his hand.

After serving the coffee, I smiled and politely left the room as was expected of me. Then I went back to the kitchen to look through the window to count how many more people were outside that I was supposed to make coffee for, and counted tens of guards standing in the cul-de-sac. I recognized one of them. It was Uncle

Arshad, Aunt Nawal's husband, and Aunt Nawal was Amo's sister. I knew them. I had even been to their house a few times. How had my parents gotten to know Amo, and why hadn't they ever talked about him before? I carried the biggest tray of coffee cups outside I could manage, only to learn guards couldn't drink anything while on duty. At the far end of the street, I noticed the entry to our neighborhood had been blocked off, and there was some sort of disturbance. It turned out that the entire neighborhood had been cordoned off as a security measure for this visit, but a teenaged neighbor was unaware of the blockade and had been arrested for trying to get to his house after curfew. Mama told me later what had happened when the security guard came in to tell the president about him.

"What would you like us to do with him, sir?" the guard had asked.

"He's just a kid, he lives down the street," Baba said. "Don't worry about him."

"Should we put him in jail just to scare him?" the guard persisted. "He was arguing with us."

Amo decided to take my father's recommendation and let the boy go, which spared him and his family the terror of a prison stay. Because my father was a friend of Amo's, he was allowed to intervene to help the boy. Of course, if he hadn't been a friend of Amo's, the boy wouldn't have been in danger of arrest in the first place. Friendship and fear went hand in hand.

After Amo left, I went into the parlor to clear the dishes. I was all alone, and I saw Saddam Hussein's cup—Amo's cup—sitting there. I remembered Mama and her friend Shaima reading coffee grounds, and I went over and picked up his cup and swirled the last bit of liquid around in it as they did. Then I flipped it over onto the saucer to see if I could make out any shapes in the coffee grounds that could foretell the future. A bird meant someone would bring you news. A fish meant you were about to get money. But all I could see in Amo's saucer was grounds.

From Alia's Notebook

I told you this story when you were little, remember?

We first met him in 1972. We were a group of friends, mostly young married couples, having a night river party on the Tigris River. We had rented a big boat with a band and we were dancing and laughing the whole night. There was nothing on our minds except having a good time. Suddenly, one of our friends ordered the boat driver to stop by an island known as the Pig's Island. We thought that we would start a barbecue there and continue our dancing.

But, when we stepped onto the sand, we were surprised to see a young man waiting there to greet us. He was wearing a white outfit. His suit, his shoes, everything was white. He was practically shining under the moonlight. We kept turning around and asking each other. Who is this man? Why is he here? Behind him were two other men who declared that he was Saddam Hussein. Saddam Hussein? Who is Saddam Hussein? We looked around at each other again, but none of us knew him. I was the one who finally asked the question out loud, "And who is Saddam Hussein?" One of the two men behind him answered that he was the vice president of Iraq. But we did not know him because we had no interest in politics.

He started shaking our hands one by one and invited us for drinks that were brought within seconds of his command from boats that had surrounded the island. He had a very charming personality that made an impression on anybody who met him. We end up having a nice time that night. He always makes sure to spend some time with each couple to get to know them on their own and part of his strategy is to start first on couples where the wife is particularly beautiful. He danced with all the blonds in the group. He drank a lot and filled the place with Champagne bottles.

Telephone calls among our friends filled the next day. Everyone was asking about him, who invited him, how he knew about us, what he wanted, etc. It turned out that one of our friends on the boat that night, Mahmood, was his dear friend. Saddam's arrival at our party was apparently in response to a request he had made to Mahmood: Would you please introduce me to the young elite of society?

4

❖

THE PILOT'S DAUGHTER

MY FATHER WAS THE CAPTAIN of Boeing 747s, then the largest commercial airliners on earth. The jets he flew were enormous shining planes with "IRAQI AIRLINES" written in green and white on the side. When we flew with him when I was little, the flight staff treated me like a princess. I would climb up the spiral staircase to the first-class lounge on the upper floor, and a stewardess would bring me an orange Fanta, and tell me how lucky I was to have a father like Captain Basil. I could see they weren't just trying to be nice. They liked him, they looked up to him, and I was sure everybody knew he was the best airline pilot in Iraq.

When I was allowed to step inside his cockpit, I was able to glimpse the world as he saw it, and I understood why he felt compelled to leave us so often. Here, high above the earth, the sky itself was round, and it was the color of the inside of a sapphire. There were no streets or boundaries. There was no nationality. We were in a free space between heaven and earth. When I saw Baba's face as he was flying, I knew this was where he belonged. Surrounded by hundreds of buttons and switches and lights and dials that would terrify most people, he was completely relaxed, master of this incredibly complicated universe. When I heard his voice on the speaker system welcoming passengers aboard, I knew hundreds of people trusted him with their lives.

"I want to be a pilot like you when I grow up, Baba," I told him once from my small seat behind his copilot.

"Then I'll have to teach you to fly someday," he said, and he took off his captain's hat with all the gold braid, turned around, and put it on my head.

Early in 1982, I began to feel tensions rise again in our home as the background sounds of our household changed. Mama stopped singing, there was no roll of backgammon dice—backgammon was a skill she considered one of the secrets to a happy marriage—and the nervous whispers were back. When Baba and Mama called a family meeting, I was afraid they were going to tell us there was another wave of deportations. Instead, they announced that Baba was getting a promotion: he was going to be the pilot of the President of Iraq. He didn't sound happy about it.

"This is not something that should be talked about outside the family," Baba said sternly. "This is not something you should brag about to your friends. This is not something that should go to your heads."

My parents were always telling us not to let things go to our heads, to be thankful for what we had, but never to brag or show off.

The best part of Baba's new job for all of us was that we were going to go to Seattle that summer to pick up a new plane for the president. We loved Seattle. We had spent several summers there when my father was attending his pilot training classes, but hadn't been able to go the year before because a foreign travel ban had been imposed as a result of the war with Iran. That summer of 1982—the last time we would go together as a family, as it turned out—was the best of all. My father was allowed to select his own presidential flight crew, and some of them brought their families, so there was a group of about fifteen of us who got to know one another well. We had picnics and barbecues together, with sparkling Puget Sound sunsets behind us. The adults made up slightly raunchy beer songs that made them double over laughing.

We spent our days sightseeing or going to the beach or shopping. We always took advantage of our summer vacations to buy clothing and whatever else we needed for the foreseeable future, because selection was limited in Iraq. My mother rented a car, and she and I and Amel, the wife of the flight engineer, went shopping together. Amel was blond and blue-eyed and talked baby talk, which I couldn't stand even then in grown women. But her husband, Amo Qusai, was one of my favorite people on the trip. A big macho bear-hug kind of man who wore his heart on his sleeve, he was madly in love with her and their little daughter and never stopped showing it. They had met when they were both in high school, and he talked about how for years he had been too shy to approach her. They were from a lower-middle-class family, and they had struggled to build a life together. This promotion was a major step forward for them, and I could see how indebted Amo Qusai felt to Baba for getting him this job.

Amel didn't know how to drive and had never been abroad before, so Mama kind of adopted her and brought her along on some of our shopping trips, translating for her and introducing her to American products. We wandered through the American department stores, buying more dresses for me than I ever thought I could wear, putting makeup on Amel, and getting clothes for my brothers. We spent a long time in one lingerie department, where Amel bought lots of lacy lingerie to bring home as a present for her sister, while I took Hassan's hand and tracked down the old lady boxer underwear that was the only thing Bibi ever asked us to bring us back except for tea rose perfume. One day we went to the Ethan Allen store to buy new furniture for the living room and parlor, and the saleslady asked how we would get it back to Iraq.

"Don't worry about shipping, we have a plane," Mama answered. She was trying to sound suave, but she couldn't quite pull it off. She turned to me, burst into giggles, and started clapping with excitement.

We didn't just have a plane. We had a brand new 747 jumbo jet. There were only four families on it when we headed back to Iraq. My father gave us a quick tour before we took off. The interior was amazing. The floor was covered in a green-and-white carpet with presidential emblems. There were separate rooms, all with ultramodern furniture: a bedroom with a huge bed, a conference room and office, a bathroom with a shower at the rear. I had never seen such a plane before. As we came in for a landing in Baghdad, I could see the huge new airport, one of the most modern buildings in Iraq, with its arched white ceilings I knew were hung inside with thousands of candle-like lights. All over the country, buildings and institutions were being renamed for Saddam Hussein—Saddam's Children's Hospital, Saddam's Theater, Saddam's Elementary School, Saddam's High School, even Saddam's City. Our airport was no longer Baghdad International. It was Saddam Hussein International Airport, and Saddam Hussein was there to meet us when we touched down.

If I were to place a marker on the moment our freedom vanished, it would probably be when that heavy jet door swung open and the hot desert air of Iraq rushed into the pressurized compartment. I watched my father step out of the cockpit and saw his expression change when hard-faced security guards with black mustaches entered in their pressed khaki uniforms with berets and guns. The happy-go-lucky look I had gotten used to in Seattle vanished and was replaced by nervous attentiveness. Saddam Hussein was coming to inspect the plane my father had helped design, negotiate the purchase of, test, and accept delivery of, the plane he had flown home. We had been instructed to remain in our seats while my father gave Amo a tour of his new acquisition, which he had named the *Al Qadisiya,* after his favorite battle against the Persians. When Baba led him down the aisle and introduced him to crew and family members he hadn't yet met, Saddam stopped to tousle my hair and say warmly, as if he really knew me, "Hello, Zanooba!" Then he looked on to the next row, and Baba introduced him to Amel.

"Ah, now this is true beauty, isn't it?" he said, looking at her and then around at the rest of us for confirmation.

Amo was pleased with the plane.

My brothers and I were grafted onto Amo's life the following year the way Baba grafted new branches onto his citrus trees: we would grow, but there would always be a scar at the joint. We would reach for the sky, mistaking our angle of vision for freedom. Then something would happen, and we would have only to look down to remember that it was an illusion, that we were not free at all, not for a minute. Our parents had known this all along, and that is why Baba never wanted to be the president's pilot.

Amo apparently wanted us to move into a house on palace grounds, but Mama said Baba used the distance from my school as a reason for us to stay in our home. None of us wanted to move, and Amo gave us a weekend farmhouse instead. Interior decorating was one of Mama's many talents, and she set about furnishing the farmhouse; she wanted to surprise us. Baba often brought her back bolts of cloth from his travels, which she kept all over the house, in various stages of progress. She was always sewing clothes or beading something or recovering cushions. Not one for patterns, she would unfold the new cloth along the designated sofa or chair and just start cutting. Or she would drape the new fabric on me and snip away, and somehow the vision in her mind would take shape on me. It was part of her magic. Then she would put a book on my head and instruct me to walk like a model in my pinned-together couture. "Always stand tall with your head raised high," she said. "Don't be shy and weak. I hate weak women. You need to be strong and confident."

Before we went to the farmhouse the first time, Baba and Mama sat all three of us down for another family meeting.

"You may see the president from time to time when we're at the farmhouse," he said. "You will call him Amo if you see him, just as we do, and you will behave as your normal polite selves. But you are never to say a word about him to anyone else. You are never to talk about how often we see him, *if* we see him at all. Not to anyone. Not even to your cousins."

Haider and I looking at each other nervously and wondered what we were in for.

"Understood?"

He looked at each of us. We each solemnly promised Baba we would do as he asked, and he seemed satisfied that we understood the seriousness of our commitment. It was a promise not only to him, but to one another. I would never violate that promise, and as far as I knew, no one else would either—even little Hassan, sitting on my lap, who was only three. Hassan had barely learned to speak, and already there were things he was being told he could not say.

Mama was excited when she took us to the farmhouse for the first time, which to the best of my recollection was shortly before I turned fourteen. It was on the airport road, and to get there we had to pass my favorite statue in Baghdad, of Abbas Ibn Fernas, our counterpart of the Grecian Icarus, who Mama told me gave human beings the idea they could fly. Abbas Ibn Fernas had been a prisoner trapped behind enormous walls, and the walls around him were so high that there was no way to escape, and he longed to be a bird so he could fly over them and escape. He began collecting feathers that fell from birds overhead and finally managed to collect enough to make himself wings. But he could not fly high enough to escape his prison when he tried, and he fell back to his death. Every time we drove by, I looked up at that statue and tried to imagine what it would feel like to be a bird with wings flapping quietly, surely, around me, and pillows of air under my arms.

A long wall lined the airport road that I had never thought about much before. Behind it was Amo's farmhouse compound. We turned into a security gate in the wall and were signaled through. We drove a short distance and stopped in front of one of three houses sitting all by themselves on a vast stretch of empty, scrub-brushy desert with a small irrigation ditch running through it. I had expected a farmhouse, something small and rustic that maybe had animals we could ride. Uncle Adel's farmhouse had gazelles, birds, sheep, cows, even a monkey. Not ours—this wasn't a farmhouse at all, I thought as we parked, it was a regular house, only surrounded by walls. When we walked inside with our overnight bags, I remember trying hard to be enthusiastic for Mama's sake, but I hated it. She had done her best to make everything look just right. She had bought new furniture downtown and upholstered it with bright fabrics. There were new dishes, a new TV set, Superman bedspreads in my brothers' room and a flowery one in mine. But, despite all her work, it felt sterile and lifeless—a little like a model home looking for buyers. I put my bag down in the closet in my new bedroom and saw that Mama had already hung up some of the new dresses I had gotten in Seattle. Where was I supposed to wear these at a farm? What were we going to do here for two whole days? Mama came in and cheerfully told me to get dressed up because we were going to meet our new neighbors. I did as she asked and walked out in a new dress and fancy shoes. There were only two neighbors to call on.

I would spend dozens, perhaps hundreds, of weekends at that farmhouse, but I absolutely cannot recall what it looked like from the outside. I only know that it was nothing like the neighbors'. The other two houses were surrounded by lush gardens that had obviously been professionally designed and maintained. These were substantial, rambling homes of red brick that looked as if they belonged in magazine layouts of desert resorts or dude ranches. They had been built by palace architects and decorated by palace decorators with lavish Italian imports. Shiny new black Mercedes were parked outside both.

A couple named Aunt Nada and Uncle Kais lived in the slightly more luxurious of the other two houses. Uncle Kais was an active Baath Party member, a man obviously accustomed to wielding influence, who seemed very rigid and aloof, at least to me. His wife was elegant and proper, the sort of woman who not only follows etiquette, but believes in it. The other couple, Aunt Layla and Uncle Mazan, were professionals who seemed more accessible and less judgmental to me, as well as less interested in politics. I had met Aunt Layla before but I didn't know her well. She was tall and gracious, far more spontaneous than Aunt Nada, and it was clear that she and Mama were close. When I saw the three women together, I was struck by how beautiful they all were. Aunt Nada and Aunt Layla were fair-haired with light eyes, and Mama was the dark-haired exception people often said looked like Sophia Loren. I was also struck by the fact that the three of them obviously knew one another well.

Between them, Aunt Nada and Aunt Layla had three daughters who were roughly my age, and these were my designated new friends. Each was beautiful and stylishly dressed. Luma was the oldest, the perfect daughter at sixteen, a vision of her mother, Aunt Nada. Her long chestnut hair was perfectly styled and sprayed. When she smiled, it was with thin lips pressed together. Following in her mother's footsteps, she had exquisitely manicured hands, and she seemed very aware of them as she spoke, gesturing with a practiced femininity. Following in her father's footsteps, she held herself stiffly and was active in the student Baath Party. I was between Luma and her younger sister, Sarah, in age. Sarah was already gorgeous and clearly knew it. She had golden brown hair, huge almond-shaped eyes, a small nose, and a beautiful mouth. Whereas Luma was proper, Sarah seemed like the younger and more daring sister who deep down inside wanted to wear her skirts short and dance all night. She was also a good Baathist, that was clear, but she seemed to have a mind of her own. More beautiful still was Tamara, Aunt Layla's daughter, whom I came to refer to with my mother as Brooke Shields. Tall, light-skinned, European in manner, she had lived for a while with an aunt in England and punctuated her Arabic with perfectly accented English words. She was the most fashionable of all, the one who turned heads. Dressed in designer-label clothing, she seemed more interested in what was trendy than what was proper, more attuned to Europe than to Iraq. Tamara lacked the air of entitlement the other two girls wrapped themselves in. Or, at the very least, she seemed less interested in flaunting it.

How would they have described me? Perhaps as a quiet girl with dark curly hair like her mother, someone who didn't pay enough attention to her appearance, someone suited to stand in the background, but not quite in their class. They traveled in the right circles. I didn't. They lived at the palace. I didn't. Luma and Sarah were best friends with Amo's daughters, and Tamara knew them too. I hadn't even met Amo's daughters. The difference in our status was clear. With every word they said, I was meant to understand that, like my parents, like our farmhouse, I was third. Only much later did I comprehend that what had brought us together was exactly the same as what divided us: our parents had met Amo the same night at a place called Pig's Island; only their parents had welcomed his friendship while mine had resisted it.

It is hard now for me to distinguish that first weekend from the ones that followed—they were all so much the same. I can't remember for certain if I even saw Amo the first time we went. He typically dropped by late in the afternoon for drinks with the adults at one of the other two houses. Sometimes weekends would go by and we would wait, all dressed up, and not see him at all. We would be instructed to sit and talk quietly in an adjacent room until and if we were summoned. Then we would go inside, welcome him with enthusiastic kisses and greetings, and array ourselves around as he convened what we referred to as our "family gatherings," though none of us were part of his family and his own family members never joined us.

"*Shlounkum ya halween,*" Amo would say to us children, taking Hassan or one of the other little kids onto his knee. "How are you doing, beautiful ones?"

"Very well, Amo, we are doing very well!" we would chorus.

A few steps behind him, always, stood his personal guard Abed, a man with intensely focused eyes and lips pressed tight under his bushy black mustache, who went with Amo everywhere. Of all the hours I spent in his presence, I don't remember once hearing Abed laugh or even speak, except into Amo's ear. I never saw his beret off his head—it was forbidden for Iraqi soldiers to wear military berets tucked through shoulder straps on their uniforms allegedly because Israeli soldiers wore them that way—and I was surprised when Abed was arrested on charges of war crimes in 2003 and turned out to be partially bald.

There was nothing natural about the way we sat or spoke at our "family gatherings." We remained perfectly still, actors in a scene that I understood even then was about the ideal family Amo had never had growing up poor in rural Tikrit. Later, historians would debate the facts, but portray Saddam Hussein as the offspring of a father who vanished from his life, a mother who married a man who abused him, and an uncle who filled him with dreams of military glory. Even my little brother, who was always so full of energy, knew better than to squirm or interrupt when we were with Amo. The other girls and I were the perfect image of young Iraqi women—utterly polite, immaculately dressed, and attentive to his every word. We were highly aware that anything we did wrong, even a wrong inflection, a hint of anything *ayeb,* would reflect on our parents.

Amo was the only one who seemed relaxed. Fastidiously groomed and impeccably aware of every person and every movement around him, he had an enormous charisma that is hard to convey if you never met him in person. I can think of no neutral adjectives for him. In these settings, he was compelling, not just affable, charming rather than nice. Maybe, like the best politicians, he just had that knack for making people, including children, feel they were being singled out for special attention. When he looked at you, it was as if he were really listening. It took me a while to realize that when he gave you his most affectionate, lingering smile, he was using that time to look behind your eyes.

My very first survival skills were manners, and I learned what I didn't know already by taking cues from my mother. When you were with Amo, you were always polite and pleasant. You had no opinions or personal preferences except those that matched his own. There was nothing you'd rather do than spend time with him. You listened to him with rapt attention, always. If you were a child, you never spoke in his company unless he asked you a direct question, and you always arranged your face to look up at him in adoration. If he showed you something new he had gotten and said, "Isn't it nice?" you would answer, "Oh, yes, Amo, it is ver-rrrrrry nice!"

Always, always, you would smile. With my mother, the only person I could ever talk to about Amo with any honesty at all, I called it my "plastic smile." Without her constant reminders, I'm not sure I ever would have been able to put it on as I did. Sometimes today when I'm talking in public, people compliment me on my smile, and I wonder how much of it is really mine. There is a certain way the muscles in my mouth feel sometimes when I smile before an audience that takes me back to that farmhouse, when I knew a smile wasn't enough; I had to stretch those muscles so as to *beam*.

Weekends were Amo's designated downtime, and we were his entertainment. Part of our job was to make him laugh at the right moment. I can still imitate Amo's laugh. He would tuck his chin slightly under and let out a deep-throated, guttural *heh . . . heh . . . heh*. If it had been a little higher-pitched or a little more spontaneous, you might have been inclined to call it a chuckle, but it had a kind of sinister undertone, like the bad guy character that always chased the good guy characters in a cartoon. When he laughed, we laughed, and every now and then I had this feeling the other girls and I, particularly Sarah, were secretly laughing at his laughter. I never felt free enough to talk to them about this, but I have a feeling they would know what I mean even today.

What I remember most from these gatherings, actually, is my parents' faces. Both of them looked nervous and helpless to me, and I understood immediately why they were so determined that we never mention Amo's name or describe ourselves as his friends. All of these adults were "friends," but I knew this wasn't the way they behaved with their *real* friends. I remember all the adults looking at Amo far more than they ever looked at the person sitting closest to them, and there were subtle—sometimes not so subtle—jibes at each other as they jockeyed for Amo's approval. In time, I came to see that each adult had a specific role to play. My father was the straight man, Uncle Mazan the joker, and Uncle Kais the parliamentarian. Aunt Layla was the spontaneous one, Aunt Nada the proper one, and Mama the ebullient one whose job it was to lighten these proceedings with laughter. Mama's eyes would fill up when she laughed for real, and the muscles in her face would tense when it was forced. Mostly, in these gatherings, it was the latter, but sometimes she would just laugh because she couldn't help herself, and she would laugh more loudly than what the culture proscribed for women. "Good God, get a grip on yourself, woman!" Uncle Kais would say, rebuking her. Yet I could see that Amo liked my mother's laugh just as he approved Uncle Kais's criticism of it, the director able to relax because each of his players knew their roles so well.

I used to wonder sometimes whether Amo had other sets of friends like this one, which he would group and regroup in repertory over the years. Only he knows the real reasons he pursued a relationship with my parents. I know that if he wanted to become a world leader, and that is what he clearly planned and craved, even when he was still a rural tribesman on his way up the military-political ladder, he needed validation by the educated opinion-setters of Baghdad, including people of money and social influence. He also needed to understand Western culture, which was second nature to my parents and their set of friends. There were other people in Baghdad who were wealthier and more powerful. But I suspect many such people—Basma's father, for example—had political opinions or ambitions of their own that presented a threat to Amo's authority. My parents were naïve to the point of ignorance about politics, a lesson in the danger of civic apathy, and presented no challenge to his career or security risk to his life. But whatever other reasons he had for seeking their friendship, I believe he genuinely liked Basil and Alia, as many people did. Otherwise, he wouldn't have kept them around. He might not have let them live.

There were times in our gatherings when Amo would get very emotional, and we were expected to show our sympathy for his sadness when we saw tears in his eyes. Usually this happened when he was talking about his love of Iraq. He practiced some of his speeches on my parents and the other adults, and when they were broadcast, Mama would look up at the television from her sketch-pad or her knitting and say, "Okay, here comes the part where he's going to cry."

I loved my mother. I wish I could talk with her now.

Unless something else was planned for us or there was a good reason—a school graduation, a funeral, or a trip out of Baghdad—I would generally be expected to spend my teenaged weekends—nearly six years of weekends—at the farmhouse. Except for talking to the other girls, usually about fashion, there was almost nothing to do and nowhere to go. There were two television stations in Baghdad, one of them a Farsi-language station run by government-authorized Iranian dissidents. The Arabic language station showed only Japanese cartoons, Egyptian films and soap operas, *Dynasty*, and hours and hours of Amo's speeches before the Revolutionary Council or his generals or at other events. One afternoon, we were watching an Egyptian movie on television at the farmhouse, and the TV went dead, then switched to another show in the middle of a kissing scene. It turned out that Baba had been with Amo when that movie was on, and Amo had called up the director of Iraqi television and ordered him to stop it because it was exposing Iraqi youth to immoral trash. My cousins would have laughed at stories like this, but it never would have occurred to me to tell them. I missed my cousins desperately. I missed just hanging out and feeling normal. Haider, for whom no playmates were available, would lock himself in his room with his video games and slowly isolate himself from everyone except my father, who, I suspect, understood. I began to think of the farmhouse as my prison, and my escape was reading. I started with the longest book I could find, *Gone with the Wind*, and kept on reading through all the familiar themes: cousins killing cousins in war, widows asked to donate wedding rings, dark-skinned people destined to live in poverty while white-skinned people danced and pretended not to see.

The adults, particularly the men, spent far more time with Amo than with us children. There is an odd picture somewhere of Baba and other men in Bavarian-style tweed hats with little feathers in them bicycling behind Amo on compound grounds with security guards all lined up on bicycles behind them. Amo always changed outfits to match the activity he had planned. At the farmhouse, he favored blue denim overalls, a red-and-white checked shirt with a bandanna tied around his neck, and an occasional cowboy hat. The fathers were expected to be farmers. Each had a plot of land in front of his farmhouse, and by the time we arrived, Uncle Kais and Uncle Mazan already had groves of established trees—olives, I think—in back of their houses that I believe were tended by the compound staff. Baba hired two farmhands of his own and a small tractor, and together they plowed the empty desert land and planted row after row of knee-high olive saplings. He always liked gardening and had actually bought a small farm a few years earlier and registered it in my name as a gift. But when we got the farmhouse, the real farm was abandoned. Over the next few years, I watched Baba's new olive trees slowly wither and die. I'm not sure what happened. Perhaps the small irrigation ditch that went to his patch of desert didn't deliver enough water to allow them to live. Perhaps he was away too often to tend them—or just gave up trying. I'm not sure. After a while, I couldn't always tell the difference between the people my parents were and the people Amo was making them pretend to be.

Perhaps half a kilometer away from our three farmhouses was the inner wall that encircled, hid, and protected Amo's farmhouse. Inside that wall was the iris that defined the eye. The men went there often, and the three women did occasionally as well, but it would be three years before that eye opened to me. I have exactly one photograph taken at the farmhouse. It happens to be of me. In it I am standing slightly off balance in dressy pants and a shirt, on the water pipe bridging the open canal ditch. I spent countless hours at that spot, and I can turn my mind's eye even now like a remote-controlled camera and see in each direction. Below me, beneath my dangling feet, were white ducks that liked to congregate in the water under the pipe. Ahead of me, across a small expanse of empty desert, was the high, impenetrable inner wall that encircled Amo's compound. Right behind me, abutting the outer compound wall and facing it in obeisant imitation, were our farmhouses. Those two walls defined our margin for error, the space in which we were allowed to live. There was a ten-minute walk between one set of guards that kept me in and a second set of guards who, had I dared approach them, would have kept me out. I sat on the bank of the canal and listened to the ducks and learned to quack with them. I thought of them as silent allies I could complain to who would never tell on me. *Quack, quack, quack,* I went. *Quack, quack, quack.*

One morning I noticed that Mama's Abbasid coin was missing from her neck. I asked her where it was.

"I gave it to Amo," she said.

I was stunned.

"Why, Mama?" I demanded. "Why?"

It had never occurred to me to tell her how much that coin meant to me. It was virtually my first memory of her, and I had assumed I would wear the coin when I grew up and some of her beauty and grace would rub off on me. It was part of her.

"It was his birthday," she said, looking down. "I had to give him something important."

Important? How could Mama's coin possibly be *important* to Amo? He had everything he could ever want. People stood in line to give him gifts he would never, ever use, let alone say thank you for. He could snap his fingers and get literally any *thing* on earth he could ever wish for. Why did he need the one physical object that probably mattered the most to me—the essence of my mother? Why had she *given* it to him?

"But, why your Abbasid coin, Mama?" I asked.

"Because I needed to give him something special, and that was the most special thing I could think of," she said awkwardly. "I did what I had to do."

I let the subject go. I had brought on the abashed look she wore sometimes with Amo, and the only thing I hated more than seeing her helplessness was seeing her embarrassed by it in front of me.

When television covered Amo's birthday live that night, we watched at home as hundreds of children sang to him. All of a sudden, it struck me as silly and stupid. Here he was, the president, all dressed up in a white suit, white socks, and white shoes sitting on a gold chair like a throne with a great big smile waiting to blow out his candles.

"He looks so childish!" I said. "He's acting more like a child than an adult."

I had said it without thinking.

"*Never* say that!" my father reprimanded me. "Don't you dare, ever, to say anything like that again!"

Baba's voice was loud and sharp, and his expression changed with an instantaneous snap, like a pilot throwing an emergency switch. I wasn't used to him speaking to me that way, and it hurt. But I got the message: I was never to criticize Amo, even in my own home, and never to question anything he said or did.

Later, my mother came to me and soothed my hurt feelings.

"You have to be careful, honey. The walls have ears," she said, consoling me. "If you really need to say anything sensitive, it is best to go into the garden."

She made me think of Radya and Abu Traib, and I got this picture in my mind's eye of the walls around me insulated with live human ears. After that day, whenever I slipped and forgot, I would look around at the houseplants or the pictures on the wall or at my mother's furniture and hope they hadn't heard me. It was as if ordinary things we had brought into our house could turn on us or remember that Amo had been here. I had seen him at our home only once, but he had a capacity unlike any other person I have ever known to leave something of himself behind in physical space after he left it. During the course of an average day, I could sense it, on the sofa where he had sat in our parlor, in the smell of afternoon coffee, even in the way our neighbors looked at us. It had taken up residence inside our home, and only later was I able to identify it. It was fear, incarnate.

Once I knew the "farmhouse crowd," as I came to think of them, I occasionally accompanied my mother to visit Aunt Nada or Aunt Layla at their homes in the main palace compound in Baghdad. I was upstairs in Tamara's room one evening, sitting on the floor with clothes spread out all around us, picking out outfits, when we heard Amo's voice downstairs. We hadn't even known he was in the house. Aunt Nada and Aunt Layla were downstairs, and I could tell that he had surprised them too. He was talking loudly, in a voice I had never heard before. He was very angry, and I could almost feel the silence around his anger get very strong and stiff. Tamara and I both knew it was strictly forbidden for us to hear anything like this; this was way at the top of the scale of those things that were supposed to go in one ear and out the other. We started picking up clothes and talking about outfits and pretending to each other that we weren't really hearing what was going on downstairs, or maybe thinking that if we could just keep talking it would go away or somehow wouldn't count.

But Amo's voice got louder. I heard him say a name, Samira, and his tone was as sharp as a butcher knife.

"Jurba!" he shouted, and his voice rang out through the house.

It was an ugly word, an angry, crude street epithet for a foreigner that means something dark-skinned and ugly. It was reserved for women, and I suddenly knew that it was my mama he was screaming at. Tamara knew it too. She stopped pretending and stared back at me. I will never forget the look on her face, her fear validating my own. Then, abruptly, the yelling stopped, and there was this awful silence. We tiptoed over to the edge of the stairs, and I breathed again when I heard my mother's voice. Amo was gone, but I could feel the cold afraidness he had left behind. Looking down below from the landing upstairs, I saw Aunt Layla put her arms around Mama and try to comfort her. They didn't see us.

"Zainab, come down please, your mother's leaving," Aunt Nada called up at us, trying to sound normal.

Tamara and I walked down the stairs trying to pretend we hadn't heard a thing. My mother's face was bright red, and her eyes were brimming with tears. She couldn't hide how upset she was, but she didn't break down until after we had driven through the palace checkpoint. Then she began sobbing as she held onto the steering wheel and I tried to comfort her from the passenger seat. My father was away, and she was so upset that for once I don't think she held very much back. Amo was mad at her because of Samira, she said, as my mind raced to make sense of this. Amel's sister? The one she had bought the lingerie for in Seattle?

Mama said Samira was Amo's girlfriend now, and Amo wanted us all to be friends. But my parents couldn't stand Samira. She was different from her sister, and they didn't want to see her. Samira had apparently said something very mean to Baba. Though Mama wouldn't tell me what it was, it must have been terrible because Amo had sent Samira to our house to apologize. Baba was so stubborn, Mama told me, that he would not go to the door. He refused to allow Samira to step foot inside our house, so Mama had to stand on our front porch and fail to invite Amo's girlfriend inside. Not inviting a guest into one's home was one of the worst examples of *ayeb* for Iraqis, who pride themselves on their hospitality, and that's why Amo was mad at Mama. She had taken the blame for Baba. If Amo had yelled at Mama like that, what would he have done to a man? Still, I wondered, couldn't Baba have set aside his pride and accepted the apology instead of risking Mama's life and flying off?

I listened to Mama that night like the best friend she needed. I was just grateful she was alive as I comforted her and kissed her good night when we got home. But my feelings were all mixed up. I felt more like her mother than her child, and a small voice inside me said I wasn't ready for this. I had wanted to be an adult so I could understand what was going on. But now that I was beginning to understand, part of me wanted to go back. It wasn't right for Mama to tell me what she had about Baba. He was my father, and I was his child.

I never talked about that night with Mama again, and I never talked with Baba about it at all. I just buried it somewhere deep in my brain.

The telephone rang one day when we were getting ready for school. We were in the kitchen, and Mama and Radya were making sandwiches for our school snack. Baba answered the phone, and I looked up when I saw him say, "No, no, no!" We all stopped and looked at him. When he hung up, tears were streaming down his face.

"Qusai is dead," he said, staring at Mama.

"What happened?" Mama asked.

"He got into a car accident when he was driving home from the airport," he said. "They say he probably hadn't slept all night and fell asleep at the wheel."

Mama looked at him and went pale, and I caught a meaningful glance between them.

"They say a truck hit him," Baba said. "Hit-and-run. They just found his body. They say they'll never know who did it."

And he left the kitchen. I wasn't used to seeing Baba cry, and I could see the agony on his face. Amo Qusai was not only a crew member, he was his friend as well.

I couldn't focus on school that day. I kept replaying that

conversation in my mind, and it was all I could do to hold back tears. I remembered Amo Qusai with Amel in Seattle and how happy they were. How could he be dead, just like that, on a road he knew so well? *They say* it was an accident, Baba had said. *They say* a truck hit him. Baba didn't believe it was an accident, and from the horror on Mama's face, I didn't think Mama did either. I asked to be excused and went into the school bathroom. I hated the bathroom in this school and tried to avoid it. It was always dirty. It always smelled bad. But it was the only place I could be alone, and I went inside and cried and cried, staring at the gray, mirrorless walls. What had really happened to Amo Qusai? Had he been killed? Was an "accident" even possible anymore in Baghdad anymore?

When I went home that day, I asked Mama to go out into the garden with me.

"How is Baba doing?" I asked her.

"He'll be all right," she said. "He's going to the funeral. I'll go over and give my condolences to Amel in a bit. She's pretty devastated. I heard she locked herself in a room and isn't speaking to anyone."

"Mama, was Amo Qusai killed, or was it really an accident?"

She looked at me as if assessing how much to tell me.

"We may never know, honey," she said softly. "Amo wanted to be friends with him, and I think Qusai didn't want to be friends."

"So he could get killed for that?"

"Zainab, I don't know," she said. "Sometimes there is nothing we can do, so it is better not to think about it. Just try to forget about this, okay? It doesn't concern you."

Of course it concerned me. Was that why Mama and Baba always looked so nervous around Amo? Because they could get killed if they didn't want to be friends with him anymore?

From Alia's Notebook

In the early years before he was president, he sometimes invited us to the Racing Club, where he would also bring his wife, Sajida, who was not particularly a social person. But most of the times we saw him, he was alone, or sometimes with a mistress.

Before Samira, there was Hana'a. He talked about Hana'a often. She was not only his friend, but the one he said who met all his desires and fantasies. In one of the evenings that we spent with him, he told us how he killed her. She had met another man, and Saddam got really jealous. He went to her home and killed her and her own mother, who was asleep in her bed. He killed them himself with his own gun, leaving Hana'a's three-year-old daughter screaming and crying that Uncle had killed her mother. The girl did not say anything else for a long period after that incident. But the case was closed with no investigation.

His friendship was not an easy one. He always made sure to talk to each friend separately and to befriend his wife as well. He never trusted any man until after he got to trust the wife. Then, he would talk about other friends in their absence. Through divide and conquer, he made sure that all the friends were suspicious of each other, but that they each thought he was their best friend. The games he played between friends to spread fear and suspicion among all of us, his nightly visits, his flirting with the wives, the inability to refuse him any request for it may cost one's life, among many other things led some to leave the country. The first of our friends to leave was Mahmood, who had introduced us to him in the first place. Mahmood was a wealthy man, but it wasn't easy for us to leave. We kept thinking that we could manage the relationship as long as we were careful.

In one of our evenings with him, he asked Bahir, a friend of ours who is a highly educated and well-read individual, about his opinion of Napoleon. Bahir innocently replied with a saying about what led to Napoleon's end was that he had no way to control his fast-moving courage. He described Napoleon as someone who never took others' opinions, who acted on his own opinion without thinking about repercussions. Saddam gave Bahir an *angry look and said, with a sharp voice, "What exactly do you mean, Bahir? Are you talking about Napoleon or someone else?" Bahir began sweating from his forehead and started swearing that he was only talking about Napoleon.*

Such an incident could not be taken lightly. We were all nervous for Bahir at that moment. There were no rules and regulations to the relationship with Saddam except that we must always please him.

5

✦

LEARNING TO CRY WITH DUCKS

I HAVE TRIED to identify a moment in which I first realized that the man I greeted with kisses on the hollows of his cheeks was a murderer, but I don't think there was one. My parents tried to protect me from knowledge of his specific crimes when I was young, and as with Amo Qusai's death, there was rarely proof. Our media was so controlled that I didn't learn of his strategic campaigns of ethnic and religious genocide until I left Iraq, though every Iraqi knew how dangerous he was, so that was never in question. I can't even remember fear as a first twinge; it was plain on my parents' faces from the day I met him. The overwhelming feeling I experienced was a deep, abiding vulnerability. Weeks would go by without incident. Sometimes, in what my mother used to call his "merciful moments," he would bestow gifts on us, like permission to travel abroad. But I came to understand that these moments would be followed by months of excruciating, often mystifying, punishment.

Why did they stay? That question haunts whole generations of people from around the world whose parents tolerated the rise of dictatorship. Now that I'm finally able to face the horror of those years I spent with Amo, the most rational answer I can think of in

our case was that my parents were trapped in an abusive relationship. I could never talk to them about this, but I spent countless
hours observing them as they struggled with the relationship, trying in their own ways to maintain some inner dignity and sense of
self in the face of the ultimate abusive master. Afraid of his brutality if they made a single misstep, even more afraid of his wrath if
they fled, they behaved as abused spouses do. They walked on
eggshells and did their best to survive.

They did talk about fleeing Iraq, especially when I was in my
early teens. I used to sit on the staircase late at night, staring at
the shattered shapes of black-and-white mosaic, trying to make
sense of painfully whispered arguments that were laden with
names I didn't know and a future that scared me no matter what
they decided. "I feel like a bird in cage," Mama kept saying. "Let's
get away, let's go to America! Mahmood got out—why can't we?"
Then Baba, the voice of logic, would say something like "You
know we can't just leave, Alia. This is our home. What would we
do? Where would we live? Do you think we can afford the same
lifestyle if we move? Do you want me to fly freight? Be practical,
Alia! Are you willing to live in a small apartment and struggle to
make ends meet? What about our family here? What do you think
will happen to them if we leave? You know how family members
get punished if someone leaves. Are you willing to take that risk?
They're watching everybody, especially me. Do you really think
they'd let me go?"

It scared me to hear Mama talk about being a bird in a cage,
but Iraq was my home. I loved Baghdad. I loved the sound of the
muezzin and the river gulls and all the familiar places of my childhood. I couldn't imagine leaving my cousins and all my relatives
and friends. There were too many good memories, despite Amo.
Hadn't we fought to be allowed to stay? Were we supposed to just
give up and leave him our country? What would happen to us if we
left? Would we have to leave our house behind and have all our belongings taken by the Mukhabarat? Where would I go to school?

I remember my parents arguing as they swung back and forth

between escape and the illusion of safety that came with submission. I don't remember any formal decision to stay; we just didn't leave. My father would fly away, and I would be left to watch my mother beat her wings against the bars around her, alternately trying to escape her cage and feather her nest. There were times I physically grabbed her wrists as she reached for pills in the medicine cabinet in our kitchen. "Stop, Mama," I would say. "You can't do that, Mama. You have got to stop." And I would do the best I could to shield my brothers from seeing her at those times. I would take her to her bedroom and we would hug each other until we fell asleep. I learned to will myself to sleep. Sleep was the easy way out, and there was always the hope that when I woke up, things would be different.

When I was entering high school and Baba was entering his third year as Amo's pilot, he and a copilot completed a record-setting flight across the globe. I still have a brittle, yellowed copy of Boeing's employee newspaper, *Boeing News,* headlined: "Iraqi Airways 747SP May delivery flight nears SAA record." The story says:

> *The delivery of a Boeing 747SP to South African Airways in April, 1976 is still the longest nonstop flight ever made by a commercial jetliner, but on May 20, an Iraqi Airways 747SP on a non-revenue flight came close. The Iraqi flight, from Tunis to Tokyo, covered 9.676 statute miles in 16½ hours, and is now considered in second place. The SAA flight lasted 17 hours 22 minutes and covered 10,259 statute miles from Seattle to Capetown, South Africa. The Iraqi flight was under the control of . . .*

They managed not only to make the flight without refueling, but to land with an hour's fuel to spare. It was the sort of thing that earned Baba the respect of other pilots. Yet he looked terrible when he returned. He stayed home from work and complained of heart palpitations. Other pilots and crew members gathered in our parlor, whispering with each other, reminding me of the family meetings my mother and her family had had when they were afraid they were going to be deported. Was I at risk of losing my father now too? I wanted to ask him what was wrong, but my father wasn't approachable in the same way Mama was. This clearly had to do with his work, but Baba never would talk to me about Amo. Mama kept avoiding my questions until one day she lost her temper and told me what was going on: Baba was under investigation because the water had run out in the plane's toilet.

"Ignorant bastards!" she said, in one of those moments I remember clearly because she was so blunt. "They thought he had let the radiator run dry, so they're investigating him for endangering the safety of the plane!"

The bastards she was referring to were Amo's tribesmen from Tikrit and others like them that Amo had rewarded with government jobs and high-ranking positions. These were the black mustache prototypes, the secret police sent along on all Baba's flights to guard him and the crew, as well as to watch all of us whenever we were around Amo. I feared these men; Mama also despised them, both for their brutality and for reasons of class that revealed her own urban elitism. Baba was facing an investigation by Hussein Kamel, one of Amo's cousins. Amo assigned one of his most trusted advisers, usually a relative, to watch each of his closest friends, and Kamel happened to have been assigned to my father. He didn't even have a high school diploma, but Amo had put him in charge of his weapons programs and military-related manufacturing. Kamel would later become infamous when he defected to Jordan in 1995 with crates of files revealing biological, nuclear, and chemical warfare programs he had overseen. I knew Kamel then only by his reputation for cruelty: he was known to carry a whip to his office and use it on engineers and Ph.D.s he supervised.

Once, earlier in his career as Amo's pilot, Amo had handed Baba an official report signed by Kamel and instructed him to read it out loud while they were fishing at a lake inside the farmhouse compound. The report called my father a "threat to national security" because he was both close to Amo and traveled abroad frequently.

"I know I am at your mercy," Mama told me Baba told Amo.

"You can execute me if you want. But you know I would never do anything to hurt my country."

Amo laughed.

"Don't worry," he said. "I know you didn't do anything wrong."

Amo was the good cop. Kamel was the bad cop. The point was to keep everyone scared and always on his or her toes. Kamel was known not only for his cruelty, but for his jealousy of anyone else who was close to Amo. Now Amo had proposed that Kamel investigate the charges of an inconsequential washroom leak, and I could see fear suffuse our household. Even Baba's friends looked terrified when they came to visit. Finally, Amo sent for my parents to attend a social gathering, and I remember how nervous they were as they whispered to each other while they were getting ready. Mama later told me that when Amo asked him what was the matter, Baba choked up.

"I have no interest in politics," Mama said he told Amo with great emotion. "I cannot handle politics. I have done nothing wrong, yet they want to investigate me for a technicality that has nothing to do with politics or national security. I know how to do my job very well. I am just a pilot, sir, and I just want to be able to do my job."

"You have a choice," Amo said. "You can choose my friendship or you can choose to be my pilot. If you remain my pilot, then you must undergo Kamel's investigation."

I imagined my father, the proud captain of a 747, standing next to Amo, petrified and near tears, completely at his mercy. Baba, who never wanted anything except to fly, chose friendship and survived. He went back to just being a captain and eventually wound up as head of Iraq's civil aviation. He had made the right choice, but it was of the Devil's making. If he had said he wanted to remain his pilot, Amo would have let Kamel proceed with the investigation, and Baba would have been at the mercy of a vengeful maniac whose word Amo could not easily ignore. On the other hand, when he chose friendship, Amo could easily have turned on him, saying, What are you afraid of, Basil? Are you trying to use my friendship to escape wrongdoing? There was no right answer, only painful life-altering decisions that were anyone's guess because they ultimately came down to whatever Amo felt like at the moment.

All of the men watched one another and were watched by Kamel or one of Amo's most trusted insiders. Amo would grow angry at them in turn, as he did at my father, and cast them out, where they would fear for their lives for a few months before being welcomed back into the relative safety of his good graces, blubbering and thankful to be alive. The lesson: no one was safe. Ever. At the end of the day, he had even Hussein Kamel, his adviser, his cousin, his son-in-law, and father of his grandchildren, murdered.

While Baba was facing investigation by Hussein Kamel, I was attending parties given by Kamel's fiancée, Amo's daughter Raghad. Amo had decided to marry her off to Kamel for political tribal reasons even though she was just sixteen or seventeen. Once they married and she had her own house on palace grounds, I found myself invited to her events the same way my mother was invited to events given by her mother, Amo's wife, Sajida. She and Amo had practically grown up in the same house; Aunt Sajida was Amo's cousin, the daughter of the uncle who had inspired Amo's political career and given him an education. She was a teacher like my mother, a strong-featured, sturdy woman who had grown distant from her husband by the time I met him. I never saw her and Amo together; they simply carried on parallel lives on palace grounds.

Raghad was the eldest of Amo's three daughters, about a year older than I was, a confident, determined young woman who taught Baathist ideology at a palace school. Rana was two years younger than I, the gentler middle sister. Hala was seven or eight years younger, the spoiled baby everyone knew was Amo's favorite. They attended a private school on palace grounds with their friends Tamara, Sarah, Luma, and the daughters of other select families, including members of Amo's tribe from Tikrit. Tikriti girls were not supposed to mix with others outside the palace, and a separate branch of a university was eventually established to educate them as they got older. I remember Raghad walking down grand hallways, expressing authoritative views on things I mostly considered silly, like fashion. The other girls and I would follow behind her just as if she were Amo and we were her bodyguards. Honestly, the body language was the same.

Other than gossip, fashion was about the only topic of conversation. As they were never allowed to leave the country, his daughters never had the chance to shop in the boutiques of London or Paris or the malls of America. But they had access to every fashion catalogue on earth, not to mention the ability to simply point at whatever someone was wearing and say, "I like that," and the wearer would be expected to give it to them. As the most fashionable young woman in this circle, Tamara found her dresses often borrowed, sometimes returned, sometimes not. One of her dresses was no longer wearable after it had been taken apart and reassembled by a dressmaker ordered to copy it. Sajida's requests for clothing would often go to my mother or other women able to travel, though from what I heard Sajida was not always good at remembering to reiumburse the buyer. Everything in Amo's life was about making up for something in his childhood—the gold, the clothes, the palaces. I almost understood that. But how did that justify the same behavior by his daughters who had grown up with nothing but luxury?

Each visit to the palace felt like a fashion show in which we were supposed to compete. It was a scandal to wear anything twice, and I joked with my mother that I felt I should wear new underwear for every visit in case someone asked me what label I was wearing. In one of his merciful moments, Amo allowed my mother to go abroad for a medical appointment, and Aunt Nada and Aunt Layla looked so excited that he permitted all three women and their children to go. He handed all the women $10,000 for each of their family members and told them to shop and enjoy themselves.

I was looking forward to buying jeans and T-shirts and some other ordinary teenaged clothing. Instead, my mother bought me stiff, preppy clothes and evening gowns from Mondi and Escada and other designers, including a plaid coat from Christian Dior I would keep for years.

There were many perks, but the price was never on the tag. Every year, he would send us a new luxury-edition Toyota; every year, the other two families received new Mercedes. He tasted a pomegranate from a friend's tree and commented how good it was, so the friend sent two crates of pomegranates, which Amo complained were insufficient, so the trees were stripped bare. Amo complained that Uncle Adel's gold donation to the war effort wasn't enough, so Uncle Adel donated more. A rich man could do better still, Amo said. Finally, Uncle Adel had to sell property to fulfill his "donation." We gave Amo expensive gifts constantly, yet never saw him use or display anything we gave him except fishing tackle. Meanwhile, he was building new palaces every few months. The principal palace compound in Baghdad was a complex of hotel-like mansions that screamed money and ostentation, which Americans would later occupy as the "Green Zone." The houses were enormous, with huge halls and chandeliers. Gold-leafed frames and gold-leafed furniture were everywhere. Expensive Persian rugs were spread across marbled halls, and coffee tables were covered with cut-crystal vases. Everything was sized inexplicably bigger than one would need.

Aunt Sajida presided over palace events with a formal imperiousness. Her eyebrows were drawn up and out on her forehead like dark stabs of surprise that contrasted with her bleached blond hair. Guests would walk over to her, and she would nod with the indifferent air of someone who needn't bother to smile back. Often she hired singers—I remember one named Suad Abedullah— who sang nationalistic songs as wives of ministers of state danced around Sajida with their marriageable daughters, displaying them in hopes they might appeal to her for her sons Uday and Qusay, who were seen in the palace circle as Baghdad's most eligible bachelors. As the adult women danced around Sajida, her teenaged daughters danced around Raghad and Rana, and Hala's little girl-friends danced around her.

"Why do I have to go?" I would demand of Mama in quarrels that often led to tears. "I *hate* it! I don't like them and they don't like me."

"Look at me, Zainab," Mama told me. "I have to dress up. I have to smile. I have to go. What else can I do? All the other women bring their daughters with them and brag about them. When you don't come, it is very awkward for me to be the only mother without her daughter. It triggers questions. What is wrong with my daughter? What kind of a mother am I for not having my daughter with me? You need to come, Zainab. You need to dress up and start putting some makeup on. You often look too pale."

So I went, my mother's daughter, and I would kiss his daughters on both cheeks with delight, as if we had just met by surprise on the street, and say, "How *are* you, Rana?" or "Oh, what a beautiful dress you're wearing tonight, Raghad!" But, in small ways, I registered my protest. I wore straight gray or white dresses instead of the frilly 1980s styles the other girls wore. I refused to wear makeup or waste my time blowing my curly hair dry. Most of the time, I would find a seat on the side and watch for hours, the different one, wondering why I was invited at all and hoping I didn't look as miserable as I felt. The women would dance together as they used to at my mother's garden parties, and my mother kept trying to get me to join in like Sarah and Luma and Tamara. Once she came over to me and ordered me to smile and clap when a patriotic song came on.

"But, I am already smiling, Mother!" I told her as I gave her my big artificial smile.

"You look more like you're smelling something bad," she said. "Smile as if you mean it, Zainab."

"Yes, Mother," I said. And I stood and danced and clapped.

Between the farmhouse and the palace, I felt like a model pasted into one pose after another for some jet-set magazine, all dressed up with a permanent smile on my face, yet completely voiceless. In my head, I started referring to our existence as "this artificial life."

Aunt Sajida and her daughters came to visit us just once. It was at the farmhouse. My mother spent all day cooking and making our house look as nice as she could. She was a great cook when she took the time, and she made Bibi's *sabazi* that day, a recipe Bibi was famous for. Rice was the base of almost every Iraqi meal, and it was usually accompanied by a sauce flavored with vegetables and meat and spices, herbs, or dried lemon, or, like *sabazi*, spinach. That night, as we were seated around the dining table, Mama was serving dinner to Aunt Sajida as a proper hostess was supposed to, and Aunt Sajida looked at Mama with the implacable gaze of someone who knew she could not be questioned.

"Oh, Alia, you made the *sabazi* the Iranian way," she observed.

I could see the droplets of sweat forming on my mother's upper lip that always gave her away when she was nervous or embarrassed. She had made a mistake.

"Well, no, not really," Mama said nervously as she continued serving the now-suspicious dish to Rana and Raghad and Aunt Nada and her family. "I just added some other vegetables to it beside the spinach."

I caught Aunt Sajida's look of authoritative dismissiveness. She knew what she had said was enough to petrify my mother. All she had to do was remind Mama that she was a "special file." I felt so bad for my mother. After all her work, the evening was stolen from her by surprise. I knew we weren't supposed to listen to Persian music or call my favorite nuts "Iranian" pistachios. But was even my mother's wonderful *sabazi* forbidden?

Well, I like it this way, Aunt Sajida! I lashed out at her inside my head, silently, the way I had at Mohammed when he humiliated me for being Shia. It tastes a whole lot better than that bland stuff you serve at the palace!

It was a perfect day all around: Raghad and Rana and I didn't like one another well enough to spend time alone, so we had remained with our mothers. Aunt Sajida had cut down Mama. And Hala had ordered her bodyguard to toss my little brother around like a soccer ball as other kids watched, afraid to intervene for fear of making matters worse. I found Hassan crying in his room after Sajida and her entourage left. He was only five or six at the time, but he knew he could not barge into the salon when everyone was there, so he had just locked himself in the bedroom and cried. When I heard the story, I was so angry I wanted to do something to teach that spoiled Hala a lesson. But I knew I couldn't. She was the daughter of the president and everyone was as much afraid of her as they were of her brothers, her sisters, and her parents.

Amo was very careful about eating anything prepared by anyone else, but he made an exception for my mother's stuffed lamb. Once, she prepared a whole dinner for Ramadan at his request, and we were all waiting for him at the farmhouse when he sent word he couldn't make it, but could she please send him her stuffed lamb? So she sent it on, and we broke our fast that night with side dishes. He had an enormous appetite for meat and had a fresh sheep slaughtered daily. When he joined us for dinner at one of our farmhouses, he brought his own cooks, food, pots, tableware, personal taster Hanna, and kitchen staff, most of whom were Christian. Like many leaders down through history, he trusted minorities with his personal care because they were unlikely to conspire with majority populations to betray him.

One evening after Amo had been at our farmhouse for dinner, my mother whispered to me with a gleeful little smile on her face, "Look what I found!" and whipped out Amo's dinner fork. His eating utensils were at least a third larger than normal and featured a crest with a taloned Iraqi eagle on the handle. This fork was nearly the size of a serving utensil you would stick in a large roast to transfer it to a serving platter. I still have it, a lone tangible souvenir in my kitchen drawer of the endless weekends I spent in that farmhouse.

Food was often a matter of controversy more than comfort. At one family gathering with Amo, Aunt Layla got really excited when grapes were presented at the table. "I haven't seen these grapes in such a long time. They remind me of the days in England!" she said.

Amo glared at her with no mercy whatever.

"What do you mean you haven't seen such grapes?" he demanded, obviously having no idea that most Iraqis didn't enjoy such luxuries. "They are from the Iraqi market. *All* Iraqis have access to this grape."

The vulnerability just below her lovely face surfaced. Aunt Layla was scared—over a grape.

I'm convinced if you understood the way he managed the competition of his "beloved ones" you would understand how he stayed in power for thirty-five years even though millions of his people hated him and there were ongoing domestic and international plots to assassinate him. Our "family gatherings" were a microcosm of how Amo not only spread but maintained fear inside the Baath Party and his Republican Guard and even our classrooms at school. He took pleasure in pitting people against one another—couple against couple, spouse against spouse, child against child. If you wanted to stay in the game—and my parents saw no choice—you had to compete for his favor just to stay even— the fathers with their obedient *yes sire,* the mothers with their coquettishness, the children with their adoring smiles. This included constantly eyeing one another and tattling on one another. I eventually came to like the other three girls, yet I remained lonely because the central ingredient missing in our friendship was trust.

Even children were encouraged to tattle on one another. One afternoon at the farmhouse when Hassan was no more than five or six, he blurted out, "There is no God but one God, Mohammed is his Messenger, and Ali is his Friend," and Sarah's little sister immediately ran to her mother, Aunt Nada, who was a Sunni and thus taught her children that it was forbidden to say the part about Ali.

"Mama, he said the wrong *shahada!*" the little girl told her.

Hassan looked up at my mother, confused.

"I got it right, didn't I, Mama?" he asked.

But, in the tense, awkward mental shuffling that went on in the kitchen between my mother and Aunt Nada, Mama was unable to give him that reassurance. Finally, the mothers each told their children they would explain later, and Aunt Nada politely excused herself and took her children back to her farmhouse. I ran to Hassan to hug him and assure him that he had said the right thing and Sunni and Shia were all Muslims in the end; we just expressed ourselves differently. I felt so protective of him. I didn't want him to be hurt the way I had by Mohammed.

Mama and Aunt Layla were very close at one point, and Aunt Layla had told her that another of my aunts, a woman Mama adored, had said something critical about her to Amo. Mama came home crying that day, and in time, she pulled back and trusted people less. I didn't like seeing her that way, but as was the case with so many other things, I later came to understand her reasons.

"Can you believe what your father did today?" Mama asked me one afternoon when she was coming back from Aunt Nada's farmhouse. "We were just sitting around and Amo went around the circle asking everyone to say who their first love was, and your father said you! Can you believe it! It was you! It was his daughter! It wasn't me, it wasn't even a girlfriend!"

What was I supposed to do? Sympathize with her because my father said he loved me? I had no idea if that was Amo's own personal kind of truth or dare or a perfectly innocent question among friends. I just knew that whatever he did was creating conflict in my parents' marriage that wasn't there before. Since no one could criticize him, he could then play the good guy as well: the patient mediator, the peacemaker. My mother later told me the term she thought of for Amo's strategy was "divide and conquer." But, if she understood it so well, I ask myself with the advantage of hindsight, why did she fall for it?

After Baba was forced to choose Amo's friendship over being his pilot, he had to cut back on his flying because he was expected to accompany Amo to public events, though he would still lean out of newspaper photos or TV cameras as other men leaned in. I would be on the phone with a friend, and the voice of a palace operator would interrupt and order me to hang up because the president wanted to talk to my father. Or the phone would ring during lunch, and my father would get a set of brief instructions for a family trip. "Be ready in fifteen minutes, pack for three days," the voice might say, and we would drop everything and get ready. A black Mercedes with darkened windows would drive up into our cul-de-sac, and we would jump in and join a small convoy of other black Mercedes speeding down the highway at more than 120 miles an hour. I have never driven so fast at any other time in my life. For security reasons, we were never told where we were going. Most of the time I didn't even know the names of the places we wound up, many of them newly constructed palaces, some lavish, some like regular houses, each decorated in different styles Amo never seemed to tire of showing off.

At one of the palaces, I saw ornamental helmets over doorways that reminded me of an enormous monument in Baghdad of a human hand, based on Amo's own, that held a net full of helmets of dead Iranian soldiers. These ornaments hung in clusters of three, like cherries, above the doorways, only they were life-sized helmets made of gold. As I stared at them, I suddenly realized that our gold donations had been melted down to make them, I was certain of it. I saw that he had forged those trinkets in the pain of the Iraqi people. Don't you know people are suffering and dying in this war? I found myself asking Amo in my head. How can you turn our donations into obscene curios? Take the Abbasid coin off my mother's neck that her grandfather had given her that bore the marks of history? Melt down wedding rings women had taken off their hands as a sacrifice to help our soldiers?

I ultimately came to understand that he took from us with uncanny precision what was so intimate to us that it hurt. Not just the Abbasid coin, which mattered nothing to him, but the qualities about us he claimed to value most: my mother's laugh, my father's wings, and very nearly what Mama said Amo sometimes called my "spirit." In return, he gave us gifts that signified only his wealth and control of the national treasury. My father had a closet full of guns he used only when he was hunting with Amo. My mother got boxed jewelry sets made in Italy—lovely, but I would have traded them all to see that Abbasid coin around her neck again.

He was running a country, a war, an army, a political party, and one of the world's largest oil economies, but he found time to keep meticulous accounts of our emotional peonage. I remember one trip we took to the old city of Mosul, gateway to Kurdistan in the north, when I was seventeen or eighteen. We drove up a winding mountain road to a modern mountain lodge with a beautiful view overlooking the city. I remember a bottle of Chivas Regal sitting in the middle of a table on an expansive modern porch and adults drinking heavily the night we arrived. When Amo drank, they were forced to drink too. Mama disliked drinking to excess, and she looked as if she wanted to cry, which was how alcohol always affected her. My father came to seek his escape in drinking as years went on, and he looked ever more tense and serious. The other adults were getting loud and slurring their words, and the men were eating pistachios with their mouths open like Amo, grossing us kids out. Exchanging glances, we older ones tried to divert the attention of the younger ones so they wouldn't have to see our parents this way.

As for Amo, the more he drank, the merrier he got. Yet I never saw him act drunk. Drinking seemed to lighten him up a bit. His merciful moments sometimes came when he was drinking, and there was the smallest opening to say something honest to him. Once, when he was talking about how he much he enjoyed his "People's Days," the days he helped resolve the problems of ordinary citizens, such as women who were having a hard time with divorces or inheritances, Aunt Layla spoke up and asked why he didn't just change the laws to protect women instead. He seemed to actually listen, and she takes credit to this day for improvements he made in family laws for women in the 1980s, though he legalized honor killings in the 1990s that allowed men to kill women family members deemed guilty of causing dishonor to their family name.

After they had been drinking for what seemed like a long time outside, Amo stood up and indicated we should move indoors. No one asked why. "Implement, then discuss"—that was the Baathist motto, after all. Once we were seated in the two-level living room, he informed us we were going to have a family piano recital. He called on me first and sat back and relaxed, ready to be entertained by his beloved ones. I had memorized the Blue Danube Waltz, and I played it that night. Surrounded by my fifteen or twenty members of this artificial family, I was nervous, but I played without a mistake. When I finished, Amo didn't just clap—I remember this vividly for some reason—he clapped slowly, with respectful pauses between each clap: clap . . . clap . . . clap. When you did something to cause Amo's admiration, he would shine his eyes on you. We all knew that shining-eye look and sought it out. It was the prize, the deposit you put in the bank against a dry spell. That night I got it, the best shining-eye I'd ever seen. After I finished, he called on Luma and Tamara and complimented them too. Then he stood up, signaling he was ready for dinner, and the recital was over.

But one other pianist, Sarah, was left behind on the sofa. Amo might as well have slapped her. Why had he deliberately snubbed her? Sarah had grown up with Amo. He was almost like a real uncle to her, and I always thought she genuinely loved him. She competed more enthusiastically for his favor than any of the other kids; she was inevitably obedient and prepared. I could count on one hand the times I had won our competitions. My most important victory was at a gold donation when I was sixteen. Sarah had stayed up all night memorizing an original poem written by her father and delivered it perfectly for the cameras. I pulled out my plastic smile, enunciated the name "Salbi" clearly for the microphone to get proper credit for my family, and spontaneously added a bit of heartfelt personal enthusiasm for the country, our soldiers at the front, and Amo. Later, Amo told Sarah that she was "good." But he told me, with that same slow syncopation, that I was "very . . . very . . . good."

I had seen her slip up just once, when we had been together a few months earlier. Her father had been publicly criticized in the newspaper, and Sarah understood nothing could appear in the paper without Amo's approval, so she had shown him how she felt by shaking his hand instead of kissing him. And it dawned on me that he had set up this whole recital as his revenge for that slight. It occurred to me, at some cost to my ego, that even his praise for my waltz was directed not at me, but at poor Sarah. Here he was, the president of a country of sixteen million people, and she was a fifteen-year-old girl! How cruel, I thought, a despot manipulating a kid—the one who probably cared for him the most.

As everyone headed out of the living room for dinner, I went to look for her and found her crying outside on the balcony. Everyone had seen her shamed, but she was all alone. Where was her mother? But I knew the adults could not leave Amo's company without his permission, and Sarah and Luma had their own competition for Amo's attention. As I walked outside onto the porch, I saw that there were soldiers nearby, and I was afraid they would see her this way and report her behavior to Amo.

For just once, I wanted this painful charade to end. I wanted something to be real. I walked over and put my arms around Sarah, and tried to comfort her as Aunt Layla had comforted Mama after Amo had screamed at her. I held her for a few minutes, until her sobbing subsided.

"It's not fair," she said when she stopped crying. Then, knowing exactly where our boundaries lay, she turned her grief into an acceptable youthful complaint and added: "I can't wait until I'm older so I can drink too."

I can't remember if it was on that trip or a later visit to the same spot that Sarah reprimanded me loudly for sipping my tea before Amo had tasted his. Amo only smiled at her and commented that Zainab was family and wasn't it nice that I felt comfortable enough to drink my tea when I felt like it? If we were all horses in his stable, which is actually not a bad analogy, I think he might have described me as the mare with the independent streak. It was to be expected that I would occasionally rear up. Unfortunately for Sarah, she had positioned herself as the steady obedient one. If she reared up, he would beat her back down.

That weekend was one of the few times I spent time with his mistress, Samira. Chairs had been arranged in a large circle for us on the lawn after dinner and each of us had a servant in full military uniform standing behind us in case we needed anything. Amo was in a jovial mood that night with Samira at his side. She was laughing and fawning over him, throwing her relationship with him in my parents' faces. Behind their facade of courtesy, I could see disgust on the faces of all the adults. Samira flirted with him endlessly as we watched, reveling in her superiority over this supposedly elite circle as she whispered in his ear and ran her fingers along his thigh. Forced to witness this overtly sexual interplay, I thought about what it must be like to be her sons who were there watching it all. Unable to get up, unable to speak, each of us sat there in our own cells of silence. Inside, I could feel a scream churning. I wanted to jump up and scream and run away into the mountains around us that smelled like wild sage and the wind. Instead, I sat absolutely still, with my hands clenched in my lap, and I prayed for a hero on a white horse to gallop in and carry me away.

———————

On some of the weekend trips we took with Amo, I was blessed to see Iraq's stark natural beauty and some of the most magnificent physical settings I have ever known. I love the wind, and especially in those days when I thought I would never get enough air to breathe, there were a few times when I felt the wind blow against my face and it revived something inside me. My mother had a way of turning her face to the wind and closing her eyes as her long hair swirled around her, and I remember thinking how beautiful she was one impeccably starry night, and how perfect that night would have been if Amo had not been in it.

We were all fishing that night. Amo loved to fish. In a land where water is more precious than oil, he took water from our rivers and flooded the desert with dozens of private lakes so well stocked Mama and I used to joke he had SCUBA divers under the water putting fish on our hooks. We were having a "family fishing contest" in which he announced he would give a thousand-dinar prize, about $3,000 U.S., to the person who caught the biggest fish. We all lined up in our chairs with our fishing rods beside one of his lakes. Luma and Sarah were sitting next to me. I remember Luma holding the fishing rod in her ladylike way, with her perfectly curled hair and manicured nails, and Sarah relaxing beside her, understanding that her role was to enjoy her privilege. It was a beautiful night with a full moon reflecting on the lightly rippled water, and everything felt very quiet and peaceful as I looked over the lake. But if I turned in my seat, I faced one man in a uniform with a huge black mustache staring at me and another ready to jump toward me to see if I was thirsty. Behind them was a swarm of soldiers, servants, and cooks, all there to wait on us or guard us. Suddenly, my line started to move around in the water, and the tug was so strong I didn't have the strength to pull it back.

"I caught a fish!" I screamed. "Help! It's heavy!"

Instantly there were three men around me, all in military uniforms, helping me reel it in. The fish was more than a meter long and so big that I started jumping up and down and screaming, "I caught a fish! I caught a fish!" I was so thrilled I forgot myself in front of Amo, the families, the guards, the servants, and everyone else. I remember Amo's smile and his shining white teeth as he looked over at me. He seemed genuinely happy for me. "Zainab is the winner!" he announced later that night.

Luma, Sarah, and I were sitting in front of Aunt Nada's farmhouse one afternoon when Amo drove up in a little red sports car. You couldn't help but notice he was wearing a racing helmet. When he learned that our parents were taking their afternoon nap, he asked us if we wanted to go for a ride. I was about sixteen.

Yes, Amo, we would love that! we all said.

"Then come with me, girls, for a private tour of my private compound."

We jumped in the car, he turned up the radio very loud, and we sped off, zipping across the flat desert road through that inner wall into a brilliant world of lush green lawns, shiny cars, and private lakes. There were security guards everywhere, but they weren't following us around; I felt free. He seemed very relaxed as he drove us around enjoying the music and the sunny afternoon. It was fun to drive with him.

Our first stop was at a fishing house, if that's the proper term for it, which was built out over one of the larger lakes. We stopped the car, and reached the house by walking across a long walkway above the water and into a huge circular room over the lake. Inside, upholstered easy chairs were arranged in a semicircle in front of the windows, which opened so he and his guests could sit inside, with their fishing poles out through the windows, and fish in comfort. Next to each chair there was a small table for food and drinks. "I like to work out here," he said, and for a moment I was jolted back to reality. Was it here, in this laid back setting, that Amo had made my father read Hussein Kamel's report?

Polite and friendly, Amo was that perfect host who made our day by giving his full attention to three teenagers and talking to us like adults. He was just Amo that day, not someone to be nervous around, just a normal guy who happened to be enormously wealthy and enjoyed showing off his real estate. He told us he had helped design many of the buildings, and he seemed proud to show them off. One of the buildings he took us inside looked like a cottage, with casual furniture. Then he took us downstairs and we wound up underground in a whole separate living area with a bedroom, living room, and small kitchen.

"This is a bunker in case of emergency," he explained casually. "I can hide in here if I ever need to. There is enough food to last for weeks."

He went into the kitchen and started showing us his food, opening each cabinet door, revealing stashes of food ranging from pistachios to potato chips to whiskey. Then he opened the refrigerator, which was filled with soda and juices, and offered us each a drink and snacks. He opened the soda cans for us himself—no servants. We spent perhaps two hours with him on our leisurely tour. His lakes were filled with boats, and he took us onto one of the biggest ones, an enormous yacht with a very ornate, fancy bedroom downstairs.

"Girls, remember this when you get married," he said, looking at us. "You can use this on your honeymoon."

Not in a million years, I thought to myself. There was no question in my mind that there were cameras behind those upholstered stateroom walls. Yet as we were driving back toward our farmhouses, I thought to myself how much I was enjoying Amo's company. It was probably about five in the afternoon when we got back. We had been gone a few hours and all of our parents were standing in front of Aunt Nada's house looking worried about us. Had we done something wrong? Weren't we supposed to have gone out with Amo? We thanked him, jumped out of the car, and ran to tell our parents how much fun we'd had on our adventure.

One trip we took started out in Amo's private helicopter, a converted Sikorsky so big it had separate rooms. For the kids, at least, this was a novelty: there was a television set, a minibar, a bathroom, a flight attendant. Less than an hour later we descended into an open field that was staged with tents to look like a hunting safari. Sarah was airsick and threw up as soon as we landed, but she managed to pick herself up, dry off her mouth, and put a big smile on her face for Amo, who greeted us in a safari outfit. He told the women and children to look for truffles and watch the exciting hunting, then directed each of his three friends and my brother Haider to a different waiting Sikorsky. The rotors spun into action with hollow whumping sounds, and the five gunships lifted into the air with their hunters. I had a stick and was dutifully poking bumps in the earth looking for the walnut-sized truffles when I heard this horrible screaming over the noise of the Sikorskys. I looked up to see a flock of wild ducks surrounded by the huge circling helicopters. The birds were trapped in the middle and flapping around recklessly, flying desperately in all directions at once. I saw Amo laughing through an open door of his helicopter as he raised his rifle and began firing, and the other men started shooting too.

"This is a *massacre!*" I half-screamed. I was shaking, looking up at the sky. "This is nothing to laugh at! This is a *massacre!*"

The ducks were *crying*. I remember thinking to myself that they were crying from the inside out, and Amo was laughing at them. Not just hunting, laughing! It was the cruelest thing I'd ever seen. I started sobbing. I must have known how dangerous and stupid it was, but I couldn't help myself. My mother heard me and ran over to me and forced my face down into her chest to muffle the sound so the security guards wouldn't hear.

"Shhhsh, Zainab, shhhsh," Mama said, holding my head down as I cried. "Please stop crying. Please stop crying, honey. Be strong for me! Do it for me, please, Zanooba? Please, remember where you are!"

Around us bloodied ducks plopped to earth. But, like Sarah, I managed to wipe my tears, wash my face, and smile for Amo when the hunters returned.

From Alia's Notebook

He often told us that rifles are the closest thing to the Arabian man's heart. After that comes his woman and after that comes his horse.

As he was arming the country, he bought all kinds of guns, rifles, knives, etc. He would show us his collection and brag about his love of them. He started sharing this hobby with his friends by sending them different weapons. I think we must have had about ten rifles in our home, each of a different kind, in addition to all kinds of knives and guns. We never used them nor did we have the interest to use them. We would thank him for sending his gifts and put them in storage. We knew how important these collections were to him.

He had many hobbies. There was a time he got into cooking. He would invite us for different dishes, mostly traditional ones. He wanted lots of compliments for everything he made, from his dishes to his palaces. If he didn't get them voluntarily, he would ask, and we would all make sure to respond with excitement about how much we liked what we were seeing or tasting. But, there was nothing that compared to his infatuation with fashion. One day he invited us to Mosul to stay with him in one of his palaces. We noticed that there were several bags following him, and in the process of transporting these bags, one fell out and opened. It was a windy day, and to our astonishment, tens of hats of all kinds starting falling and flying away down the road.

We saw him go through many phases There was the time he was into architecture and psychology. There was the time in which he was a military strategist and spent hours talking to us about his strategy and how he would kill generals who suggested alternative strategies or commented that his strategy might lead to the loss of many lives. After he visited a different Arab country, he would come from that trip inspired to build a palace better than what he had seen. He loved decorating his bedrooms, each in a different color and design. He spent millions on Italian furniture.

6

BOXES

I NEVER WITNESSED what he did to people. I never had to put together the body of one of my family members like a puzzle after it had been hacked apart. I never had to spend years going from prison to prison in hopes of finding alive a son who had been snatched away from our dinner table by the Mukhabarat. I was one of the lucky ones, one of his "beloved ones." I was guarded by the very secret police Amo used to terrorize others. There are times I cannot stop sobbing when I think about the crimes he committed against the Iraqi people. But I couldn't cry then. I couldn't even imagine being able to express any feelings at injustice. I just processed such horror stories as information. We were surrounded by stories of people going to prison for simply making a joke about someone in Amo's family or for criticizing a single thing he did.

Any society that stops questioning its leaders is vulnerable to dictatorship, and Amo used our own traditions against us to help instill and perpetuate fear. To the traditional concept of *ayeb,* which dealt with things that were forbidden by cultural courtesies, and *haram,* which dealt with things that were forbidden by religion, Amo seemed to add a third, *mamnu'a,* which just meant forbidden. Forbidden by government? Forbidden by Saddam Hussein? Forbidden by law? It didn't matter. We couldn't tell the difference. We lived *in* fear. Fear had spread through our society the way color does when you put a single drop of tint into water to dye eggs for Norouz or—a better metaphor—the way a single drop of blood does when it drips from your finger into a dishpan.

I remember one perfect cloudless winter day at school when I was sitting outside, leaning against a volleyball pole in the sun with four other girls, and one of them started telling us with very wide eyes a story that could have put her and her family at risk had we repeated it. It was about a man who had been executed in the street the night before in a poor neighborhood. A semicircle of men with rifles had gathered around him, and they were cheered on somehow by someone else, and they all started firing at the man and kept on firing *until his blood was spurting out of his body like fountains*. I knew I couldn't show sympathy for the person who had been executed because I could have been associated with whatever it was that had gotten him killed. So I remember listening with no expression on my face at all, impassive on the outside, as I took in this awful image of blood squirting out in all directions from a man's living body. As I got older, there were more stories. I remember hearing about a businessman who had been executed for raising his prices in violation of a law no one understood. The amazing part was not his murder, but the fact that the Mukhabarat had apologized to the family afterward, saying they had made a mistake because he hadn't violated the law after all. This gave the family the right to mourn him and give him a proper public burial, because such things were normally denied to families of persons who had been executed.

My private hell and that of my family was that we spent so much time with Saddam Hussein himself. Amo could never know I had heard such things—neither could his daughters or even the girls who were my friends at the farmhouse. Never having mastered the art of making such dangerous thoughts fly out of my brain as my mother had tried to teach me, I learned to hide them. Each time a horror story came in, I put it in a box and locked that box away in my brain—I could almost hear the sound the box made when it clicked closed. The good "Amo" things stayed in the front of my brain; I needed access to those. The bad "Saddam Hussein" things I buried in those boxes deep in the back of my brain behind a wall so thick Amo couldn't see through it.

My mother's way of staying alive under the gaze of the man who caused all these horrors was to shut off her mind, and I learned from her example. *Thinking* was dangerous, so I learned not to think or form an opinion. I learned to numb myself with novels and forced sleep and mental tricks. As for my emotions, they got checked into storage like so much baggage I would have to pay to claim later. But, every now and then, those boxes would rise to the surface and pop open and I would see the spatter of a man's blood on a neighborhood wall. Or the body of the husband of a friend of Mama's that had been left at her front door after she had begged Amo to release him from prison, and Amo had promised he would be home the next day. I tried to push these thoughts back down into my brain, only sometimes they wouldn't stay there and I couldn't stand it and I would step into this room of buzzing white light that was so blinding it was like walking straight into one of those lights over your head in a dentist's chair with your eyes wide open. And finally I couldn't see anything anymore.

It was hard for Mama to hide her feelings. Amo had known her for a long time, and her large, wonderfully emotional eyes, and a generous mouth that tended to give her away. When Aunt Samer kept telling Mama horror stories about Amo and complaining to her about the way Tikritis were taking over Baghdad, Mama finally had to ask Bibi to intercede. I remember going to Bibi's apartment and seeing Mama lying with her head on her mother's lap, the supposedly liberated daughter seeking comfort from an old woman who smelled of tea rose perfume.

"Please tell her to stop, Mama, she'll get us all killed!" my mother pleaded to her mother. "She doesn't understand that Amo is the Devil in all its meaning. He charms people, he seduces them, and then he harms them."

Bibi just listened. So did I.

"Samer doesn't understand," Mama said. "Amo knows how to read eyes!"

Amo would stare at you with such intensity, even as he smiled, that I instinctively got into the habit of casting my eyes down, knowing my gesture would be taken for a young girl's modesty. After watching her with Bibi that day, I became even more protective of Mama. I still asked her questions that came as a result of our family gatherings. ("Mama, why does Amo have pierced ears?" "Because in his tribe first sons were coveted and sometimes disguised as girls in early childhood to protect them from the evil eye.") We were best friends, and sometimes we had only each other to talk to. But I spared her the horror stories I heard from time to time at school, as I knew she had spared me hers.

Bibi died in 1986, not long after that afternoon, when I was not quite seventeen. With the help of a woman at the cemetery who performed such services, her three daughters washed her body and wrapped her in a white shroud as Islam requires, and we buried her in the sand outside our family mausoleum in the vast cemetery in Najaf. I remember how many headstones there were, many of them marking new graves of young soldiers who had died in war. The headstones were jammed chock-a-block in the sand, thousands and thousands of them, and it seemed like we had to walk around them forever through scorching desert to reach the mausoleum that had been in our family for years. Finally, rose water was spread over Bibi's grave. Candles were lit as we cried and listened to recitation of passages from the Quran. I had thought of her as the tent under which we found shelter. Now, she was gone.

Bibi's death changed Aunt Samer. She gave up complaining about Amo, and she began to pray.

Baghdad has always been a city of political intrigue, a trading crossroads that was fought over by armies of invading ethnicities for centuries. Amo inflamed these ancient rivalries, tipping the delicate balance among autonomy-minded Kurds in the north, with their own culture and language, fearful Shia in the south, whose loyalty was always questioned, and a mostly tribal area north of Baghdad that Americans would later reduce to "the Sunni triangle." By the late 1980s, the entire atmosphere of Baghdad had changed. As Amo's cement palaces crept out over our riverbanks, he distributed to Tikritis jobs and whole neighborhoods of apartments around his palaces, a sort of protective tribal moat. Baghdad used to be a city of riverside parks in the 1970s, and our family used to stroll along the Corniche, eating *masgoof* fresh from the Tigris as children played and women in *abayas* sat comfortably next to women in short skirts. But Amo and his tribesmen transformed those riverside cafes into male drinking hangouts. Pig's Island was no longer a quiet sandbar where we had family barbecues; it was a tourism casino complex called "Bride's Island," with townhouses for honeymooners forbidden to travel abroad.

I remember playing slot machines once when I was a teenager. Gambling, smoking, and drinking were encouraged in the name of modernization. Later, when I went to America, I saw that Amo had actually won points in the West for these changes. American obsession with the way women dressed helped dupe Americans into believing that because Iraqi women looked more like them, they also had greater freedoms. Behind this façade there was almost no freedom to travel or speak or pray, zero tolerance for any public views at all that conflicted with Saddam Hussein's. Informers were everywhere. Women were reportedly raped by the Mukhabarat on videotapes that police threatened to release to blackmail women into informing on family members. Neighbors informed on neighbors. Children informed on their parents as they innocently answered their teachers' questions like "What does Baba say about Uncle Saddam?"

War was the inexorable backdrop of our lives. As I drove back and forth across the city, between palace and school, thoughtless wealth and working class fear, the streets of Baghdad reflected

Iraqi militarism. There were men in uniforms everywhere. Baath party members, soldiers, young men in Civil Defense who had been trained in "defense" and issued Kalashnikov rifles. Iraqi television was filled with images of dead Iranian soldiers, and Baghdad's streets were lined with black cloth as families hung up the traditional banners announcing the Iraqi war dead and women assumed the black of mourning that is traditional for forty days and up to a year following the death of a family member. Mourners strapped caskets to car rooftops and one day we found ourselves waiting in traffic behind a car with a wooden casket covered with an Iraqi flag. But the casket wasn't fully closed, and I let out a scream as I recognized that the dirty bluish thing hanging out of it was a foot. "Calm down, honey," Mama said, though she was clearly shocked at the sight as well and immediately began reciting prayers from the Quran asking for God to have mercy on his soul, as was our custom when we passed by anyone who was dead.

The war was very personal to girls I went to school with. Many had fathers and brothers who were being sent to the front. I remember in particular when a tall girl who had been nice to me came to school wearing black and told me her oldest brother had been killed at the front and her mother could not stop crying. I comprehended my privilege when I realized that no one in my family was fighting in the war. As in families of means everywhere, my teenaged male cousins managed to avoid the draft. But even they paid their own special price. Dawood, Uncle Adel's oldest son, was sent to study in England. He was cut off for years from everyone he had known and loved, because his family was not allowed to travel abroad, and if he had come home, he would have been drafted. Our family managed to visit him once when we were abroad, and it touched my heart that he asked about so many simple things: what his sister looked like, whether his little brother had a girlfriend, what everyday life was like for his family.

Most Iraqi families didn't have that option, of course. I remember the sun-browned fingers of Radya's mother hanging onto the windowsill of our car one day when we picked Radya up for work as her mother sobbed and begged my mother to intercede to save her son. It was her oldest son who had been drafted, the one on whom they had pinned all hopes for a brighter future for their family. "Everything will be okay," my mother tried to reassure her. As we drove home, I in turn told a sobbing Radya, "Please don't cry, he'll be okay." But the truth was no one knew it would be okay. He was headed for the front lines. Hundreds of thousands of families like theirs would lose sons; our family would lose none. The unfairness was implicit, but as gaping as fate. I came to see the poor less as living in poverty than as marginalized, shut out of the options that allow human beings to shape our own lives. If you were Shia, religious, and working class, there was always a whiff of suspicion about you. For security reasons, Radya was not allowed to come to our farmhouse even to clean. We passed Radya's neighborhood when we drove to the farmhouse, but I never mentioned to the other girls that I had spent time there with a servant's family.

There were times I felt that not the smallest, most ordinary event in my life was free of Amo. I wanted nothing more than to be just an ordinary teenager doing ordinary teenaged things. When I was in high school, my cousin Naim invited me to go with him and his friends to a disco party for teenagers at the Hunting Club, a large private club where middle and upper middle class families went to swim, play tennis, watch movies, and eat. My cousins and I practically grew up there. It was the place where my father first whirled me around a dance floor and my mother sneaked extra servings of hummus when she thought no one was watching after lights went out for movies. It was in the middle of the noisy Hunting Club swimming pool that Aunt Samer criticized Amo. Excited at the prospect of an evening free with people my own age to just enjoy myself, I put on a purple disco dress with huge earrings and let my curly hair down, and I let Mama put a little makeup on my face for the first time that night. She was surprised, but this wasn't a palace party.

When Naim picked me up, my parents were happy to see their daughter's first night out on her own as a teenager. To me, it felt as if it were a reward after all my weekends at the farmhouse. When we entered the Hunting Club hall, it was full of teenagers our age, disco lights were flashing on and off in different colors, and everyone was dancing. Midway through the evening, a friend of my cousin's I thought was cute asked me to dance. I was thrilled to be out dancing, both trying to look cool though we were too shy to even get close to each other. When we finished dancing and I sat down next to my cousin, a murmur spread through the hall. The music kept pounding, but people began turning around in their seats at the far end of the room to find out what was happening. We were at one of the far tables in the hall, but word eventually reached us. Something was wrong.

"Uday just arrived," someone from the next table whispered. "He has ordered that no one can leave the party."

Uday was Amo's son, who dominated the social pages of the newspapers with his ridiculous outfits, fancy cars, and womanizing. Naim and I looked at each other. I had promised my parents I would be home by 11:30, so had he, and we were both worried that on my first night out, we wouldn't be home on time. He got up to check out what was happening and came back a minute later.

"Uday ordered every door to be locked," he said. "Get your purse and coat, but don't put your coat on. Just put it over your arm as if you're strolling. I think I found a way out."

He led me to a small window near the floor of the hall, and I bent down and squeezed myself through it, wishing I were wearing pants instead of my new purple dress. It was a good thing we knew the layout of the Hunting Club so well, because Uday's guards were everywhere. We located a back door, crossed the frighteningly huge backyard and found a way through the outer wall to our car, and escaped, victorious. When we got to my house, I noticed that my father's car was not in the garage. When I told her how we had gotten away, my mother looked very upset with me, even though we had gotten home on time.

"But, Mama, I didn't do anything wrong! I'm not late! Why are you mad at me?"

That's when she started crying and screaming.

"Can't you understand, Zainab? We were really worried about you! Baba went crazy when he heard Uday was at that party. He drove to the club to look for you. He's still there now."

Why was she yelling at me? I had done nothing wrong. I only knew that Uday had taken away my one night of freedom. All I wanted was to just be a teenager, and Amo and his family were taking over our lives. I cried myself to sleep that night as Baba questioned everyone at the club to see if they had seen me. Mama told me later that he drove home trembling with fear and went into my room after I was asleep to make sure I was really there. The next morning the phones did not stop ringing as my aunts and my mother's friends called one another petrified that the notorious Uday had invaded the one space everyone had thought of as "safe."

The women of Baghdad knew what I did not fully comprehend at fifteen or sixteen: Uday, the elder of Amo's two sons, would later become infamous worldwide for his "rape palaces" where he raped and tortured women. He had finders who tricked young women into going to his parties. Some were drugged and ordered to strip and dance naked for him before being raped. In Iraq, a virgin is no longer considered marriageable material if she is raped. If she has an understanding family, they will embrace her and help "cover her honor" by arranging for her to marry the man who raped her. But if the rapist was Uday, no such negotiation was possible. The woman would be completely at his mercy, forced to join the "harem" of other rape victims who would be handed down to his friends and bodyguards and remain forever vulnerable to his wishes and fantasies. About a year after that incident at the Hunting Club, Uday invited the daughter of a friend of my mother's out on a date, and her parents were so upset they arranged overnight for her to be married to a cousin in Dubai. She left the country almost immediately. At her engagement party her fiancé was just a picture on a chair next to her.

I was taking tennis lessons at the Hunting Club one day when Uday stopped and watched me from the sidelines. My father was an excellent tennis player and had given me the lessons, along with a racket and tennis outfit, so we could play together. I remember becoming suddenly conscious of my short tennis skirt as my instructor tried to figure out the rules of what to do. If we stopped the game, that meant we could be accused of fearing him. If we ignored him and continued playing, however, that would be impolite. So we continued hitting briefly, then my instructor called me to the net under the guise of giving me a tip and quietly told me to go back inside after the next rally. He went over to talk to Uday while I avoided his eyes and walked safely off the far side of the court.

Until that day, I had felt I was immune. I was a "friend" of Uday's sister. My mother was a "friend" of his mother. And, most important, my father was a friend of his father. I spent time with girls who fantasized about marrying the man. I know Luma thought that marrying the president's son would mean power, wealth, and permanent residency at the palace. I don't know how many times I saw young women at the palace gatherings blushing as they talked about Uday. Hadn't they heard about his cruelty? Did they actually like the idea of imprisonment in the palace? Did they care so much for power that they were willing to sacrifice their own freedom for it? I didn't know, and I couldn't ask. I could only try to hide the horrified look on my face when I heard the other girls talking about him.

One night my family was going to meet another family for a Thursday night party with an Iraqi and a Western band playing. I got dressed and went downstairs to tell my parents I was ready.

"That's too revealing, you need to change," Baba told me when he saw what I was wearing.

I had on a perfectly decent dress with cap sleeves, but I was accustomed to doing as my parents asked, so I went upstairs and changed into something more conservative still. When I came back down again and he told me crossly to change again, a switch in me flipped.

"What is wrong with you?" I demanded. "*You* bought me these clothes. *You* are the liberal father who brought me up this way. *You* are the one who taught me to eat with a knife and fork and keep my mouth closed when I eat, and now you even eat like them and drink like them. What is happening to you, Baba? You're a hypocrite! You're becoming someone else!"

That was an enormous act of *ayeb,* if not *haram,* because the Quran did not allow us to disrespect our parents, and I ran upstairs with him asking me how dare I talk to him like that. I had never talked to my father that way. I remember Mama explaining to me that he was just trying to protect me from Amo's Tikriti police who were going into the Hunting Club and ordering waiters and patrons around at gunpoint. In fact, the next time we went out of the country, I noticed that Baba didn't care a thing about what I wore. But I barely recognized this other man as my father. It was as if he had walked deeper and deeper into a desert of sand until he was buried by it. Baba used to insist on proper table etiquette. He was the one I remember teaching me how to set the table. Now, with Tikriti tribal power on the rise in Baghdad, he was beginning to eat with his hands. What had happened to the Baba who used to rock and roll with me? Who swam with me, tickled me, and promised to teach me to fly? I could hardly see that man anymore. He was becoming someone else, someone conservative who no longer smiled or told jokes or sang funny songs, but was always strict and afraid. Mama explained all this by saying that Amo had ridiculed Baba for growing up as a spoiled city boy who went to the best schools and spoke fluent English, and that Baba was just trying to fit in because it was safer that way. I'm sure she was right. I could almost see him struggle with this new image he was trying to create for himself. But what I also saw was this: after so many years of resisting, he had finally surrendered to Amo.

I think I remember the day it happened. We were at the farmhouse. Instead of greeting Amo with kisses on both cheeks as Middle Eastern men do, Baba kissed Amo on each of his shoulders instead. I had noticed that officials had started greeting him this way in public ceremonies on television, but it was so degrading to see old friends treated like this. Had anyone looked, I'm sure they would have been able to tell by the look on my face how upset I was. Was this some new order by Amo? Or had Baba volunteered to kiss Amo in this way?

"Why did Baba kiss Amo on his shoulders instead of his cheeks?" I asked Mama later.

"Amo's afraid of germs, so he made it a requirement to have everyone kiss him on the shoulder," she said, a weak answer.

I knew Amo was always washing his hands and sometimes made strangers wash with antibacterial soap before meeting him. He was a fanatic about washing. But that didn't explain why he still let women and children kiss him on the cheeks. Amo screamed at women, but he needed to degrade and emasculate men, even in private. It was almost as if he thought he were some sort of god who stood above them.

I caught a small glimpse of his hubris one night at Aunt Nada's farmhouse during Ramadan. The weather was nice, and the guards and cooks set up the *iftar*, the Ramadan feast table, in her garden. We all recited the opening prayer around the table, "God, I have fasted for you, I have depended on you, and I have made the intention to fast tomorrow. God, please forgive the men and women believers and Muslim men and women and forgive my own sins, oh, please God."

Then, before we could break our fast with lentil soup and dates dipped in yogurt, we had to wait for Amo as he said his prayers in front of us. I always viewed prayer as a reminder of our own humility. We had to take off our shoes, do our ablution, and wear clean clothes when we prayed. Every time I have ever kneeled to pray and leaned my head down to the floor, I have tried not only to thank God, but to remind myself of my own insignificance, as if I were an ant in the presence of God. Bibi taught me that everyone is equal in front of God. Yet as Amo prepared to pray, he stood in his military uniform and raised his foot to Hanna, who removed first one shoe, then the other. I saw no humility at all. Didn't having a servant waiting on you contradict the very notion of prayer? He reminded me of the way I used to pray in front of the family with the television set on, in front of the mothers laughing and the other children playing, showing off that I knew my prayers, instead of focusing on God. Was that what Amo was doing? Putting on a show? What sort of man was it, I wondered, who didn't need to be humble even before the magnificence of God?

After we all broke our fast, Amo started drinking his Chivas Regal as usual. That shocked me even more. Even very secular people like my father who drank regularly didn't touch alcohol during the month of Ramadan as a matter of respect for that holy period. Ramadan was supposed to be a contemplative time when one slows down and reflects and connects with one's family and the community at large.

The next morning, as my mother and I were taking a walk, I asked Mama about why Amo didn't take off his own shoes to pray.

"Amo has a back problem," she said. "He can't bend."

But, in the end, he had bent over to pray, I thought. Could that sort of pain be any different than taking off your shoe?

"Why does Amo drink whiskey during Ramadan?" I asked.

"I don't know, Zanooba, I just don't know," she said wearily.

People compare Saddam's megalomania and terror to that of Hitler and Stalin, which I think he would like, since I know he kept their books on a rollaway trolley he sometimes had a servant bring out so he could read after dinner. Occasionally, he would drop their names into conversations, along with historic Arab figures like Saladin, who fought the Christians during the Crusades, and Hammurabi, the ancient Mesopotamian king famous for his code of law. Saddam had come to see himself as their equal and was

trying to outdo them. He spent three years rebuilding King Nebuchadnezzar's Hanging Gardens of Babylon, one of the seven won-
ders of the ancient world. He was really excited about this latest of
his construction projects and couldn't wait to show it to us.

We were invited to opening night. It was a huge event, like a
premiere. Entertainers and musical troupes were invited from all
over the world. Baba was away, and we went with Uncle Kais and
his family. Television cameras were pointed at us as we walked into
the Babylon Festival, with its Bulgarian dancers and Russian bal-
lerinas, and were led toward seats in the front row. Uncle Kais was
some sort of a celebrity, and his daughters walked ahead with their
heads held high, as if they were used to walking on a red carpet and
enjoyed the attention. I followed behind them, stunned to realize
that we were supposed to be VIPs. My parents had so drilled into
our heads that we should not tell anybody about our relationship
with Amo or let anything at all "go to our heads" that I was surprised people stared at us. I didn't want anybody staring at me like
that. I would rather have been invisible.

But the most amazing part of that evening was Babylon itself. I
had been to many historical sites, from Athens to Rio. I understood something of the importance of preserving history. I knew
that the beauty of a historic site is in its age, in the accidental grace
with which stones cling precariously to ruins, in the texture and
even the smell of ancient bricks. But this city was entirely new. In
his determination to one-up Nebuchadnezzar, Amo had destroyed
the ancient ruins. As Mama and I walked through and realized
what he had done, we didn't know whether to laugh or cry. On top
of the ancient bricks, which had a historic inscription on them saying "Built in the Time of Nebuchadnezzar," he had cemented
thousands upon thousands of bright new yellow bricks inscribed
"Built in the Time of Saddam Hussein."

I left that night with a better sense of what my parents had
given up in their struggle to resist Amo. Aunt Nada and Uncle Kais
publicly exhibited their relationship with Amo and had taken advantage of their contacts to start businesses and grow wealthy.

They could afford extravagances our family couldn't on the salary of a professional pilot, even with my mother's inheritance offsetting the growing expense of keeping up appearances. We were a professional middle class family caught between two worlds. The people who watched us walk in that night considered us palace insiders, and palace families considered us just part of the people. We were members of Amo's circle of friends, and yet members of the Shia community he persecuted. We didn't belong to either the world of the powerful or the world of the powerless. I traveled between them, unable to talk to either about what I had witnessed in the other.

The financial pressure to keep up was enormous, and one night my parents had such a huge fight over how to deal with it that my mother took me and my little brother and moved to the farmhouse while Haider stayed home with Baba. I was almost eighteen, ready to start college, and I found myself living in the farmhouse, utterly trapped in the middle of the parched desert compound, in summer. Mama and Baba hadn't talked for a month when we finally drove home to get more clothes, and they started fighting again almost immediately. As if on cue—did the walls really have ears?—the phone rang and it was the palace saying Amo wanted to see them both at the farmhouse immediately. I hadn't even unpacked and couldn't stand the thought of turning right around and going back. So my parents left immediately in separate cars, and my mother promised to send a driver back to pick me up. Alone in the house that had once been so happy, I looked around at the familiar surroundings I hadn't seen for a month and felt that nothing was the way it used to be. We hardly had friends anymore. I hardly saw my cousins now—we had to be at the farmhouse, and I was beginning to feel some of them were looking at us as if we were truly "friends of Saddam." I just wanted to escape. I missed Bibi and I got her *abaya* out of the closet and put it on and walked down to a crossroads near our house. I signaled a taxi and got in. As we drove off, I felt a small, scary thrill of adventure. I was breaking the rules. I was disobeying my parents. I was a young woman going out to a public place by myself; my palace friends, even Mama, would be scandalized. I told the driver to go to the Kademiya Mosque, which was one of the emblems of Baghdad itself, the holy site we had been driving by when I first heard my mother mention Amo.

When I arrived, I walked inside the courtyard and stayed there for two hours in the comfort and anonymity of hundreds of other women dressed just as I was.

"Please God, do something, please save my family, please do something," I prayed. "Please get me out of my prison, God."

While I was at the mosque, Amo was trying to save my family. As it turned out, the reason he had called my parents to the farmhouse was to try to get them back together. Amo, who went through many phases, saw himself as a marriage counselor. When the driver my parents sent called them to say I was missing, Amo immediately told them, "Zainab is trying to send you a message. She ran away to get your attention. She wants you to be back with each other. You need to do it for her if nothing else."

All I wanted that day was to be with other people and free of Amo, free of the guards and the scrutiny. But I learned later that Amo had sent search parties out for me. Police apparently even searched the mosque, but didn't pick me out. Later, I wondered how many times Amo's soldiers had been in that mosque picking up poor Shia young men to deport them to Iran or draft them into the army, or put them in prison and torture them for praying. Had the search for me caused pain for anybody else? Had I put anyone else at risk as my father had put the boy in our neighborhood at risk the night Amo came to visit? Was my privilege a blessing that saved me from losing loved ones like my classmates, or a curse that made it impossible for me to simply disappear like other people?

When I finally came home on my own, my parents were both there waiting for me. They started hugging me and apologizing for their arguments and said we were all moving back home. At the end of the day, was mine the act of a spoiled kid? I wasn't sure whether I had brought my parents back together or whether Amo had, but they never reprimanded me for running away that afternoon.

Amo never said anything to me about it at all, but I apparently scored points with him for daring to make myself vulnerable to save my parents' marriage. Mama told me he liked my "spirit."

From Alia's Notebook

Saddam got into building mountains in Baghdad during that time. He built about three mountains. He would compare these mountains to the Nebuchadnezzar's mountains in Babylon. He built a new palace every three or so months, and we would be invited to parties opening each of these new palaces so he could show them off. There was a point where he claimed that he designed 150 of his palaces. He built new lakes all around his palaces and ensured that they were filled with fish. If he couldn't catch a fish, he would throw a hand bomb into the lake to kill as many fish as possible.

During that time, he often talked about the universe and God. He claimed that God was not fully satisfied with his creation of mountains, trees, and even animals. So, God created humans and ordered them to worship Him day and night. God's satisfaction increased more and more as He ordered humanity to call his name and pray for him day and night. Saddam compared God's feelings with that of a leader. A leader without people to follow him and worship him is not a master, he claimed. A leader needs his people to worship him so he can exercise his power and his strength and finish perfecting the earth.

7

❖

A WHITE HORSE

THE IMPORTANCE OF EDUCATION had been drilled into me ever since my father used to squeeze fresh juice for me and bring it to my desk so I wouldn't have an excuse to interrupt my homework for a snack. By the time I was ready to graduate from high school, I also saw university not merely as education, but as a way out of the life I was living. All the young women I was spending weekends with were going to college—that was a given—but they seemed to see it as a personal ending point. Our mothers all went to university and pursued careers. Many had continued to work all their lives; even Saddam's wife worked after her husband became president. Yet most of the young women I knew seemed to see university as a place to find husbands, after which they would settle into lives that revolved around children and social schedules.

That was not what I wanted. By the time I was a senior in high school, I dreamed of a career that I was not only good at, but that I could be passionate about, something that would allow me to travel, meet people from around the world, and be exposed to foreign literature, arts, and cultures. Thanks to travel and years of study, I was fluent in English and knew a little French, so I planned to major in translation in college, take my father up on a long-standing promise to send me abroad to study for my doctorate, and perhaps work for the Iraqi foreign ministry or a United Nations agency. A Ph.D. in languages would be my passport to freedom, and I made a vow to myself to have it by the time I was twenty-six.

High school students couldn't simply apply to the universities of their choice or even choose our majors. We could express preferences, but our fate was based on a strict numeric system that awarded bonus points for Baath Party membership and family members killed or disabled in the war. I qualified for no bonus points at all, so I was relieved when I tested high enough to qualify for my first choice: the language school at Mustansiriya University, the second largest university in Iraq. I would specialize in Arabic, English, and French.

The first day of school felt like a fresh new beginning to me. I had a new uniform, my mother gave me her old car, and I drove myself to school. I felt a rush of independence pulling into the big, modern campus with thousands of new students I had never met before. New students were assigned to older students as guides, and my guide, known by his Baathist title Rafeeq, which means a friend or comrade, was a handsome young man who turned out to be a leader of the student Baathist Party. The party was active on campus, and when I got a call "inviting" me to a Baath Party meeting, I knew I had to attend. When the teacher started talking about the Baathist slogan, "Implement, then discuss," I raised my hand, smiled, and asked a question.

"Why?" I asked in a pleasant voice. "I need to know what I'm implementing before I can implement it, don't I?"

The room hushed. The teacher tensed and smiled a rigid smile. I could see he was trying to be patient with me. I was new.

"If everyone needs to discuss every order, then we will never get anything done," he said. "We have to trust in our leaders to make decisions, so we implement their orders quickly and avoid delaying important actions."

I had assumed that there would be some opportunity for discussion on a university campus, but I was wrong. I soon learned that there were at least two Baathist spies in each classroom; many university professors, including the one who lectured me that day, would wind up fleeing the country. Still, for the first time in years, I felt the world was opening up to me. There were new possibilities at school and a new sense of calm at home now that we were all living together back in the Airlines Neighborhood. Mama relaxed. Baba wasn't away as often, and we hired a cook, ending a low-level source of friction between my parents stemming from the fact that Mama always wanted to go out when he was home from a trip, and Baba wanted to stay in and eat home-cooked food. When I came home from school, I walked in the door to the smell of wonderful food and lunch served with garnishes and table linen.

One day over *timen bah gillah,* I was babbling on about all my classes and all the new friends I was making when Baba started quizzing me testily. Where did these new friends live? Who were their parents? Had I given anyone my phone number? For a few blissful weeks, I had allowed myself to forget the rules. I should have known better.

"Remember, your friends are your friends because of who your father is," he said.

We were at the end of the meal, and he said that over his shoulder, almost as an afterthought, as he left the table. I put my fork back down on the plate and could feel Mama look away, knowing instantly how I felt but unwilling to meet my eyes. I will never forget that one sentence. He really hurt me with that, all the more so because he spoke so casually. Just when I was beginning to think there was a chance I could create my own identity, he was stealing it back from me. People liked me at the university, and I thought it was because I was cool or because I was a good student or maybe even just because I was me. But he erased those silly assumptions with a single remark. Was it naïve to think people liked me for myself? How could I tell the difference? And as I thought about it, I realized with a sinking heart that it was no accident that I had gotten a Baath Party leader as my student guide. He knew who my father was. They knew who everyone was.

It didn't matter that my father was no longer Saddam Hussein's pilot, or that he had only been his pilot for a few years in the first place. The sobriquet had stuck. People still called him the "pilot of Saddam." They referred to Mama as the "pilot's wife," and they called me the "pilot's daughter." An awful wave of fatalism washed over me. No matter how hard I worked, no matter who I became, I would always be defined by my father's passenger, or former passenger, the man millions of people feared.

I have a picture of me in my university uniform at a ceremony in which Amo honored Iraqi women who had donated gold my first year in college. In it, he is smiling at me warmly with his hands on both my shoulders. I am smiling as well, but my hands are at my side, clenched into fists. I knew what a sham it was this time; the very pin he put in my lapel that day for donating gold was itself made of gold. The next day at college, everyone was pointing at me and checking me out as I walked through campus. They had seen how he had greeted me, and seen me smile back. "There's the one, the pilot's daughter," people whispered.

I had seen the change come over my parents as they had become more and more like the farmhouse crowd. Would that happen to me too? Would I finally give up fighting and find a way to fit in? I knew they would never be true believers like Uncle Kais and Aunt Nada. But the more they seemed to accept their fate, the more determined I became to fight my own. Studying seemed the only way out. French was the newest and weakest of my languages, so I signed up for intensive lessons three nights a week at the French Institute in addition to my full load of classes at the university. I was focused intensely on the teacher's lesson the first night when a young man sitting next to me kept nervously shaking one leg, and the movement made it hard for me to focus because our desks were connected. I poked him politely with my pen and said with a smile, "Please stop that." He did. Over the break, he and I and two other students, an older man and woman, started chatting with one another in a small patio where an Egyptian man ran a little refreshment stand.

The young man's name was Ehab. By the end of the first semester, the older two started drifting off, clearly interested in each other, and Ehab and I found ourselves continuing the banter by ourselves. He was tall and thin, with chestnut hair, a few years older than I was, and he carried himself with utter confidence. He was good-looking and dressed well, not because he wore designer jeans or had the money to buy fancy labels, but because he had an instinct for what looked good on him and how to wear it. We sat on our white plastic chairs in the little patio and discussed literature and poetry. He always carried a book of poetry, and we started reading poems together aloud. I couldn't help but look at his lips, which were sort of pouty-looking and naturally deep red. There was an incredible intensity about him. He lived in the world of books, and I did too. Now we shared this precious world with each other. He was enchanted by British romantic poets like Byron and Shelley, novelists like Gabriel García Márquez, and Arab writers like Mahmoud Darweesh and Najeeb Mahfouz. He loaned me his books, which I devoured at the farmhouse, and we began having regular discussions that fed my lonely brain. While Luma and Sarah and Tamara chatted about Luma's latest prospects for a proper husband, I read *Love in the Time of Cholera*.

I have never been flirtatious. I'm too focused on my goals. But before I returned *Love in the Time of Cholera*, I went into my room and sprayed my perfume on the pages. The next time he lent me a book, he tucked in a poem on a piece of paper. One thing led to another, and we began skipping that last hour of class after the break in order to continue our literary discussions. Then one night he read a love poem describing the features of a woman, her beautiful eyes, her mouth, the smell of her. It was one of the most romantic things I had ever heard.

"I wrote it," he said shyly.

He didn't say it was for me, but I knew.

"Oh, thank you, Ehab," I said. I reached over and put my hand on his and felt the warmth of his hand under mine. It was a very daring move, and I kept my hand there, touching him for the first time, feeling my heart flutter. We looked into each other's eyes for a very long time. We both knew we were in love.

Technically, a proper young Muslim girl wasn't even supposed to be alone with a man. Dating was not sanctioned in Iraqi culture and Arab culture at large—it still isn't—until the couple is betrothed. Most of my friends were dating anyway—"underground dating" I sometimes called it. Boys and girls would find places to meet in private or in groups, politely getting to know each other, though stopping short of sexual relations because virginity was still expected of brides. No one I knew told their parents about such dating. But as soon as I got home that night, I ran to Mama's room, excited. She was still my best friend, and I knew she believed in love, in bending rules. All through high school, she had asked me if I had a crush on anyone and always seemed disappointed when I said no.

"Mama, I think I am in love!" I told her.

"Oh, how exciting, *habibiti*," she said. "Tell me! Tell me all about it!"

"He wrote a poem for me and it was so romantic!" I said. "He is very good-looking, Mama, and very smart . . . and I held his hand."

She was happy for me. Later that week, she dropped me off at the institute as students were going in, and eagerly asked me to point him out. "Which one is he, Zainab? Tell me!" she asked, giggling, more like a girlfriend than a mother. When I pointed to the tall young man going up the steps, she said, "Oh, he's cute!"

I'm sure she thought it was a passing infatuation.

It was assumed I would grow up to marry a prosperous, secular, university-educated, cosmopolitan man. Ehab was none of those things. His father was a shopkeeper, and his family was large—eight brothers and sisters. Neither of his parents had a university degree, and though he was adamant he would one day, he still had not finished his first year of college. He was a practicing Sunni from Samarra, an area northwest of Baghdad that Americans would later dub the "Sunni Triangle," and through him I was exposed for the first time to the tribal culture that still dominates much of rural Iraq. His tribe was one of the most powerful in the region, and he had been raised to give utter loyalty to the sheikh and tribal elders who resolved disputes, determined policy, helped arrange marriages, protected their own from outsiders, and negotiated alliances (and, historically, wars) with other tribes or governments. His tribe's principal rival was in nearby Tikrit, and this generations-old rivalry had been inflamed by its most prominent member, Saddam Hussein, who had poured government resources into Tikrit's infrastructure while ignoring Samarra, which was far larger and boasted an internationally known historic site. Ehab hated Amo. For the first time I had met someone who felt more strongly about him than I did.

"They are all crazy criminal idiots!" he said of Saddam and his tribesmen. "Vulgar, stupid, all of them! They have sex with their own animals!"

I had never in my life heard anyone talk like this, and soon realized that Ehab was a closet dissident who trusted me enough to say things that could easily have gotten him killed. He had a friend, a disenchanted Baathist like Aunt Samer, who had been imprisoned for eight years over a policy difference with Amo, and he knew another man who had been imprisoned because he objected to Mukhabarat flirting with his wife. I listened intently to everything he said, but dared utter no criticism of Amo. When it came to Amo, I trusted no one, not even Ehab. I said nothing of our relationship to Amo, but there were times the palace operator interrupted our telephone conversations, and after a while Ehab put two and two together.

"You are friends of Saddam's, aren't you?" he said. "Your father was his pilot."

I was scared at what he would say, but I finally nodded and waited to see if he would still love me.

"Please be careful when you're around them, *habibiti*," he said, taking my hand. "The Tikritis know no boundaries. They are rapists! They are known for rape, *igh tisab*. When they see meat, they are like dogs! They're not used to women in these short sleeves and skirts. They will jump on any woman! They will take a sister, take a wife. They feel they can just take any woman because they have power. Saddam is so powerful, he thinks he is Pharoah!"

I knew no Tikriti I happened to meet would rape a friend of Saddam's—at least not without his approval. But, out of respect for Ehab and the interest in Islam he was rekindling in me, I began to dress more conservatively, in line with Islamic belief that both women and men should wear modest clothing that is not revealing. Many young people were growing more religious at this time, though I was never sure if it was in reaction to secular parents or part of a low-key rebellion against the corrupt and dissolute regime. A friend of mine decided to wear the *hijab*, a head scarf, and this simple decision was an ordeal for her family because they were afraid her decision to cover her hair would categorize her as being "too religious" and therefore open to being accused of affiliation with a religious party and thus government prosecution. I have often found it curious that many Western women fail to notice the forces that make them dress as they do, yet they pity Muslim women wearing the *hijab*, unaware that covering their heads is sometimes a choice that educated women make on their own.

I didn't want to cover my head, but I started wearing long sleeves and skirts that fell mid-calf, and my father now feared I had gone too far the other way. The point was that in the regime that ruled Iraq, our freedoms were so limited that a head scarf, a prayer, a long skirt, a single word of Farsi dropped into an Arabic conversation—all could be taken as proofs of disloyalty to the state. The Mukhabarat conducted surprise sweeps of mosques, arresting young men on suspicion they belonged to the outlawed Dawa religious party. During this time, an older cousin of mine was swept up this way with some of his friends and tortured before his family was able to negotiate to allow him to leave the country, and we later heard reports that some of the friends arrested with him had been executed. One night my cousin Naim had gone to a mosque to pray, and his father, Baba's brother, called him in a panic. Naim later told me Baba and my uncle took him straight out to a bar, bought him beer, and finally convinced him it was too dangerous to go back to the mosque.

While I was secretly falling in love with Ehab, I knew Luma's parents were evaluating suitable husbands for her, and she would accept without question whomever they selected. Sarah was a different story. She wanted to run and dance and break with tradition when it came to social rules.

"When I marry, it is going to be for love," I declared one day as we were sitting around Aunt Nada's kitchen table.

"Zainab, love comes *after* marriage—don't you know that yet?" Luma said, taking it upon herself to reprove me, as if my liberal mother hadn't managed to get into my brain the mantra that Iraqi women had handed down to their daughters for generations.

"I don't care if he's poor," I went on, speaking of this theoretical future husband. "We are going to build a life together from scratch, starting from the ground up, brick by brick."

"Marry someone rich and you won't have to bother!" Luma retorted.

"Well, I want to marry for love," Sarah said. "But I am not willing to marry a poor man. Living comfortably is very important. It would be dumb to marry a poor man, Zainab. How would you eat? Love someone rich. That's how you can have your cake and eat it too."

I could almost see Sarah's brain, as sharp as a lawyer's and just as calculating, reasoning that surely it was possible to find a rich man to fall in love with.

At that time, wealth presented itself almost as a trap to me. I was reading *Wuthering Heights* for an English literature class, and I escaped the farmhouse to the wild moors of Emily Brontë's nineteenth-century England, where her star-crossed lovers, the brooding dark-haired Heathcliff and the fair-haired, impulsive Catherine Earnshaw, struggled with issues of class. Young Cathy was privileged and educated. Heathcliff was poor and swarthy; he had been abused as a youth and grown up ignorant. Instead of following her heart and marrying Heathcliff, however, Cathy did what was expected of her; she married an insipid, landed young gentleman. Heathcliff, brokenhearted and obsessed with jealousy, took his revenge by abusing everyone around him. She married for money, and everyone in the book lived—or died—in misery.

The differences between us made Ehab more compelling to me, not less. For me, true love was all wrapped up in overcoming obstacles, especially those imposed blindly by religion or class. The Iraq I had grown up in tolerated intermarriage, and intermarriage went on despite the anti-Shia sentiment whipped up by the Iran war. People I knew didn't ask each other what their religion or sect was when they first met, any more than people did in Europe or America, though sometimes it was obvious. There were several Sunni-Shia couples in my family. The two friends I had initially met at the French Institute with Ehab were a Muslim man and Christian woman who wound up falling in love and getting married. Naim fell madly in love with a Kurdish woman, and at this time I was playing the romantic role of go-between because her parents opposed the idea of her marrying a non-Kurd. I would call up and ask for her, then pass the phone to Naim, or cover for them on secret dates.

My favorite new university friend was a Kurdish girl named Lana, the daughter of hardworking professional parents. We were together on campus one day when another student made a silly joke about the vice president, Ezzet Al-Douree. Another quickly hushed her, pointed at my earring as if it were a secret recording device, and started singing one of the patriotic songs we had learned in school. "May God protect the president!" she sang, using the chant like an amulet to ward off evil. "May God prolong his life!" The others laughed at the joke, but I couldn't. I was more afraid of them than they were of me. I wanted so badly just to tell them how I really felt, but I couldn't, and I knew I never could. That was the way informers worked. They played Devil's advocate and got you to say something you weren't supposed to. I knew I wasn't an informer, but as I looked around that day, I realized that one of my new friends might well be. So I buried my feelings and stayed silent, letting them think what they would.

One of the things I liked about Lana was that she found it hard to filter her emotions. She was one of the three or four students I was friendly with whose homes I was able to visit, and we were sitting on her bed one day studying for an exam when she leaned over and whispered very fast in my ear.

"Zainab, I have to tell you a secret," she said. "It's so awful! The government dropped chemical weapons on the Kurds in the north and thousands and thousands of people are dead. They just fell where they were standing. A whole town was killed in a matter of minutes."

She told me what she had heard, and pictures flashed across my mind of Kurdish families fallen in narrow streets, children heaped on one another, babies without breath, in their mothers' dead arms, a whole village of people inhaling gas so poisonous they died *while they were moving*. A father was found dead with his children around the kitchen table, killed in the middle of a meal, *as they were eating*. I heard her describe these awful things, and yet I couldn't respond. I couldn't say anything to her at all. I just went stiff, and I remember her almost jumping backward on the bed at my silence. I always suspected she reacted that way because she suddenly remembered she was talking to the daughter of a "friend" of Saddam's.

We both looked back at our books and made a pretense of resuming study of our English composition. But later, when I was alone, the images kept assaulting me, a hail of arrows shooting over the walls I had built up around that part of my brain that I had hidden off so I wouldn't have to think about the horrendous things Amo was doing to his own people. Thousands of people died? *Thousands?* Lana probably had relatives in the Kurdish region, so she must have heard it from someone there. I doubt even my father had heard about this; he was in civil aviation, not the military. This was the most dangerous thing I had ever heard. I knew I could not repeat it to anyone, not even my mother. I had seen how desperately Mama pleaded with Bibi, scared to death that she wouldn't be able to hide one more horror story from Amo. But every time I closed my eyes, I kept seeing that father and his children. I couldn't cry for them. I couldn't be angry for them. I couldn't keep their pictures in my mind. I had to disinfect my brain of their existence. Finally, I just stepped into that painfully bright white space in my brain that had the power to burn them away like overexposed film.

As Amo's acts of despotism increased, virtually unrecorded inside Iraq for lack of independent media, I went on about my life as normal. I took pottery lessons, tennis lessons, painting lessons, and piano lessons with a French Catholic nun named Massier Camel. *"Sabah al-kher!"* my mother would say cheerfully at 7 A.M. "Good morning!" She was almost always happy in the mornings, before the events of the day would remind her of our cage. She would breeze in, open the curtains, brush the back of her hand lightly against my cheek, and kiss me awake. Sometimes she would sing, and if I complained about the farmhouse or a palace party, she would remind me to be grateful for what I had and suggest I look harder to see the beauty that was all around us. I had taken piano lessons since I was twelve from Massier Camel, and I took to practicing the piano for hours when I was home. Tick, tick, tick, tick, the rhythm of the metronome numbed me, yes, yum, yes, yum, and I was able to find escape in music as Baba did in his cockpit and Haider did in his computer games and household electronic appliances, which he patiently took apart and put back together. It was my mother's dream that I learn to play the piano, which she had never studied, and she brought me stacks of sheet music, romantic songs mostly. Her favorite was "Love Story." She asked me to play it over and over again.

Sometime in my sophomore year, my father told us that we were to pack for two days—bring tennis shoes, bathing suits, and homework if you've got it. The driver was on the way, so my brothers and I rushed upstairs to pack. I opened my top drawer and stared at my three bathing suits. I picked up the red one, then told myself I wasn't going to swim. It wasn't proper. I put the bathing suit back, packed the rest of my things, and ran back downstairs.

I don't remember where we wound up that weekend except that the house was enormous, and each family had its own wing. We had dinner by the lake—almost all Amo's palaces had lakes—and he said, "Okay, everybody get their suits, let's go swimming." It was a beautiful night, and the water of the lake was a midnight blue, as smooth as a mirror until everyone came back a few minutes later and jumped in. Amo came back in his bathing suit, and I watched as he stood at the edge of the water and waited for a servant to remove his swimming robe and the group formed a semicircle so he could dive in. He stood there for a moment, and I remember thinking he was heavier than my father, who was still trim and athletic. Then, with a small flourish, he dove in. He was a strong swimmer. Everyone was splashing around in the water; then he turned around and looked back at me standing there on the shore in my long skirt.

"Zainab, why aren't you swimming with us?" he said.

"I forgot my bathing suit!" I called back, using my planned-out excuse.

"How could you forget your bathing suit, Zainab?" Sarah said. "How silly of you! We were told to bring them!"

"Doesn't matter, Zanooba, just go up to my room and put on one of mine with a T-shirt!" Amo said.

That stopped me. The thought of going into his room and putting on Amo's swim trunks made my skin crawl. I couldn't imagine pulling his clothing on my naked body, then coming back out with everyone looking at me.

"No, thank you, Amo." I kept my resolve and called back politely, "I'll just watch tonight."

"Well then, just put on my dishdasha if you're shy about wearing mine! It's beautiful out here, isn't it, everyone? *Yala!*"

"*Yala! Yala!*" everybody chimed in. Come on! Come on!

I saw my parents' apprehensive faces in the water behind Amo. They were the only ones who weren't calling to me, and I appreciated their silence. I'm not going to fall for this, I thought. I am not going to wear his clothes, not even an ankle-length dishdasha. A bathing suit was respectable for swimming. A dishdasha or a T-shirt would cling to me in the water. I was a young woman now, and I knew what that meant. I was not going to wear Amo's clothes.

"Amo, I just really can't swim today," I called out finally, coming up with the only way I could to end the conversation. There was nothing he could say to a woman's excuse.

But after the swimming was over, he came over to me later as he toweled off. "You missed a very nice experience tonight, Zainab. The water was beautiful."

In August 1988, Amo declared victory against the Persian enemy, and eight years of war with Iran ended.

"So we got our territory from Iran?" I asked my mother.

"No, not really," she said. "The borders are the same."

"So nothing changed? What was the point of all those people dying?"

She made her opinion clear with a raised eyebrow.

Still, that was the most joyful day I ever saw in Baghdad. The city forgot to be afraid. People flooded out of their homes and into the street. There was music everywhere. People were dancing. You could hear the din all over the city. We drove downtown, and women were throwing water on the ground to usher in safety and *baraka*. A stranger from the crowd splashed water on our windshield and said, "I'll wash windows all my life if I have to, anything not to go to the front! Thank you, God! Thank you it's over at last!"

There was an official victory celebration at the palace, where two separate areas had been set up in the garden, one for the men's celebration hosted by Amo, and another for the women's celebration hosted by Aunt Sajida. There were huge long tables of food—stuffed meats, Iraqi dishes, and exotic fruits like mango, kiwi, and pineapple that I hadn't seen in Baghdad in years. I happened to be standing near Amo's daughter Raghad at the table, watching the entertainment and eating *bourak,* a famous Iraqi pastry filled with cheese that is a mix of Persian, Turkish, and Arab cuisine. Gypsy women were singing and dancing onstage in brilliant dresses of shiny greens and reds and yellows and purples. Their hair was black and straight and hung to their thighs as they danced to the music of drums and tambourines and string instruments I couldn't name. Plump, with rounded bellies, they wore the heaviest makeup I had ever seen. Their cheeks were very red, and their lipstick thick and dark. Their eyes were almost black with shadow and mascara. Heavy gold earrings hung from their earlobes, and their arms and necks were ringed with bangles and jewelry that clinked as they danced.

Then they finished their routine and packed up their instruments and headed for the men's area for their next performance.

"God only knows what they'll do now," Raghad commented as she watched the women walk off.

"Sing and dance?" I asked.

Raghad gave me a look that made me feel more naïve than I ever had in my life.

"Men *like* gypsy women, and my husband is in that men's party," she said. That was the only confidence she ever shared with me, though we had been together many times and were enrolled in the same college.

Amo had married her off to Hussain Kamel, the Tikriti man who tormented my father and terrorized much of Iraq, when she was just sixteen or seventeen. Everyone knew she had conditioned the marriage upon being able to complete her education. The uneducated Kamel had agreed, adding a condition of his own: a child a year for every year she spent in school. She was only two years older than I was, but she already had three children. I felt sorry for her that day. I asked my mother about the gypsy women later, and she explained to me that gypsies were nomads, so Amo had granted them citizenship. They too were "special files" open to a special kind of intimidation, I thought. He had sent the men to the front lines and kept their women in Baghdad to sing and dance in the palace.

One night when we were talking as usual on the back balcony of the French Institute, Ehab slowly pulled me toward him by the hand and hugged me. I looked up at his face, and he kissed me. It was my first kiss, and I had never experienced anything like it before. His lips were soft and incredible, and I felt almost weak with my first sense of what passion could bring. We had been together a year and a half before that first forbidden kiss. After that evening, we started talking about marriage, the children we would have and the life we would build together. We made a plan: I would open a translation service as soon as I finished school, and he would open a fabric store like his father, next to my office.

Baba, who had not even known about my relationship, was instantly and vehemently opposed once he heard. I was too young, the contrast between our two backgrounds was too large, Ehab couldn't support my lifestyle. He hadn't even finished his first year of university, though he was older than I was and I was now a sophomore. To my surprise, Mama failed to back me up. I cried for days on end. I refused to eat. I told Mama and Baba they would never see my smile again because without Ehab I would never find happiness.

"You always told me that I should marry for love, Mama!" I told her angrily after a month of suffering. "Now that I've found the man I love, you've changed your mind. Tell me, Mama, do you believe in love or not? Do you still want me to marry for love, or have you turned into Aunt Nada and want to marry me off to a rich man like Luma?"

I must have hurt her terribly with that. I had seen how hard she struggled to keep something of the old Alia alive inside her, and a part of that core was a belief in love.

Finally, she changed her mind, and though it took two months, she somehow managed to get Baba to invite Ehab to our house. I waited nervously for Baba's verdict after they had tea together alone in our garden.

"He wears way too much cologne," Baba declared. "I don't like him. I think he is the wrong man for you, but if you're going to kill yourself if I don't approve, then you give me no choice."

Hardly a resounding endorsement, but I had his approval. He said he had to ask Amo for his approval, and Ehab and I had to wait nervously for six weeks before he cleared a security investigation.

In Iraq, the engagement process starts with the women of the groom's family paying a formal visit to the home of the bride and asking her mother and other women of the family for the bride's hand in marriage. Special pastries called klache, made of dates and cardamom, are served by the future bride, who is expected to be demure and polite and represent her family with dignity. Mama ordered the klache and flowers and made a freshly squeezed pomegranate juice for the occasion.

When the day came, my aunts arrived in their latest fashions, perfect makeup and hairdos and perfumes. Ehab's mother and three sisters and several aunts whooshed into our house in old-fashioned black, baggy clothes, full abayas, and no makeup. Ehab's mother, a chubby, not very tall woman with a bland face, rushed forward and grabbed me in her arms. I fumbled as I tried to kiss her politely on each cheek, while she blanketed my face with unrestrained kisses. She was far more expressive than my mother and my aunts, who welcomed my future in-laws with greetings that were polite, but reserved. There could scarcely have been a bigger difference between women who spoke the same language, I thought, while I watched glances darting back and forth across the room, as the two sets of women studied each other.

I took my seat between them and served Turkish coffee as Ehab's mother began the traditional appeal requesting my hand in marriage. I had heard these appeals before. Strangers had come to our house before asking for my hand, and Mama and I had politely entertained them because we were expected to, only to laugh later at the thought I would consider marrying a man I didn't know. As Ehab's mother promised to guarantee my happiness, spoil me like her own daughter, provide whatever I needed or wanted, and support me in the lifestyle to which I was accustomed, I noticed Ehab's eldest sister surveying the furniture and staring at the family photographs on the wall. She had never been in a house such as ours before, and it was clear to all of us that our family would have to support us if we were to live in the manner to which I was accustomed. Aunt Samer looked over at me quizzically, and we exchanged surreptitious glances. See? I told her with my eyes. I heard what you were telling me in the pool at the Hunting Club; Amo didn't poison my values after all.

Aunt Najwa came up to me afterward and asked me a single blunt question: "What on earth are you getting yourself into, Zainab?"

A few weeks later, a caravan of cars drove up into our cul-de-sac and out stepped a dozen men, including tribal sheikhs. They strode into our house with a sense of command, in traditional dishdashas, shoulder *abayas* of fine handmade wool woven with gold, and white head cloths held in place with black bands. They shook hands with the men of my family, all in suits, and seated themselves in a circle in the garden. I watched nervously with the other women through the parlor window as Ehab's father and the highest ranking tribal elder completed the men's part of the ceremony that would seal our engagement. Each man recited poetry and Quranic verses about marriage that he knew by heart, including the Quranic phrase "And among his signs is that he has created spouses from among yourselves so that you may rest in them and initiate love and mercy among all of you." Baba, looking polite but ill at ease, wasn't equipped with memorized verses. Instead, he told them that I was dear to his heart and that he wanted nothing but my happiness and for God to bless my marriage with Ehab. When they finished, all the men ran the palms of their hands over their faces, read *Al Fateha*, the first chapter of the Quran, and shook hands, which was my signal to go out to serve each one a special juice from a large tray. As I served Baba, I saw on his face how hard it had been for him to go through with this. When I smiled at him reassuringly and gave him a kiss, he looked away.

For the engagement party, our garden filled with the smell of cooking and flowers reminiscent of my childhood. Radya came back to help. We had become good friends over the years, and I had been excited for her as she told me about the neighbor she had fallen in love with. She had finished high school, gotten married, and asked my father to help her husband get a job as a clerk at the airport. My mother was so excited about her wedding that she gave Radya her own wedding gown to be married in. Yet when I saw her that day, she was pregnant with her first child and was struggling with her-in-laws in the small house where she and her husband lived with his siblings. "Love is beautiful but life is hard when you and your husband don't have money," she told me.

The engagement party is traditionally a woman's event, and when it began, I stood with my aunts and friends in the garden as children came in bearing a Quran and my engagement ring, as well as a necklace, earrings, bracelet, and ring that Ehab had chosen for me as an engagement gift. Then came Ehab himself, handsome and elegant, followed by seven women from his family, each bearing traditional baskets of symbolic gifts for me of fabrics, perfumes, flowers, and sweets. Ehab and I danced together that night for the very first time, in front of everyone. Then he picked up the microphone and recited a love poem he had written for me. He looked over at me as he spoke, and I welled up with love and emotion. All my girlfriends were in tears at how handsome and romantic he was.

"Zainab, you did it!" Sarah said, congratulating me with a real hug. "You're marrying for love!"

On the other side of the garden, past the women in the black *abayas,* I took in the looks of disapproval on the faces of my mother and her friends. Ehab's poem had scandalized them. It was virtually a public admission of illicit dating. Nothing about him—his family, his financial prospects, his lack of a university degree, his seemingly backward tribal ties—matched their expectations. I didn't care. I will *not* be like you, I told them with a look. I will *not* live my life as you live yours.

I was happy that night. Mama was miserable.

"Zainab, do you know what Aunt Nada told me?" she said the next day. "She said, 'Alia, how could you even think of marrying your daughter to such a man? What are you doing? You've gone too far with your liberal ideas. It's your daughter's *life* we're talking about.'"

She smiled at me, then asked one more time, "Zainab, are you *sure*?"

I took it as just another sign she was capitulating to the farmhouse crowd.

A week after the party, a palace guard drove up with a new light green Mitsubishi. Baba brought in the keys in and registration papers and gave them to me.

"Your engagement present from Amo," he said. "The only pistachio-colored car in Iraq."

Automobiles were imported by the government, and almost every one of them except the black Mercedes was white. No one except my family and Ehab knew who had given the green car to me, and I loved driving it around Baghdad; it quickly felt like my signature. When I took Ehab out for a ride one day, however, he told me we should sell it and use the money to open his fabric store.

"But I don't want to sell it, Ehab," I said. "It is a gift to me."

"I will buy you a smaller, older car and we can use the money to invest in our future," he said.

"But it would be impolite to sell it so soon after receiving it," I insisted.

After our engagement was formalized, we were now expected to appear together as a couple, and Ehab grew more assertive in his role as my future husband. The first night we went out to a social engagement together, with a Cuban doctor sent to Amo by Fidel Castro, he got suddenly jealous and insisted on sitting next to me. He wasn't accustomed to seeing me laugh with another single man. He wasn't accustomed to seating arrangements.

He had simply been brought up differently than I had. One evening we got into a serious discussion about Sunni and Shia history and who had the right to rule Muslims after the death of the Prophet Mohammed, and I said I didn't understand why an event that happened thirteen hundred years ago should continue to be a source of hatred between Muslims. My mother had taught me—and Shia believe—that Ali, a cousin of Mohammed and his favorite son-in-law, had been tricked out of his right to lead all Muslims and later killed so the trickster could take over.

"If Ali got tricked by politicians, then it was his fault," Ehab told me. "All politicians play tricky politics, and how you win doesn't matter. If Ali lost, then he just proved he didn't deserve to lead Muslims. You know, lots lot of people think Shia have tails."

Tails? I couldn't believe I was hearing this from him. Just as some Christians in the West used to think Jews had horns, some Sunni apparently thought Shia had tails. Aunt Samer had just told me she had been in the sauna with friends at the Hunting Club and one woman, who had no idea she was Shia, casually mentioned that Shia were known to have tails. Aunt Samer stood up, dropped her towel, and bent over.

"Here's my butt," she said. "Take a good look. I am Shia. Look! Do I have a tail?"

I didn't understand such hatred and ignorance. Shiites were the ones who had been oppressed and victimized, and they didn't hate Sunnis with the same sort of passion some Sunnis hated them. Ehab obviously didn't believe such stories, but he had little respect for Shia. Samarra was a tribal Sunni stronghold that was best known, ironically, for a historic Shia mosque. The mosque is dedicated to Al Mahdi, the only one of twelve descendants of Ali and Fatima who was not believed to have been murdered. He is a Messiah-like figure to observant Shia, who make pilgrimages to the mosque to pray for his return. Some Samarra Sunni resented the constant pilgrimages of Shia into their midst, and Ehab apparently was one of them.

"I hate the Shia!" Ehab said in an outburst one afternoon. "They should all be killed! I'd like to go to Najaf someday and just kill them all off."

His sudden expression of hatred shocked me. I had spent time with many Sunnis, and I had never heard anything like it. I knew Amo hated Shia, but even he didn't talk this way, at least not around me.

"I am a Shia, Ehab," I said angrily. "So, you think I should be killed too?"

He immediately took my hand and said, "Oh no, my darling. Not you, you are different. You are special."

To this day, I am angry at myself for letting that moment pass and not standing up to his zealotry, but I was so in love I didn't see that the man I was engaged to was not quite the student poet I had fallen in love with. In our romantic trysts at the French Institute, he used to condemn Amo and the palace insiders I was anxious to escape. Now he was anxious to meet them. I had been willing to overlook the class differences between us, but he clearly hadn't. As I prepared to leave for America with my mother to buy my wedding dress, he handed me a long list of gifts I was to buy for all of his family members, neighbors, friends, and colleagues. While we were in Chicago, Ehab kept calling and asking me to stay home rather than go out with my family. He kept adding to the list of gifts he wanted me to buy, even including presents for friends' wives. He seemed to think he was entitled as my future husband to tell me what to do even though I was thousands of miles away, and I began to resent it. When he called and I wasn't there, he would leave angry messages on the answering machine.

When I stepped up to model a wedding dress in a three-way mirror, Mama kept needling me about him.

"Such a pity for all of this beauty to go to a man who does not deserve you," she said.

"Please, Mama, leave me alone," I begged her. But inside I was starting to feel afraid. Did he really think he had the right to control my movements? What about my thoughts? What was the point of marrying him if the freedom I so desperately wanted would be taken away in the name of love?

"He's crazy, Zainab," she said. "He's obsessive. You've got to break this off! Never let any man control you or abuse you!"

I had been hearing that line ever since I was small and a cook's daughter had confided to me that her stepfather had molested her. As I grew older and Amo's control over our lives became ever stronger, Mama had become more adamant. One afternoon, when we got back from shopping, I finally heard Ehab's obsession on the answering machine. This time there were seven messages, the last one ordering me to return home immediately. His tone of voice actually scared me. I imagined what it would be like to have a husband who talked to me like that for the rest of my life. He was like Heathcliff after all, obsessive and controlling and jealous.

I told Mama I was calling off the engagement and burst into tears. Had I been so desperate to escape Amo that I had run from one captor into the arms of another? That I had allowed myself to love a man who hated if not me, people like me, people like my grandmother? I couldn't believe how bad my judgment had been. When I called Ehab from Chicago to tell him of my decision, he went mad and refused to accept a breakup. I agreed to meet him in person to give back his engagement presents, but when I met him in Baghdad, he threatened to take me to a cleric near Samarra who would perform the wedding ceremony against my will. Then he started stalking me around Baghdad. Everywhere I went, he would follow me, and my family grew worried for my safety. Baba decided to ask for help. He gave up only after Baba went to talk to him with one of Amo's security guards.

I have never been so grateful for loving, supportive parents as I was after that breakup. I was devastated after the engagement fell through. I was so despondent I didn't want to leave the house. I had publicly humiliated myself, my mother, and my father. No-body ever said I told you so, but that's what everyone else I knew was thinking. People were polite enough, but they looked at me as if to say, Okay, you had your fun, your little experiment, and it didn't work. We knew it wouldn't all along, but you had to learn the hard way and embarrass your whole family as well. Now you've come back, and you realize you're just like us—which made me feel lonelier than ever. The only escape route I knew had turned out to be a mirage, and I completely lost faith in my own instincts. I was tired of arguing and tired of being the one who didn't fit in.

"Mama, will you help dress me up for Uday's engagement party?" I asked her. I planned those words out in advance so as to make her happy, and it worked. Baba had brought me a bolt of yellow silk from Thailand, and we took it to a dressmaker. It was the late 1980s, and excess was fashionable. When I put on the yellow dress the night of the party, I felt the big pouffy sleeves sticking out from my shoulders and the stiff new fabric of the waltz-length skirt sticking out around my legs. I sat down at my mother's vanity table for her to put makeup on me, and I remember looking at her in the mirror the way another woman might, appraising her care-fully applied foundation, her dark eye shadow, her shiny dress, and her freshly set hair. Why had she stopped wearing her hair long? I missed her long free-swinging hair. I felt her hand steady my chin as she applied mascara on my eyes and blush on my cheeks and a touch of lipstick on my mouth. I looked at myself in the mirror, but the smile I saw was hers, not mine. I felt I was taking the first step toward my own surrender.

When we walked into the hall that night, I felt like a champion horse she was showing off to the world, saying, Here is my daughter. Look at her. She is beautiful. She fits in. She is not different from you after all. All around me, women were clapping to the music with lipstick smiles and hair-sprayed hair and shiny faces and dresses. I looked like them, but I felt like a gift package all wrapped up in bows, delivered to the wrong address. I could feel the weight of the makeup on my face, like a mask hiding the real me underneath. I saw Mama laughing and dancing and wondered whether she was really enjoying herself or just pretending. When Uday walked in wearing his white tuxedo, women flocked around him like fans around a rock star. His future bride looked beautiful and innocent as she danced around him. I knew her. I liked her. She was a decent person. But she was also the daughter of the vice president, and her father had arranged this engagement for political reasons. How could any man do that to his own daughter? I wondered, knowing my own father would never do such a thing. How could these people celebrate her betrothal to the rapist of Baghdad? I knew most of them were family, his aunts and sisters, but didn't they take any responsibility for raising such a son? How could they ignore what a monster he was?

Uday later broke off the engagement. I was silently grateful it had happened, for her sake. But what people gossiped about was this: what had she done wrong to lose such a catch?

One day when I was still recovering from Ehab, my mother told me with a great deal of excitement that she had gotten a call from Fakhri's mother in America: her son wanted to marry me. She was so excited. Her eyes were shining. I hadn't seen her look this happy in a long time.

"Fakhri? Who is Fakhri?" I asked. I had no idea who she was talking about.

"Oh, you remember! You met him in Chicago!"

She reminded me of an older man I barely spoke to at a large gathering I had attended when I had gone to America to get the wedding dress.

"La, la, la, Mama," I said, lightly at first. "No, no, no, Mama."

She couldn't be serious. But she was.

"Mama, I don't want to go through that again," I said. "I just want to focus on my studies and that is all. No men for now."

"Oh, *habibiti*, don't let one bad experience color how you look at all marriage proposals, especially good ones like this," she said.

"What are you talking about, Mama? I can't just jump into another engagement. I need a break, Mama. I was with Ehab for two years. I need some time for myself before I can think of this whole marriage thing again."

"He lives in America, Zainab," she reminded me.

"But, Mama, I don't even know him!"

And it began to dawn on me how very serious she was. She looked at me imploringly, so very sadly. As if she had invested every ounce of energy in this offer to help save me from winding up as she was now.

"Look around you, Zainab," she said slowly. "Can't you see the bars?"

And I followed her eyes as she scanned the walls and the furniture and the glass patio doors leading out to our garden.

"They're invisible, but they are everywhere. It is a big country, but every day for the past ten years of my life I have felt the bars of this prison around me. This is your chance, honey. Take it. Don't stay here and be like me. Escape. This is your chance to be free."

That was such a painful and confusing moment. She was urging me to go against everything she had ever taught me to believe about love and marriage, but she was also showing me that she hadn't surrendered the core of her being after all. She had long ago stopped begging Baba to leave. But she was still aware of the hell we were living in. She had surrendered her own hopes of freedom, but she had never lost hope of helping me find mine.

"Who is he, anyway?" I asked.

And she started going on about how he was a successful businessman with a master's degree who lived in Chicago, a man from a good Shia family who had fled Iraq in the early 1980s, when I was just starting junior high school.

"How old is he?"

"Well, he's a little old," she admitted. "Thirty-three."

"Are you kidding, Mama? He's thirteen years older than I am!"

"Zainab, you tried the love route and it didn't work," she said. "Has it occurred to you that maybe that was for the best? You deserve more out of life than the future you can have here. You want a career, you want to see the world, you want freedom to do what you want to do and to say what you want to say. How can you ever find any of those things here? Trust me, *habibiti*. Take this chance, Zainab. Live the life I can't."

And I felt tears of confusion come into my eyes.

"Just promise me you will seriously consider it, all right, honey?"

Because she was Mama, I told her I would.

Luma had gotten married by this time, and she had met her fiancé only once, in her parlor, before agreeing to marry him. Now all she talked about was furnishing her new house. Was that what lay in store for me if I stayed? A rich husband and a big house to decorate? Yet she did seem happy in her marriage, and I found myself wondering if maybe the old ways were best. Maybe there was a reason for daughters to trust their parents' judgment when it came to something as important as marriage. Should I just listen to Mama and do what she asked of me? Fulfill her dream? Be a good daughter and make her happy for once? Where was I supposed to draw the line between being a good daughter and being true to myself? I couldn't tell. I had failed so completely at love that I didn't trust my own judgment anymore. I couldn't imagine falling in love again. And yet what if I did, and I got it wrong again? Mama was right. I had tried the love route, and it didn't work.

The only good part of the whole Ehab fiasco was that it had brought Baba and me closer than we had been for years. Baba had been kind and gentle to me during that time. He had always shown his love for me with gifts; one night he brought over a new tennis coach to the house, along with a new racket, in hopes of drawing me out of my depression and getting me out of the house. He had been right about Ehab since the very beginning. I wasn't used to talking over personal things with Baba, but I honestly wanted his opinion.

"I want to ask for your advice, Baba," I told him. "What do you think about this marriage proposal? Should I accept it?"

"It is your choice, Zainab," he said. "Not mine and not your mother's. You choose."

"No, Baba, I tried that before," I told him. "I failed, and I embarrassed you and Mama too. I don't want to do that again. You two make the decision for me. I trust your judgment to do what is best for me, and I will go along with it. I want to be a good daughter to you and Mama. I was so wrong before. I don't want go through that again and repeat the same mistake. Please, Baba. I want your advice. I really do. Tell me what to do."

"I could never do that, Zainab," he said, though it was clear he didn't want me to leave Iraq. "I can only tell you that you should not let your mother pressure you into accepting it. If you want to accept it, accept it because you want to. You need to live your own dreams and not your mother's."

I stayed up the whole night weighing my parents' arguments. Baba was right. I should not try to live my mother's dreams, but Mama was also right. I didn't want to stay here and live in her prison, either. I had been a witness to her suicide attempts, her tears, and her flights to her mother in Karbalā'. I had witnessed her pain. Was that what lay ahead for me?

So many things good and bad have happened to me as a result of that proposal that I cannot look back on it clearly and say why I ultimately made the decision I did. I loved visiting the United

States, but it was not home. I loved Iraq and couldn't imagine leaving my family and my whole life behind. But years of weekends at the farmhouse had taken their toll. I was deathly afraid of being trapped like my mother, both physically and emotionally. In the end, I didn't say yes to Fakhri, I said yes to Mama. She had been right about Ehab when I had been wrong, and I trusted her far more than I trusted myself to do what was best for me.

"Hamdelillah!" Mama said when I told her. "Thank God!"

Things moved quickly this time. Amo apparently gave grudging approval, and Fakhri's mother flew from the United States to formally request my hand. I served her Turkish coffee and *klache*. A small woman with a bony nose, she raved about her son, and handed me his picture. I studied his face. He looked very thin, with hollow cheeks and thin lips and a nose like his mother's. There was something cold about him, I thought, but then photographs were often misleading. One day the phone rang, and the face in the photograph had a voice, formal but friendly. Then there was a small engagement party with a few of my aunts and cousins in our parlor. I felt completely defeated that day—I, who had argued so vehemently for love, at my own engagement party had an empty seat next to me where my fiancé should have been.

Mama spent hours designing my dress, buying gifts for the wedding guests, and planning my trousseau. Mama and my brothers would fly over with me for a couple weeks, and Baba would come as soon as his schedule allowed. I surprised my teachers when I told them I was dropping out; I was one of their best students. But I explained that I had already bought my textbooks for the following year, and would return for finals. I already had a return ticket and planned to graduate on time.

"You will not come back, I know it, you won't come back!" Lana told me, crying.

"I've got to finish my fourth year," I told her, hugging her. "Of course I'll be back! I'm not even taking my albums or journals with me. When I come back, I'll be staying for a couple months to visit, and we'll see lots of each other then."

There was no big send-off at the airport. What I remember most is sitting in silence with my family and our driver at the VIP lounge inside Saddam Hussein International Airport. My father had tears in his eyes. My brothers looked tense and downcast, and even our driver was trying to stop his tears. Everyone looked sad but Mama. She looked as if she were on a mission.

Baba was captain of the first leg of the flight that carried me out of his life. As he lifted his jet into the sky, a song played on the audio system that was a tribute by Lebanese singer Fairuz to Baghdad's beauty and rivers and poetry. From the window seat I stared down at my city. It had been darkened for war for eight years. Now, just as I was leaving, it was all lit up. It looked like a beautiful carpet of twinkling lights, each with its own story. Down there somewhere were my cousins, my school, my home, and friends whose kisses had melted my heart when we said good-bye. I pressed my face into the window and tried to stop my tears as the lights turned to pinpricks and disappeared.

At least Amo was no longer going to be able to control my life. I had seen him just once since my breakup with Ehab. He had put a big hand on my shoulder and looked at me for what felt like a long time. That was one of those times I thought he was reading my eyes, and he seemed to see that I had been punished enough by the broken affair and said nothing about the breakup. Since my new engagement, there had been silence. No engagement present, no congratulations. Mercifully, I thought, I was being punished for leaving. Yet my sadness was profound. Was I crying because of where I had come from or because of where I was going? I didn't know. I felt as if I were flying into a black hole, and I willed myself to sleep.

I stepped off into crowded American daylight. Fakhri's family and some friends were there to greet us at the gate. I quickly scanned the crowd for Fakhri and recognized him from his picture. I greeted every other person first, beginning with kisses for his mother and his father, a nice-looking man who greeted me warmly, then a sister who looked me over the way Raghad and Rana did when I arrived for their parties, and other relatives and friends. Finally there was no one left.

"How long did you think you could avoid greeting me?" he asked.

I smiled politely and shyly shook his hand without responding to his question. I didn't want to kiss him on the cheeks and feigned shyness. When I finally looked him in the face, I recognized that there was no chemistry between us. There was no skip of a heartbeat, no connection at all. There was no softness in his eyes, no invitation to love. Standing before me was a tall, older man who looked like his mother.

When he picked up my two suitcases off the baggage carousel, I felt as if he were literally holding my whole life in his hands. I sensed the power he held over me, and I felt vulnerable as I followed him out the airport door to the parking lot, where he opened the trunk of a big American luxury car, black.

"I bought this car in your honor," he said. "What do you think?"

"It is very nice," I said and smiled politely. Was he trying to impress me with money and a used luxury car? It had a broken side mirror. "It is very nice of you to buy it in my honor."

"I bought it at auction," he said, adding, "I can get the mirror fixed."

From Alia's Notebook

Samira was the only one who called him by his first name. It is worth noting that Samira is a 35-year-old blonde woman with blue eyes.

He first developed his relationship with Samira during the summer of 1981. Samira was a teacher in Al Makasseb Elementary School. He was a frequent visitor to that area as he had a swimming pool near the school which he often went to with his friends. Samira tried to get close to him in many ways. She claimed that she wanted his help in her divorce case from her husband. He helped her get her divorce from her husband and she became his full-time mistress, joining him in all the parties he hosted, even the exclusively male parties. Samira never left his side. He often talked about how much he liked the fact that sometimes she behaved as a teenager and sometimes as an adult woman. He talked about how comfortable he was with her, for she did whatever he asked of her. He would send her for a medical checkup now and then to ensure that she was in good health and free of all diseases. She would be the only woman drinking with him and his male friends and would go with him to his van in the middle of the party to come back after few moments filled with the smell of sex and lust.

Samira, like Saddam, came from a poor family. But unlike him, she grew up in Baghdad and came from a larger family that overall had a respected name. She shared his vengeance on those who enjoyed a good life. They often started cursing with each other around those with whom they felt comfortable. He changed a lot during that period. Prior to knowing Samira he was trying hard to imitate the elite in their behavior and lifestyle. He would ask us to teach him how to eat with a fork and a knife. He would never curse and always talked attempting to change his accent to a city one. During his relationship with Samira however, he dropped his attempt to behave properly and switched to vulgar talk with her and everyone that was surrounding them.

One day, she hit him jokingly. That caused his head piece (from his traditional Arabian dress) to fall on the floor, the thing that is considered an insult for an Arabian. He immediately started to hit her with all his strength using his head piece, which can be as hard as a leather belt. In the process she started kissing his hands and feet, the thing that gave him a great level of pleasure. So he continued to hit her and she continued to kiss him and we were all witness to this until they went to the van to make up.

8

❖

COLLATERAL DAMAGE

I WAS TO BE A JUNE BRIDE IN AMERICA, but the wedding was to be conducted in the tradition of Iraq, in two parts. The first part is an Islamic religious ceremony, after which the couple is generally allowed to get to know each other more intimately than they would be permitted to do on their own, as a kind of sanctioned trial run. If this fails, the marriage is annulled. If not, the couple is deemed formally married when they are presented to their community at a large public reception—a wedding party. Often there are many months between these two events. In our case, the public ceremony would follow soon after the religious one.

On the morning of my Islamic wedding, I let my mother dress me in the gold-and-white creation she had designed for me in Baghdad, a stunning traditional Iraqi *sayya,* a full-length dress topped with a long vest that she had embroidered with flowers and poetry in gold thread. I don't remember feeling much of anything as our wedding party set off on the highway in two cars for Fakhri's house. I was a backseat passenger on my way from an Iraqi past to an American future. We had been driving for about thirty minutes when the car in front of us pulled over to the side of highway, and ours followed. My father got out of the first car and

stalked back toward us as cars and trucks whizzed by at frighten-
ing speed to our left. My mother gave a heavy sigh of exasperation
and lowered her window.

"This is wrong, Alia!" my father shouted angrily over the sound
of traffic. "We cannot let this marriage proceed. We cannot do this
to her!"

"I am *not* taking her back to Iraq!" my mother said, and burst
into tears. "This is her chance at a future. This marriage must go
through. I will not allow her to go back to Iraq! I am *not* taking her
back there!"

It was a continuation of an argument that had started the
night before. There had apparently been some disagreement over
the terms of the dowry, and Baba felt Fakhri had treated him with
disrespect. Baba said he didn't trust Fakhri because he had gone
back on his word. Mama's argument had little to do with the
bridegroom and everything to do with making sure the bride
stayed in America. My mother fighting to leave Iraq, my father
fighting to stay in Iraq—the same argument I'd heard since I was
twelve. The only difference now was it was my life they were arguing over, not theirs. I thought about how heartbreaking it was, the
two people I loved most, each convinced the other was trying to
ruin my life on my wedding day. I was the only one who wasn't crying. I remember just staring out at the shoulder of the road, a dirt
strip littered with dried up weeds, and wanting desperately for
them to stop.

"Zainab, I *beg* you not to do this," Baba said, finally turning to
appeal to me directly, tears in his own eyes. "You don't have to do
this. Don't let your mother impose her choice on you. It is *your* life,
honey, not your mother's."

I loved him very much at that moment. Despite our disagree-
ments, I had never, ever doubted how much he loved me. Part of
me thought he was right. How could I marry a stranger I felt no at-
traction for? But I also understood Mama's point, and the one
thing I felt good about was that for once I was being the good, dutiful daughter to her. I hated to see her cry. Besides, what were the

alternatives if I went back? No one was talking about that, really, but there it was. Was anything better waiting for me there? If I went back to Baghdad now, I would embarrass my whole family. People would think there was something wrong with me—twice engaged, twice failed.

"I will take responsibility for my own marriage," I said finally, coming up with the only answer I could find that avoided taking sides. "I will have a talk with him, and then I'll make my decision."

When we got to Fakhri's home, where the religious ceremony was to be held, guests were already gathering downstairs. We went upstairs where we could be alone, and I had a serious talk with him for the first time about my expectations for this marriage. I told him that I expected respect, a college education, a meaningful career, and financial independence. I told him he should not expect me to cook and clean—or to do anything at all just because I was a woman. I wanted to be clear, given what had happened with Ehab, so that there were no misunderstandings. I was almost surprised to find that he listened to me.

"I promise that I will love you and cherish you, Zainab," he said. "I respect what you are asking for, and I assure you I will try to give you a happy life."

He still wasn't handsome, with his small eyes and long nose, but for the first time I saw the possibility of love coming after marriage. In that upstairs room, with his family waiting below, he was gentle and respectful. He told me he understood and that he would support me in becoming whatever I wanted to be in life, and it occurred to me that maybe we just hadn't had enough time to be alone together. When we walked back downstairs together, I was nervous, but relieved.

I could face my father and mother and tell them both in good conscience that I was willing to go forward.

As I came downstairs in my *sayya*, I saw my brothers, Haider looking out of place, and Hassan, not quite ten, standing very close to my father, who had clamped down the disapproval on his face. Other than my family, I knew only a few of the two dozen people assembled there. I sat down next to Fakhri on the sofa as we had arranged, with the imam in front of us, and prepared to witness my first traditional Iraqi religious marriage ceremony—my own. It was a beautiful ceremony, rich in the symbols of Islam from all the cultures that contributed to Iraqi culture, from Iran, Turkey, and the Middle East. Two happily married women—one of them my mother—held a swatch of fabric over our heads while two others rubbed sugarcanes together to sweeten the marriage. My feet were dipped into a silver bucket filled with mint and rose petals, a Quran was placed in my lap, and cardamom seeds were tucked between my fingers. I felt as if I were watching a play.

"Zainab, do you accept this man to be your husband and to marry him in front of God and his prophet?" the imam asked.

I didn't answer. Mama had told me that he was going to ask me this same question twelve times, once for each descendant of the prophet Shia believed were the rightful leaders of the Muslim nation, before I was supposed to respond. Fakhri had already said yes, and it felt like an eternity each time the imam repeated the question to me, an eternity to consider and reconsider, with everyone in the room quietly staring at me, my head filled with voices frantically arguing with each other. What would happen if I just said no? Was it too late? I saw my father, looking miserable, across from me, and I felt the weight of Mama's presence above me, giving me blessings for a happy marriage when she no longer had one herself. I wanted to scream, No! How could I possibly do something so *ayeb*? Hadn't I just had a perfectly nice discussion with him a few moments ago? Again and again, the imam asked, and finally against all my instincts, I heard myself say "Yes."

Fakhri looked at me with relief and kissed me on my forehead. I couldn't look at him.

Hassan ran out of the room screaming, and Baba ran after him.

"Well, this isn't a funeral!" Fakhri's mother commented to her son, as she kissed him in congratulations. "This is supposed to be a happy occasion!"

We signed the standard marriage contract, a form with blanks for the dowry and signatures and, ten days later, on the arm of my new husband, I walked into our wedding reception. Two hundred people celebrated in a rented hall. I knew very few of them. I put on my plastic smile, greeted them, and danced with my husband. He had a victorious look on his face, as if he had caught a big fish.

We had a suite in a hotel that night and planned to have breakfast with our parents the next day before leaving for a honeymoon in Hawaii. I was nervous about the wedding night. I went to him in my new nightgown feeling shy. I had never had sex before, but I also knew how a kiss can melt the heart. He asked me to lie on the bed and spread my legs apart. I did. Then he suddenly was on top of me, an uncomfortable stranger pressing into me. He didn't say anything. There was no kiss, no caress at all, no tenderness or effort to help me relax. There were just humiliating shoves and then he stopped. I felt hurt and invaded, but there was no blood on the sheets; we each looked. I knew that in some parts of rural Iraq, men still had to produce the marital bedsheets with virginal blood or the bride's entire family was shamed. Our family was far more sophisticated than that, and my mother the biology teacher had explained to me that there isn't always blood.

"What's wrong with you?" he asked. "Come on, open up! I'm sure you know how."

"What? What are you talking about?" I said. "How could you say that to me, Fakhri?"

"Well, you're not a virgin," he said. "No blood came out."

"I *am* a virgin, Fakhri," I said. "But, just so you know, there doesn't have to be blood to show you're a virgin. It depends on the woman."

"Well, I don't know what you are, but you are not a virgin," he said, and he turned over. "I'm going to sleep."

I can't even describe all the feelings that passed through me in waves that night. Alone, wide awake, I lay there in the dark trying to figure out what I had done wrong. My mother's anatomical drawings had not prepared me for this. I was a virgin. The closest I had come to sex was kissing Ehab. But I remembered hearing stories of girls losing their virginity through sports accidents, and I searched back through my memory, trying to think of a time I might have injured myself without knowing it. Was there something else I was supposed to do? I moved as far away from the man next to me as I could and curled up on the edge of the bed like a child, holding my confusion and fears within as I realized that this was only the first of thousands more nights to follow.

The next morning, when our parents came to have breakfast with us and take us to the airport, I managed to take Mama aside.

"Are you sure what you have told me about blood is correct, Mama?"

"Yes, honey, but from what you are describing, I don't think you had sex."

Only a virgin would have failed to understand that her husband had impugned her innocence to cover up his own inability to perform.

We flew to Hawaii for our honeymoon, but the only beauty I saw there was a deep blue horizon that made me wish I were far away. Other newlyweds, langorous and in love, celebrated with tropical drinks and intimate hugs in the Jacuzzi. Their happiness only made me feel sad and isolated. Almost the only time Fakhri was kind to me was when we were in front of others and they took pictures of us and made *ooh* and *ahh* sounds when he told them we were on our honeymoon. When we were alone, I felt as though I had married an entirely different person than the man who had listened to me so attentively before the religious ceremony. They had buffets at the hotel, and he lied so we could eat free, claiming he had lost complimentary tickets that came with some show. Then he told me to eat as much as I could at the buffet so I could get all the food I needed for the day. I was shocked and embarrassed. This was not the world I had come from. I had been taught honesty since birth and trained never to lie or steal. Now I was married to a man who did both of these things and was rude and cheap as well. At night, he started telling me I wasn't "womanly" and didn't know how to please a man.

The third or fourth night of my honeymoon I couldn't even stay in the same bed with him. I lay on the sofa and cried. Love comes after marriage, I kept reminding myself. If Luma and others had managed to be happy, I told myself, why couldn't I? It was just getting to know each other that was hard. I tried and tried to think of a way out of my quandary. I contemplated my own failure to be womanly. What was I doing wrong? I felt none of the pleasure my mother had told me about, and I certainly wasn't wearing the kind of smile on my face that I came to recognize on hers after I knew she'd had sex with my dad. I thought that if I could just prove to him that I was a virgin, he would treat me better. I tried imagining that this painful trial period was over and that I had somehow learned to love him. What would I do when that day came? How would I behave? A small, logical answer came to me: I would kiss him. The next night, I went to the bed, kissed him, and tried as hard as I could to *imagine* that I loved him. By the end of the evening I had my proof; there was blood on the sheets.

He was happy when he saw that blood.

"So you are a virgin after all," he said with a laugh.

I was relieved, but confused. I actually looked at the bedsheet with spots of blood and considered taking it with me as proof, doing the same thing that my mother and I always ridiculed Amo's village family for doing. But I couldn't bring myself to do it. He never mentioned the subject of my virginity again, and he began treating me more nicely.

We talked for a while about how to make marriage work. I was nervous about the impact his parents, particularly his mother, might have on our marriage. I had often heard stories about in-laws interfering in a couple's life, and I wanted to make certain that didn't happen to us. Fakhri agreed, and we promised each other that we would abide by a rule in our marriage: to keep our problems to ourselves and not involve our families. But I was surprised when we got back to Chicago to find he had other rules in mind as well. He informed me as he was dressing to go to work for the first time that I was to get up with him, make him breakfast, and press a shirt for him each morning. He brought the iron into the bedroom and began to recite my wifely duties as he plugged it in. He gave me a twenty-dollar bill and told me that was my allowance for the week.

"Twenty dollars?" I asked, staring in shock at the bill in my hand.

"That should be more than enough for your needs."

He kept the keys to the car he had presented me at the airport and handed me keys instead to a car that turned out to be so old and battered it barely ran. We also had an argument about my education. I told him that I wanted to enroll in certain classes to help me prepare for my exams in Iraq, and he told me he thought it was a waste of time for me to get a college degree and recommended that I get a real estate license instead so I could start making money.

He was going back on everything he had promised in our little talk before the religious ceremony, and I had no proof it had ever even happened. I reminded him of our agreement, and he responded that he was abiding by it; I was welcome to do whatever things I chose to do as long as I performed first the wifely duties that we both understood superseded them. I was to be his wife, keep his house, and start giving him children as soon as I got my real estate license. I argued and I protested, but what was my alternative? If I called my parents, they would just get into more fights with each other and suggest I at least give the marriage a chance. We compromised on the education front. He agreed to give me enough money to enroll in two classes at a local community college, and I agreed to take a real estate course along with an English writing course in preparation for my finals in Baghdad.

Finally, I theorized that if I could prove I could do the housework the way I had proved I was a virgin, he would meet me halfway. My shirts never looked like Radya's, but I ironed. I cooked, though he ridiculed my painstaking efforts every night at the dinner table, sometimes in front of guests. I felt poor and vulnerable and utterly dependent on him, both financially and emotionally. When I asked him for more money midweek, he made me recite everything I'd spent the first twenty dollars on and criticized me for wasting money on two greeting cards for friends in Iraq.

I began to feel I had escaped prison in Iraq only to wind up in solitary confinement in Chicago. I felt depressed and trapped. I looked around my apartment and thought of the farmhouse and did now what I had done then: I read. With no money and no one to talk to, I turned to Danielle Steel. There were so many of her paperbacks in the used bookstore near our house, I could only hope they would last me until I learned the secret of how to love a husband who didn't seem to care about loving me. Danielle Steel wrote about women in abusive relationships, and in the end she rewarded them by setting them free. Actually, I'm not sure now if that's what her books were about; I do know that is what I read into them.

We had been married a little over a month when Saddam Hussein invaded Kuwait, whose oil fields Iraq had historically laid claim to, setting off an international showdown that would lead to the Gulf War five months later, in January 1991. I found out about the invasion over dinner at Fakhri's parents' house. Instead of launching another invective against Amo across the dinner table in my direction that night, my father-in-law announced that he had just called the Iraqi embassy and left a message saying congratulations! Kuwaitis are the Arabs that Iraqis and many other Arabs love to hate. In Baghdad, what we saw of Kuwait was arrogant rich sheiks who came to Baghdad to spend their ill-gotten gains on Iraqi prostitutes and Iraqi property, driving up the prices for both. This resentment of Kuwaitis was so ingrained, it trumped even Fakhri's father's hatred of Saddam. There would be time enough to get rid of Saddam after he did the dirty work of retrieving Kuwait.

All I could think was What? Another war? We just finished one!

So many people were dead, so *many*. I believed you when you said loved Iraq, Amo. But if you do, why are you taking your people into another war? What's the point? Why are you doing this?

Almost immediately, the White House began issuing ultimatums. Iraq was on the news almost every night, and Fakhri and I were watching television when a news report came on talking about a secret gassing that had killed thousands of Kurds a few years before. As the scenes I remembered from Lana's description flashed across my mind, Fakhri pointed a finger at the television set and stared at me as if I were responsible. "Look what a criminal *your* Amo is!" he said. I didn't say anything. I was fresh from Iraq. Fakhri still did not understand—or did not care to find out—that I called him "Amo" not out of affection, but because I was afraid to say his name—*Saddam Hussein*—out loud. I knew Amo had spies everywhere. I didn't know who his spies were in this community. I didn't trust anyone, including, for that matter, my husband.

A few weeks after the invasion, my father was able to call me when he was on a trip outside Iraq. Fakhri answered the telephone and immediately began complaining about me to him, about how I wasn't a good enough housewife or something to that effect—as my anger boiled. It felt as if he were complaining to a merchant who had sold him bad produce. How dare he do that to my father? To me? What had happened to our agreement to work out our marital issues on our own?

I had never heard anything as gentle and warm as Baba's voice when Fakhri finally handed me the phone.

"Are you all right, honey?" he asked me. I just wanted to fly into his arms for protection. If only I had taken his advice and refused to marry Fakhri, this nightmare wouldn't be happening. But I couldn't tell him how miserable I was. Fakhri was sitting nearby, and I felt strongly that I had to take responsibility for making my marriage work. There was nothing Baba could do to help me.

"I miss you a lot, Baba," I said. "I wish I could come and visit you in Baghdad."

"You can't right now, honey," he said. "They've closed the borders. You can come visit once things have calmed down again."

Then he paused and said, "All new marriages are hard, Zainab. Just be patient and take care of yourself until we see you again."

Then, to lighten things up, he jokingly added a comment he used to make about marriage in Iraq.

"You know what I always say, Zainab. Marriage is like a barrel that is filled half with honey and half with shit," he said. "You can start by eating the honey and then deal with the shit part later, or you can start with the shit and end up with the honey part. I suggest you mix them up. That's the secret of a successful marriage."

I giggled politely. He was famous for that bit of advice, which often made adults laugh. Now he was giving it to me. When I hung up, I tried to remember to be patient and look for the honey. How patient, though? Love may come after marriage, but how long does it take? I set a deadline: a year. I would give the marriage one year. If it didn't work then, no one would say I hadn't tried.

Looking back on it, I realize I was also in culture shock. I had assumed the transition to America would be easy; I felt comfortable with Americans, and after all my father's summer training at Boeing, I considered Seattle my second home. But the people in Fakhri's community were like neither the Americans nor the Iraqis I knew. They were Shia businessman and professionals like Uncle Adel's neighbors, who had been deported, leaving their dreams behind to rust in the rain with boxes of factory machinery. Some had lost everything. Others, like Fakhri's family had managed to flee before being dispossessed. A decade later, this was where they had wound up, heels dug into round-the-clock jobs, doing their best to educate their children, and embracing, more fervently than most ever had in Iraq, the religion for which they had been persecuted.

The only person I found to talk with was a young Iraqi woman about my age who had come to America from Iran. Also lonely, also married to a much older man, she came from a prominent family that had been deported from Baghdad not long before the Mukhabarat came after my mother's family. This was the first time I had ever heard a firsthand story of what had happened to a deportee, and I absorbed her tears like a sponge. Secret police had shown up at their door at midnight and given them fifteen minutes to pack a suitcase. In the dark they were boarded onto buses for the Iranian border along with hundreds of other Baghdad residents "of Iranian origin." They were force-marched for days in freezing weather so they could be "returned" to Iran. When they bedded down at night in the freezing desert, Iraqi soldiers sauntered among them with rifles, singling out young girls and women to rape. The young woman's parents tried to hide her and her sister under blankets. Soldiers found them anyway, and her father bribed them to spare his daughters. After leaving her family penniless, the soldiers just moved down the line and raped other girls whose fathers weren't rich enough to save them. Faced with a sudden refugee crisis ignored by the outside world, Iran housed the Iraqis in makeshift refugee camps for months before finally allowing them to go to Tehran to try to make a life for themselves among Iranians who saw them as citizens of the country with which they were at war. This young woman's family had scrimped for years to send their daughter out of Iran. Her salvation was an older man she still barely knew who was about to be the father of her child. She might have been me, I thought. Amo had saved us and punished her instead.

Fakhri's community had good reason to hate Amo, and his family in particular was very bitter. To them I was a "friend of Saddam" who had shared his palaces while they suffered. Fakhri never let me forget that. He would pick up one of my things and sneer in a whiny voice, "Oh, did you get *this* as another perk of being Saddam's friend?" The sad part was that I could see other professional couples who had made successful, loving marriages out of engagements facilitated by their parents or elders. Fakhri, on the other hand, seemed to see me as a kind of mail order bride, like the lonely girl from Iran, like thousands of other young immigrant brides streaming into the United States from oppressed countries worldwide. I was supposed to be not only obedient and amenable to spousal training, but grateful for the opportunity—a toxic mix of American arrogance and Arab machismo.

I sometimes felt that when he looked at my face, he saw Saddam Hussein's instead. I began to suspect he was using our marriage to make up for that inequity. *Your friends are your friends because of who I am,* I thought one night as my tears dropped into the dishwater, making a crinkling sound in the suds. My enemies are my enemies because of who you are too, Baba, I thought bitterly. I was the daughter of the pilot of Saddam Hussein, and Fakhri was doing to me in bed what the whole exile community wanted to do to Amo. I tried to put out of my mind the short ugly English swear words he used each night as he *fucked* me. *Fuck you, fuck you,* he would say as I prayed for morning. To him I might have been a piece of wood, stiff and dry.

I understood the concept of a wife meeting her husband's sexual needs. That was culturally Arab. I later found out that there is enormous confusion between cultural and religious issues and that Islam is very explicit about sexual pleasure being the responsibility of both marital partners, which was what my mother had told me. I tried to talk with Fakhri about sex, but he only got angry. Finally, I called his mother, feeling that if he had violated our one marriage rule, I could too, especially if it was in the name of helping our marriage succeed. I thought that as a woman she would understand and explain to him that a woman needs to be treated gently. She invited me to tea, and I broached the topic obliquely after the traditional courtesies. But my woman-to-woman tact yielded only an outburst of exclamations accompanied by arm waving. "What are you *talking* about?" she scolded, gesticulating dramatically over the teacups, her voice sliding up and down. "It is your wifely *dooo-ty* to satisfy my son's needs! As a good wife, you must be prepared to satisfy your husband's sexual needs at any time. His needs come first—did your mother not teach

you this? Tell me, do you bathe before bedtime and put on perfume? Do you do up your hair and put on sexy lingerie before you
walk around the bed seven times to offer yourself to him?" This
went on for two hours, until she finally ran out of breath. The only
thing I could think of to say as I left, as politely as I could manage,
was "I'm sorry, but I disagree."

Was she kidding? Walk around the bed seven times displaying
myself to Fakhri? What she was describing was slavery. I learned
later that there apparently are places where this circumnavigation
of the marital bed is actually practiced, but I doubted it was in my
mother-in-law's own bedroom; she complained constantly about
her husband behind his back when I went with her to some
women's gatherings. So very different from my mother's parties,
these gatherings were all about religion and wifely duties. Sometimes I thought they were discussing a different religion than the
one I was taught. Where was the dividing line between being a
good wife and allowing your husband to control or abuse you?
Were women worth less than men? How many men gathered to
discuss their husbandly duties?

Three months after our wedding was my twenty-first birthday.
My present from Fakhri was $50 and a new bedtime accusation I
didn't even understand: I was now a "whore" who was no longer
"tight" in my vagina. The next time we quarreled, I refused to have
sex with him. He screamed at me and threw me down on the bed.
Then he flipped me over onto my stomach and forced my head
into the pillow. He held my head down and started penetrating
me from behind, hurting me as he had never hurt me before.
"Fuck you," he cursed, again and again. I cried into the pillowcase
until my voice disappeared. I couldn't breathe, and I was afraid I
was going to die of suffocation. I vividly remember how powerless
I felt. Finally, I consciously stopped resisting and took my soul
away, leaving my body an empty shell for him to abuse so he only
had the illusion of power over me. In some painful faraway place, I
counted each second until he finished. Then he got up, put on his

clothes, and walked away as if I were a piece of dirt he was leaving behind.

I hobbled out of bed and turned on the shower. I stayed in the white plastic enclosure for an hour, sobbing and trembling in pain. *Ightisab,* I thought in Arabic. Rape.

When I finally came out, Fakhri told me to get dressed because we were going out to dinner with his mother. That was when I broke. I hated him! I would *never* love him! I screamed at him. I flailed at him with my fists, and when he tried to hold my arms down again, I bit him on his forearm. "Domestic violence!" he shouted and called 911. He really did. I didn't know what domestic violence meant. It just seemed ludicrous that a grown man, much larger than I, would call 911 and say, "My wife bit me" after what he had done to me. I ran into the bedroom, locked the door behind me, and packed one bag with my best clothes, my mother's jewelry, and my $400 in cash. When the police arrived and I finally came out of the bedroom, his mother was actually sitting in the living room, waiting for us to go out to dinner. Fakhri tried to tell them I had attacked him, that *he* was the victim.

"Look, she bit me here," he said, trying to show the police a bite mark on his arm that hadn't even pierced the skin. "You need to take her to the station so she can learn a lesson."

"Yes, I bit him," I told the police. "I'm ready to go with you."

On the way out to the police car, the policeman asked me gently if I was in love with someone else. "No" I answered. "Did he hurt you, then?" he asked. I didn't answer immediately, then murmured a soft no. I wasn't about to tell a strange man, let alone a policeman, about my sex life. It never occurred to me to talk to police; the only police I had ever met terrified me. I just asked to call my mother's friend when we arrived at the station, and she came to pick me up. The next day, while Fakhri was at work, she drove me back to the apartment. We packed my clothes, my Persian rug, and the wedding china my mother had given me. Everything else, including all the wedding gifts, I walked away from.

"Take the bedsheets," she said.

Why do I laugh remembering this when it was really so tragic?

"What am I going to do with the bedsheets?"

"Okay, just take the pillowcase," she said.

"Why?"

"To be mean to him, to remind him when he comes home that you're gone and that it was you that left him."

A small, satisfying act of revenge only a woman would think of. I liked it. I walked over to the bed and stripped my pillow of its beige-flowered pillowcase and green border. Taking it was the only act of my marriage that honestly gave me pleasure. I still have it. A reminder that I had learned the lesson my mother had taught before I left Baghdad: never let any man abuse you; always be a free spirit.

When I walked out of Fahkri's life, I was injured and angry and I hated men. All men. I swore to myself that I would get into no more relationships with men. Both of the men I had become involved with had promised to love and care for me, and I had trusted them. But they both had hidden agendas. Neither was what he appeared at first. Both were hypocrites who had lied to me to trap me and control me. The other two major male figures in my life were Amo, who had controlled and abused millions of people, and my father, who was a loving man, but whose wife felt so caged in that she had tried to kill herself to escape. Did I mention that there were more suicide attempts than just that one when I was little? That I worried about her sometimes when she went near the medicine cabinet?

I really, really, really wanted to go home. I felt so homesick it hurt. I just wanted to go back to school where I belonged and pretend these awful months never happened. But I couldn't even contact my mother to tell her I had left Fakhri. All communications had been cut off. I tried to call home hundreds of times, but the calls wouldn't go through. Mail service was cut off too, so I couldn't write. I still had my return business class ticket, but no international flights were permitted into Iraq. (Baba, I later found out, had flown his fleet of civilian airliners to Tehran for safekeeping in case the airport was bombed.) The only way I could get home was through Jordan, but I knew no one there and was afraid of being stranded with no money. With nowhere to go, I finally called an uncle of my father's in Los Angeles, and he invited me to stay with his family. I wrote a letter then to Mama telling her I had left Fakhri and where I was going. I sent it the only way I could think of: with an address in Amman, Jordan, on the front in English and a message on the back in Arabic saying, "To the people of Jordan: I ask for your generosity and kindness for delivering this letter to my beloved mother at this address in Baghdad, with many thanks from her loving daughter, who is stranded in America."

When I arrived in Los Angeles, I went to the Immigration and Naturalization Service because my tourist visa, acquired on the assumption I eventually would be admitted as the spouse of a green card holder, was about to expire. After hours in many lines, I wound up talking to an African-American INS agent who was so gentle and motherly to me I can still remember her face. She listened to me and made me feel I would be okay. "You can get a job," she said, and when I walked out that day I had a temporary work permit available to foreigners caught in America due to political crises. I got two jobs, one selling clothes at The Limited and another as a cashier at a Hallmark stationery store run by a kind Italian family my father's uncle knew. As soon as I got a paycheck, I filed for divorce and bought a car. The car was a battered two-tone 1978 Chevy that cost $600. It was the first thing I'd ever bought with my own money, and I was ecstatic driving it off the lot.

Meanwhile, the United States and Iraq were on the brink of war. Amo was on the news constantly. I remember watching a little British boy who was one of hundreds of people taken hostage as human shields in the days leading up to the war. Amo allowed cameras in to document how well he was treating them. The little boy was on his lap, and Amo patted his head. "Did Stuart have his milk today?" he asked. And I thought of poor Hassan watching this in Baghdad; he had been made to sit on Amo's lap, looking as scared as little Stuart did now. I cringed as I remembered Amo holding a glass of whiskey to Hassan's lips and forcing him to drink, thinking, no doubt, he was helping make a man of him.

American news commentators recoiled at the way Amo treated this little British boy—an affection which, incidentally, I saw as genuine. (I knew that Amo saw no conflict between feeling fondness for people and killing them.) They talked about the perversion of a man who would pat a child on the head one moment and send him off for use as a human shield the next. They were right, but why couldn't they take it one more step? If Americans could feel so much sympathy for that one child, why didn't they even mention the millions of Iraqi children who didn't have their milk today? Or take the logical next step? All Iraqis were that little boy. All of us were hostages. By the time I had met Amo, I was too big to sit on his lap, yet I was there for ten years. So were my mother and my father. Americans were a generous and empathetic people. Why had they remained silent about all the crimes Amo had committed when he was one of America's best friends and the U.S. government was sending him money? There had been years of torture, years of ethnic cleansing and corruption and mass deportations. Why, now that everyone was aware of his tyranny, was the White House talking about bombing his victims? Why was the FBI harassing Iraqi-American children at school? Sending agents into Iraqi-American homes and questioning their loyalty to America? Even considering putting exiles into internment camps as they had Japanese-Americans during World War II? The way the U.S. government was demonizing Iraqis reminded me of the way Amo had demonized Iranians, dehumanizing them in preparation for war. "Never tell anyone you're Iraqi," one Iranian-American I met advised me. "Trust me, you'll just be harassed. Say you're from Saudi Arabia." I decided I would rather be harassed. My family had suffered too much trying to prove its Iraqi citizenship. I was a citizen of Iraq. I was proud to be Iraqi.

Soon it was Christmas. Shopping season. Lights twinkled in Southern California malls. Children sat in Santa Claus's lap and made wishes. Sometimes a mother would sneak back into the Hallmark store and buy her daughter something she had had her eye on when they had been in together. I was so lonely for my mother. It had been three months since I'd had any communication with home. I was so, so lonely. Finally, on January 2, 1991, my mother got a call through to me. Someone in Jordan had forwarded my letter to her, and she said she just stared at the message on the outside in tears before opening it. She sounded drained and hurried, as if she had just managed to stop crying and didn't know how long we had. I could only imagine what she had to do to get that call through.

"Our garden is dry, honey," she said, talking very fast and crying.

That was the secret code we had decided she would use to get past Amo's listeners to let me know something was wrong. She talked fast. "There are some things you need to know in case anything happens to us in this war, because you are the only one who is safe outside the country. You need to know what we own so you will know what to do."

She told me to get out a pencil and paper, and she began telling me about her inheritance and what was registered in whose name. Tears streamed down my face. I didn't take notes. I didn't care what we owned. I just listened and cried and wished I were there, no matter what sort of war was going to happen. We'd been through it before, right? She had been the brave one who made us laugh and feel normal. But now she was afraid, and I was afraid I would lose her. I told her I loved her. I told her again that I loved her. Then the connection was lost. I was afraid I would never hear her voice again.

The Gulf War began the next night. Like many Iraqi exiles, I watched the war on television aching because I wasn't there with my family. For Iraqi exiles, every building that exploded in bursts of light had a name, military targets had civilian employees, and bridges blown up were routes we took to school and home. It all looked more like a video game than what I knew war to be. I saw nothing on CNN of the people who waited at the other end of this war, ordinary people wondering if they were going to die; nothing of the families whose lives were being shattered by death or disrupted by the destruction of the power grid that allowed them to cook their food and light their houses and keep their schools and hospitals and businesses running. I went through my days at work like a zombie, worrying about my family as the war went on. When the Pentagon finally acknowledged "collateral damage," we feared that the people under the rubble were people we knew. The irony for many Iraqi-Americans was heart-sickening; many were Republicans who had voted for President Bush and lobbied for years to get the U.S. government to do something about Saddam Hussein. Now that Washington had finally gotten the message, it was their families who were suffering, not Saddam. But this message didn't seem to be getting out to the American people. If they only understood, I kept thinking, we could find another way to change the dictatorship and spare our families. I kept wishing there was some way I could help the people in Iraq.

I was asked to join a friend at a press conference that the Iraqi-American community was holding at a mosque in Los Angeles, to ask for a cessation in the bombing. The mosque was just a converted house with no gold or Quranic calligraphy, but as I waited for the press conference to start, I prayed as intensely as I ever have in my life. I asked God why he was keeping me away from my family when we needed each other the most. I started crying and couldn't stop. Why are you doing this to me? How could you do this? You're supposed to save me. Why did you leave me here all alone? Why won't you let me be back home with my family? But I didn't hear an answer, and I got so angry I stopped praying.

A reporter from the *Los Angeles Times* noticed my tears that day and asked to interview me. I told her my family was in Baghdad, and I didn't know if they were dead or alive. She asked how I had come to be in the United States. It was a simple question with such a complicated answer I didn't know what to tell her. I didn't even know how to describe myself. I wasn't a refugee. I wasn't a tourist. I had come here as a bride, but I wasn't a wife. I couldn't tell her that I had wound up here because my parents were friends of Saddam Hussein's and my mother had sent me here to try to make a better life for myself. So I told her half of the truth, which was that I had come to the United States on vacation, on a tourist visa, and gotten stranded when the borders were closed. She wrote a story and told a friend of hers from CBS News about me, and I wound up as a kind of national poster girl for the "Iraqi side" of the story, innocent victims caught up in war. People would recognize me in the Hallmark store and say, "Oh, you're that poor girl from Iraq, aren't you? Have you heard from your mother yet?" I was the lucky one, the innocent, nonthreatening Iraqi who got to see only nice, kind people while other Iraqis I knew were being called "sand nigger" and having their cars smashed and houses attacked, even though some of them had been born in the United States. The harassment brought back memories of our passports, stamped generations later with "of Ottoman origin" or "of Iranian origin." Why were these people being demonized?

No one had any reason to connect me with the man who had been Saddam Hussein's pilot. In these stories, my name was Zainab Rasheed, not Zainab Salbi. I didn't lie about it; Amo had changed it. People were upset that he had been giving top jobs and properties to his tribesmen from Tikrit, but instead of stopping nepotism, he ordered everyone to start using their grandfathers' surnames on the premise that then nobody would know who the favored people were. I'm sure the official pronouncement sounded more reasonable than my recollection of it, but the result was the same. Our last names were officially changed to our grandfathers' first name—the paperwork alone must have been enormous—and by the time I came to the United States, my passport said Zainab Rasheed.

In the waning days of war, I saw the bombed tanks and troops that lined the highway leading back to Baghdad from Kuwait. Many bodies were burned to a crisp, and I thought of Radya. How many of her cousins or neighbors had been forced to fight this time on Amo's pointless battlefields, only to be seen as enemies and killed by Americans? What choice had those young men ever had? Thousands of young men were dead, many of them no doubt conscripts whose mothers and wives would probably never know for sure what had happened to them.

I got word my family was alive just as the war was ending. Mama had managed to send a letter with a British doctor who was leaving Iraq for Jordan. He had mailed it from London.

> *My lovely daughter,*
>
> *I wish I could see you now and kiss you. You are the light of my life. What a misery we are in. We thank God that, to this day (Saturday), we are safe. Perhaps somehow, the best can come of things that are the hardest for us to bear.*
>
> *Thank God you are not here. We do not wish for God to show the face of this misery to anyone else. I worry and cry continuously. I don't know what the future bears for us. But you know me; I always worry about everything. There were other ways; it is so sad there had to be war.*
>
> *I last talked to you on the 15th. On the 16th, the bombing began. We left Baghdad for a Al Khalis [a town about 60 miles from Baghdad] to stay with a relative of a relative. The room was very, very cold—like ice. We had the radio on all night. Then, because that home was full of people fleeing Baghdad, we left and stayed in an abandoned building.*
>
> *There was no toilet. The place was full of roaches and bugs. The smell was terrible, the smell of animal things. Dirty, filthy, rotten, smelly. We used the broom to sweep away the human waste. It was dark, it was cold, but for a while we felt safe and free from the threat of the war. Then bombs fell around us there too. We stayed one terrible week. I had a nervous breakdown and we came back to Baghdad. I prefer to die in my house than to live as we were. The war with Iran was nothing compared to this one.*
>
> *Now we have been in Baghdad 10 days. Every morning and every evening the sky is full of fire. It looks like Star Wars: airplanes, jets, rockets, missiles. Every second the house shakes. We get used to the shaking, but not to the being afraid. We are living back one full century*

now. At night we use the lantern. We forgot about the refrigerator. All signs of civilization have been forgotten. There is no electricity, no water, very, very little gas, and no heating oil.

My daughter, please don't worry. I ask you to remain strong, keep your ethics strong, and do whatever is right. You are a strong woman. Listen to your elders and heed their advice. Keep your self-respect. Hopefully God will reunite us again. Love to everyone in America. In two days we are going to another town above Tikrit and below Al Mawsil. We do not know when we will return. God willing, we will see you again. We are proud of you.

Mama.

The *Los Angeles Times* ran a copy of that letter as the war ended, along with a quote from me saying, "My mother really is my best friend, and I am her only daughter. I just want to go home." I also said I was worried about my father and my older brother because Mama had barely mentioned them in her letter.

Amo had lost the war. It was an unprecedented, humiliating defeat. I didn't think his ego would be able to handle it. I honestly thought he would step down or even commit suicide and leave some grandiose statement to ensure his legacy. It actually surprised me when he didn't, and I found myself talking to him in my mind as I drove to work in my Chevy. If you ever believed one single thing you said on all those nights about how much you loved your people and your country, why don't you resign? Haven't you taken enough lives already with your senseless wars? If you can't leave, Amo, please have the decency to kill yourself! Wouldn't death be the punishment you would mete out to anyone else?

But he stayed and fought—this time against his own people. Iraqis in the United States cheered when we heard through the media and the Iraqi-American grapevine that for six days Iraqis all over the country rose up against him. Kurds were fighting in the north. In the south, planes had dropped leaflets promising U.S. support if Shia rebels rose up against Saddam, and Shia did rise up, struggling to overcome decades of oppression by Saddam.

Then, somehow, a deal was cut, and Saddam Hussein was back in control. Kurds were given certain protections and self-governance by the United States; the message about the gassing had come through to the American people. But the Shia in the south were afforded no such protection. Saddam Hussein was allowed to violate a "no-fly" zone over the region and massacre thousands of Shia. He sent gunmen into the holy cemetery in Najaf and attacked the shrine where rebels had taken refuge. He bombed the ancient marshes of the south where insurgents had hidden. To make sure they never hid there again, he ordered his engineers to divert the Euphrates River itself and dessicate their villages, floating settlements of reed and mud that had occupied that delta for five thousand years.

In the context of such suffering and death, who would even notice the toll the war took on one family who had lost no one? I found out later that during the bombing, my father had sat in a corner, almost paralyzed in sadness at the destruction of his country. "Iraq is gone," he kept saying, and numbed himself with whiskey. Mama was hysterical, unable to cope, until she began worrying about how to find food for her family during war, as women do, and learned to bake bread over a portable heater. It was in those few chaotic days after the war ended that Mama saw a small opening to finally leave her cage. She figured Amo had more to worry about than a few friends moving to Jordan. "I'm leaving," she told my father. "You can come with me or not." But he couldn't leave Iraq and she couldn't stay. My brothers, forced to choose between them, split up. Haider, who was always close to my father, stayed with Baba. Hassan, who was very attached to my mother, left for Jordan with Mama.

The love, the singing, the smiles and happiness I remembered during the first ten years of my life—all that was gone. Amo had torn my family apart. My mother blamed my father for staying in Iraq and my father blamed my mother for my failed marriage. As for their three children, we were now living in three different countries, all going in different directions, not knowing when we would see one another again, and not knowing why our parents had allowed this to happen to our family.

When Mama left for Jordan, Aunt Layla went with her. The story of the two women leaving Baghdad reminds me of the American movie *Thelma and Louise,* about two women escaping abusive husbands. Iraqi roads were tightly patrolled, Amo's agents were armed and loose, and the borders were closely guarded. My mother and aunt packed Hassan in the backseat, tossed in an autographed picture of Saddam Hussein like an amulet in case they needed to prove their loyalty, and headed for Jordan. At check stations, they turned the radio to a patriotic channel and uttered the requisite "Amo Saddam, may God preserve him!" Many hours later, after driving through flat desert, they finally asked a Bedouin man where the Jordanian border was. "Ladies, you've been in Jordan for an hour!" he told them. Laughing, they pulled over, got out, turned up the car radio as loud as they could, and lit up Virginia Slims.

"I am free!" my mother shouted to the empty desert. "I am finally free!"

But Aunt Layla hadn't told Mama her husband was joining her, and Mama wound up starting over alone. When news reached Amo of my mother's escape, Mama later heard from Aunt Nada, Amo started referring to her as "that Persian traitor" and "that foolish woman." He apparently never forgave her for fleeing, but did not deem her worthy of punishment.

When Mama came to visit me in America after the war ended we were both women in the process of divorce. I didn't tell her what Fakhri had done to me. I couldn't. She had gone through enough already. Instead, we talked about the future. I told her how much I was enjoying working and earning my own living and going to school at night. For the first time, I was in charge of my own life. She told me about her new apartment in Amman and a restaurant she planned to start.

"Why don't you come back to Amman with me?" she asked me, excited. "You can finish college there. There are some families who have expressed interest in asking for your hand when they learned you left Fakhri."

"Are you kidding me, Mama?" I told her in amazement. I had finally gotten a taste of independence, and there was no way I was going to give it up. "You want me to marry again? I am not going with you, Mama. I am staying in America and finishing my school here. If I go with you, I will be trying to live the life you want me to live instead of the one I want to live. Please, Mama, let me go. Let me make something out of myself, and I will go back to Iraq someday. I want to help the people there. Let me go, Mama."

Her eyes filled with tears, but she said yes.

From Alia's Notebook

One day in December 1989, Saddam called for us and when we arrived at his compound he was watching TV. He was watching the news about Americans who were invading Panama to overthrow the government of Manuel Noriega. He was very, very upset to see this. He asked us, "Can you believe what these Americans are doing to Noriega? He was their friend and now they are invading his country and taking it away from him." He was very upset and angry at this.

The last time I saw him was a year later, on December 28, 1990. That was two weeks before the Gulf War. We had just been in the States a few months before and it seemed to us that the Americans were serious about war. We expressed to him our concern. I remember he was fishing that night and he started laughing and ridiculing the Americans and all their military equipment and satellites, etc. He didn't expect a war. As a matter of fact, I asked him directly if he was expecting one and he said that the Americans would not strike Iraq because they feared the reaction of other Arabs. He also didn't believe American soldiers could handle the heat of Iraq.

He was relaxed that night. He even cooked for us and made traditional stuffed lamb. He talked about how he would lead the Arab world in war if America did dare to attack. He talked about a dream he had had recently where he, along with Hussain Kamel, were followed by barking black dogs. In that dream the dog had tried to attack him but Hussain Kamel hit him with one blow, killing the dog and saving Saddam. He said he had another dream in which he was standing and thousands of Muslims were praying behind him. In this dream, he said a man with headgear—referring to a religious cleric—turned to him and asked him to lead the prayers. In Saddam's mind, that implied that he was going to lead all Muslims. He truly believed in these dreams and drew strength from them in those days.

The day I left Baghdad, which was soon after the war, I felt I was finally liberated from my chains. It wasn't an easy decision. He was mad at me for leaving the country but I didn't care. I needed to leave and free myself and my children. I had forgotten myself in these years. I need time to decompress and recompose myself. I need time to find the me inside myself again. My life, as well as the lives of so many Iraqis, had been stolen from us not only by the Gulf War, but by Saddam himself. It had been a long time since I had a good night of sleep without having to deal with fear and nightmares from him.

9

❖

BECOMING ZAINAB

ON CHRISTMAS NIGHT of 1991, I surrounded myself with my
most valuable belongings and boarded a train for Washington,
D.C. At my feet was a Persian rug. Around my waist were pieces of
jewelry my mother had given me as a wedding present and all the
money I had been able to save working for eight months as a
cashier, sales clerk, and accounting assistant. It was vividly cold,
and I wrapped my plaid Dior coat around me as I tried to sleep, a
poor person with a rich person's baggage. I had made a vow to myself never to let anyone hurt me or control me again. I was in what
I thought of as my "survivor mode," and if anyone had asked how
I visualized myself, the answer would have been as a castle with a
moat around it and guards on top with their weapons pointed out.
I would have no romantic relationships with men at all. I would
tell no one about my life in Iraq. No one in my life now knew anything about the pilot's daughter I had been or the arranged marriage I had escaped, and they never would. I was starting over.
Whatever I made of my life from here on out would be my doing
alone. If anyone asked how I came to be in America, I would give
the same answer I had given the newspaper reporter: I was here on

vacation and had been caught by the Gulf War. No one would ever ask why I hadn't chosen to return.

I had a job waiting for me in Washington as an assistant to the ambassador in the League of Arab States, and my priority was to get my college degree. After I arrived, I found an efficiency apartment located in Adams Morgan. It was so tiny, I barely had room for a bed and a small table, but I was so proud of it. I enjoyed every step I took exploring the streets of my eclectic new neighborhood. Around me were Guatemalans, Ethiopians, Thais, and other immigrants and citizens—all with their own histories and aspirations. I found myself invited to a New Year's Eve party with a whole set of people my age, and I realized that was the first party I had been to where no one knew me. I played games and laughed with people I'd never met, and we stayed up until after dawn the next day. It was the most fun I had had in years. I felt free. Everything around me felt free. There was a mix of young men and women from different countries, and one of them was a tall, thin young Palestinian-American named Amjad Atallah, a recent University of Virginia graduate who was working in the publications department of a student exchange organization. He had the most beautiful eyes I had ever seen, and I couldn't help staring at them. He asked if I'd like to go out to lunch, but I refused without a second thought. No men. I was going to clear my head and get my university degree and then consider my options.

I enrolled in evening classes and began hanging out with this new crowd, playing games, cooking, and just enjoying ourselves. It turned out that Amjad and I worked in the same building, and I didn't have a car, so he began offering me a ride when we were getting together with friends after work. One night a friend offered to give us all Tae Kwon Do lessons, and we were joking around and laughing as we practiced the movements he taught us. At one point, he chose me to demonstrate.

"Hit me on the chest, Zainab," he instructed me.

I laughed and gave him a light jab.

"Not like that," he said. "Hit me harder."

I giggled and hit him again.

"Harder."

"But I fear hurting you," I said.

"You won't. Trust me."

His voice was firm and focused. I hit him with real force on his chest. He didn't move. "Harder," he kept saying, "Harder." And finally I hit him.

"Harder."

And I focused my eyes and hit him for real. I hit him as hard as I could, and I kept on hitting him, and somehow, in front of all these people I barely knew, I felt my anger and hate of Fakhri come out through my fists. I hated him for hurting me. I hated him for humiliating me. I hated him for raping me. And finally I burst into tears and ran out of the room with my new friends looking after me. A near-stranger had crossed the moat and broken down my defenses less than a month after I arrived in Washington. I sat down near a piano in an adjoining room and was sobbing uncontrollably all alone when Amjad came in and sat down next to me. He put his hand on my hand and didn't say a word. I don't know how long we sat there. I was embarrassed to cry in front of him, but I was also comforted by his unjudging presence. He drove me home in silence without asking any questions.

He stopped by my little apartment a few weeks later, and we wound up chatting on the floor because I had no chairs. It happened to be Valentine's Day, an American holiday I knew because of its greeting cards. I found myself talking to him about Fakhri because, despite my vow to leave my past behind, I felt he deserved an explanation. I remember looking at his face for some reaction: a rejection? But I saw only kindness in his eyes. So I kept on talking. And little by little, I told him about what Fakhri had done to me and about why I had come to America in the first place. He listened. For the first time, I realized what it felt like just to tell someone openly about my own feelings and my own life. I cried at some points and laughed at others. It was healing and reassuring, and it felt so good that I found myself telling Amjad almost everything I had vowed to myself to keep secret, so he would understand how important it was for me to start over on my own.

"My father was the pilot of Saddam Hussein," I said finally. "We were his friends."

And I waited again for signs of rejection.

"Thank you for trusting me," he said. "I am honored, really."

"So you don't hate me?" I asked.

"No, of course not," he said. "That was not a life you chose. It was chosen for you. I think it took great courage for you to leave Fakhri. I don't hate you. I am proud to be your friend. You make me understand what the Iraqi people have gone through."

He promised to keep my confidences, and I knew he would never break that promise. I trusted him, and we began spending time together. When I mentioned that I missed Iraqi food, he took me to an Iranian restaurant, the closest thing to it in Washington. When I told him I missed hugging my family, he brought me a teddy bear. When I told him that I couldn't take lunch break at my work, he brought me lunch at my desk. I had only been in Washington for six weeks and out of my marriage for just over a year, and despite all my resolutions, I began to wonder if I was falling in love. I knew how dangerous that was. What did Amjad's kindness mean? One night on the way home from a movie with friends, I asked him to stop the car to talk. It was late, nearly midnight, and we walked along the Potomac River in Georgetown. It was so cold we could see our breath in the air.

"Amjad, you have been nothing but nice to me, too nice in many ways," I said. "I don't want to be confused, so I need to ask you. Are you nice like this to all women around you or are you being nice to me particularly? I just don't want to be hurt. Whatever your answer is, it is all right with me, but I need to understand, Amjad. Are you just a friend or are you more than a friend?"

He took a deep breath, looked at me with those magical eyes of his, and said, "Zainab, I want to spend the rest of my life with you if that is okay with you."

I felt this tremendous rush of love for him. I had no idea he was going to say that, and I hugged him and lost myself in his wonderful warmth. He told me then that he had fallen in love with me the night we talked. I felt the unfamiliar wool of his fabric against my cheek, and I wished to myself that I were falling in love for the first time, that I could wipe away the men that had come before. My heart was racing, but I kept hearing a voice in my brain saying, Careful, Zainab. Careful. Slow down. Don't make this same mistake again.

"I don't know about the rest of our lives," I finally told him. "Let's take it a step at a time, and we can revisit this whole thing in two years."

He didn't question the time. He just said, "I understand."

"And you have to understand a few things," I said. "This is not going to be an easy ride for me. You should not expect any kissing or sex for that matter. None of that. And if it ever works out between us, you need to know that I don't want to have children."

He looked at me for a while, and I could see him taking all this in and processing it.

"If I have to make choices," he said, "then I pick you."

I hate the cold, but life was beautiful that night. We stood there holding each other until our feet grew numb.

Amjad never expected to meet, let alone fall in love with, a "friend of Saddam." He was a political activist who had regularly demonstrated against U.S. support for Saddam Hussein in the Iran-Iraq war. In some ways, he knew more about the current history of Iraq than I did, because we had had no free media at all and, ironically, because I had seen Saddam Hussein from so close up that it was hard for me to put him in the proper perspective. When Amjad and I talked, I was shocked to learn that some facts I had been taught to believe my whole life were simply wrong. I learned from him that Iraq, not Iran, had started the war and one million young men from both sides died for nothing. Though my mother had shared with me her sense of the sheer loss of life and the futility of the war, the enormity of Amo's fraud was staggering to me. It had all been a setup, not a defense. By declaring war on Iran when he did, Amjad felt, Saddam had galvanized Iran in its most vulnerable revolutionary stage and ensured the control by hardliners when many factions were still fighting to determine future control of the country. None of this surprised me, really, and yet the more I learned, the sicker I felt about the time I had spent with Amo. My mind kept swinging back and forth between images of Amjad and me at the time of the Iranian war. While he was protesting the war in front of the Iraqi embassy in Washington with a *kafiyeh* wrapped around his face to protect his identity from Mukhabarat retaliation, I was all dressed up at the farmhouse at the beck and call of the man who caused it all. Through him, I became interested in learning more about Iran. Who had our enemies been anyway, and why had they risen up? What was the story behind Persian women; what was their role in the revolution and what had they been through since the revolution? Amjad became my mentor and political soul mate. I told him that I felt very guilty about my on-again, off-again attempts at faith, and confessed that I had stopped praying or even fasting for Ramadan after the Gulf War and my experiences with Fakhri.

"I felt so angry at God," I told him. "I felt God betrayed me."

"You wouldn't feel betrayed by God if you didn't love him in the first place," he said. "You had to have a relationship with him to feel that anger when something went wrong in your life, right?"

That one comment, logical and generous like Amjad himself, lifted a huge burden from my shoulders and ultimately enabled me to begin a larger quest for spirituality. He reintroduced me to that part of Islam that was not confused with rule-bound ancient cultures, that part of Islam that was beautiful, my mother's faith. Amjad came from a Sunni family and had an undergraduate degree in religion. His knowledge of Islam was based not only on faith, but on history and contemporary politics. His parents had been dispossessed in Palestine and were finally able to immigrate a few family members at a time to the promise of America. His father worked at a mill as he got his college education and his mother worked in the school cafeteria. Little by little they built their lives. His father became a translator and his mother a sales clerk. Starting from zero, they had sent both their sons to college; both sons were now in Ph.D. programs.

I was in love with a wonderful and intelligent man with whom I could talk, laugh, and enjoy myself. I had a great circle of friends, an interesting job, and though I was able to get credit for just one year of college of the three I'd had in Iraq, I was finally back on track to get my university degree. Everything felt new, including me, and I felt free in every single step I took. That was one of the happiest times of my life. I was learning to breathe again.

Then I got a call from my mother in Jordan. She was panicked. I had been talking to her on the telephone every week or two, mostly about how hard her divorce was and how she was losing money on her restaurant business. I never mentioned Amjad—the last thing I wanted was Mama's advice on marriage. But one of Amjad's relatives had told me she was going to Amman, and just to be friendly, I had given her my mother's number. The two had gotten together and, of course, Amjad's relative had told Mama about Amjad and me.

"Oh my God, Zainab, you're dating a man!" she said, quite upset.

The rules hadn't changed just because I was living in America. I was openly dating a man I wasn't properly engaged to. I was every immigrant parent's nightmare, a divorced woman living on my own outside traditional cultural norms in a foreign country. I had even allowed Amjad to kiss me, though she didn't know that. But that wasn't what scared her the most.

"Why haven't you told me, *habibiti*?" Mama asked. "Have I finally lost you?"

"It's okay, Mama, calm down," I told her, trying to think of a way to assuage her hurt feelings. "His name is Amjad. He is wonderful. It all happened very fast. I was just going to call and ask you if it was all right for him to go to Jordan to meet you and ask for your approval to marry me."

As soon as I hung up, I called Amjad and told him he needed to go to Jordan to ask for my hand. He was thrilled, and his parents were thrilled; one thing led to another, and I realized my two-year waiting period was gone. Once again, I had let Mama's emotional needs take precedence over my own. I called her back.

"Mama, there is something I want you to know," I told her. "I want your blessing, but I love him, and I am going to marry him even without it."

Baba agreed to drive to Amman with Haider to meet Amjad. I watched in admiration as Amjad planned his request for my hand with every respect for cultural tradition, as well as for my family personally. Two close friends joined him to speak for the men of his family.

"I love your daughter," he told Baba after a few visits to get to know them. "I know she has been through a lot. I want you to know that I will do anything I can to make her happy. From the bottom of my heart, I promise you I will give her the best life I can."

Amjad told me Baba cried as he gave his blessing. I knew Baba felt he had failed in his traditional paternal role as protector. The Gulf War had prevented him from coming to rescue me, leaving me all alone to fend for myself. Now, for the first time, he was agreeing to entrust his daughter to someone he liked and re-spected during their few meetings, but a man who came from a world entirely separate from his own. Amjad was still learning Ara-bic, and much of their conversation was in English.

"I am giving you my daughter, whom I love more than any-thing in my life," Baba said. "I can't be there for her. You can. I only ask you to make her happy, and I trust that you will do so. Re-member that behind every great man is a great woman, and be-hind every great woman is also a great man. Zainab is the jewel of my eye, Amjad. Take good care of her."

I wish I had been there. I wish I had been able to run into Baba's arms. But unlike Amjad, I wasn't a U.S. citizen and couldn't get the proper visa. And because of visa restrictions on Iraqi men entering the United States after the Gulf War, Mama was the only one from my family who was able to come to the United States for my wedding. When it came to dividing our family, the global political issues spun off by Saddam Hussein's invasion of Kuwait would seal the division that Amo had started. It would be nine years before I would see my father again, nine years before I would step foot in Baghdad—and I would barely recognize either one.

Amjad's adviser from the University of Virginia, Dr. Abdul-Aziz Sachedina, was the religious cleric, or imam, who was to perform our Islamic wedding and help with the marriage contract. Amjad and I had already discussed the dowry and had agreed that it was to be symbolic, a single old coin from Jerusalem.

"This is good," said Dr. Sachedina, when we met him in his office in Charlottseville. "But you have a lot more rights to discuss besides the dowry, Zainab. You need to put down all your conditions."

"Conditions?" I asked. I knew almost nothing about the legalities of Muslim marriage. When I married Fakhri, the only issue I knew about was the dowry. A piece of paper had been put in front of me and I had signed it.

Dr. Sachedina sighed.

"Unfortunately, this is a very common problem," he said in a calm, professorial voice. "People don't know Islamic law, and they assume cultural practices stem from Islam. You have a lot more rights to discuss than the dowry. When a woman marries in Islam, she has the right to stipulate all the conditions she wants to have in her marriage. Then, the husband needs to sign if he agrees to those conditions. This is your chance to put whatever conditions you choose as part of your contract for marrying Amjad."

"Anything I want?"

"Anything from the kind of lifestyle you want to the way you want to raise your children," he said. A kind of prenuptial agreement.

"Here's my computer, Zainab," he said, standing up and offering me his seat. "Just type in all your conditions for the marriage contract, and if Amjad agrees, they're binding. Good luck."

And he left.

Oh my God, I had no idea! I had just learned about a whole new right nobody had ever explained to me I had as a Muslim woman. Another thing we hadn't been told about in Iraq! How many women knew about this? Even my mother, who had just finalized her divorce, didn't know! If I had only known about this when I was marrying Fakhri. Instead of going around the house trying to obey him and be a "good wife," I would have been able to look at the contract and say, Here, you signed this. I would have had proof in writing of all those promises he had made me right before we got married.

I didn't know how to type or use a computer at that time. So Amjad typed and I talked.

"You may not stop me from pursuing any career or educational path," I dictated.

"Agreed," Amjad said as he clicked away on the keyboard. I was so excited, he got excited watching me.

"You must share with me all household duties fifty-fifty. You must do half of the cooking, you must do have of the cleaning, you must—"

"Before you add vacuuming, don't you think it is clear when we say *all* household duties that that is implied?"

"Hmmm," I said hesitantly. He had a point, but I went through every other possible condition I could think of. I didn't want to leave anything out. "Okay."

"The most important thing," I said at last, looking at him as if waiting to catch him in a lie. "I want to share the right to initiate divorce."

"Absolutely," he said. And typed it in.

Oh my God, this actually works, I thought to myself.

"I can't think of anything more now," I said.

"Well, you can always add to this contract if you want," he said. "At any point in the marriage."

Later that day, we had a small and intimate religious ceremony at Dr. Sachedina's house with Amjad's family, my mother, and a few friends who had been with us the day Amjad and I met. I couldn't wait to show my mother the contract that evening. I was proud to have learned something so important and to have a wonderful man who was so supportive.

"But, Zainab, a woman doesn't have the right to divorce the husband!" she said. "The husband must agree to the divorce first."

"All the more reason to have a contract," I said. "No one told us we had that right."

"But even so, honey, are you positive you want to put all these conditions in?" she persisted. "You don't want to risk your marriage with Amjad, after all."

"Mama, what's come over you?" I asked. "Are you really suggesting that I give up rights that might have protected me in my marriage to Fakhri? I don't understand! Why?"

I was *very* upset. What was wrong with her? I had never told her what Fakhri had done to me. First, there was the war, her nervous breakdown, then the divorce from my father. But even if she didn't know about the rape, it felt like she was a different person now than the strong, independent woman I knew.

"I'm sorry, Zainab," she said. "Do whatever you want. I'm sorry I said anything."

"It's not just the marriage contract, Mama," I said. "Ever since you've been here, you've been giving me advice about cooking and housekeeping. You used to call yourself a strong and independent woman, but I can feel the difference in you, Mama. I don't understand."

Then she sort of broke down. It had been several months since Amjad had seen her in Amman, and in that time, she had finally given up on her restaurant business for financial reasons and returned to Baghdad, where at least she had a free place to live. But the society she had returned to wasn't as open to single women, especially divorced middle-aged women, as it had been in the 1970s or 1980s. She tried having dinner parties and inviting couples she knew, only to be scolded by some women who felt it was inappropriate for a divorcee to be holding "mixed" parties. She was striking up some of her old friendships, but instead of dancing, she and her friends read and discussed the Quran.

"Some of my friends blame me for our divorce because I was the one who initiated it," she said. "As I think about it at the end of the day, I wonder if maybe I have been wrong. Maybe it would have been better for me to stay with your father."

"Mama, don't give up!" I said and instinctively hugged her. "You have to be strong. You're beautiful. Your marriage with Baba may not have worked out, but you'll find someone else."

"I don't think so, *habibiti*. I no longer trust the advice that I gave you on love and marriage. I no longer trust in myself. Maybe what I taught you about being a strong woman was wrong. Maybe it is better to be a good wife."

She was looking down at the floor, not meeting my eyes at all.

A few months later, my mother flew over with the wedding dress she had made for me, a gold-and-white dress she had embroidered with love poems and our names. Amjad and I were married in January 1993. His family arranged the ceremony, which in Iraqi Muslim tradition is hosted by the bridegroom's family. Amjad and I had rented a hotel suite for our wedding night, and Mama and I checked in early to dress for the wedding. She looked beautiful that day. We combed each other's hair and were giggling when the makeup lady came to our room. She thought we were sisters. When she left, I put my arm around my mother's neck when we were still in our bathrobes and giggled. "We are two sisters!"

When my mother helped me into the dress, I worried about how low-cut it was.

"Oh, honey, don't worry about it!" she said, kissing me on the forehead. "Just enjoy your wedding and your life. I love you, *habibiti*. Amjad is a good man. Take good care of him, and be happy. Don't ever forget to do that! Be happy!"

I was happy that day. I was really happy. Mama looked like a bride herself, and everyone commented on how beautiful she was. I felt a spark of her old self shining through. That was my mama. The beautiful Alia. I could hear her laughter through the crowd as she enjoyed herself. My wedding was the best party I have ever gone to, though I didn't really care. I spent practically the whole time just dancing with Amjad, reflecting on how much I loved him and how lucky we were.

Little by little, I came to trust him sexually, as he undoubtedly knew I would. Amjad was a healer, the most patient, understanding person I have ever met. There were times we stood in my little apartment kissing for hours—so long my knees would quiver—but I was afraid to lie down, and there was no place to sit. Then, later, we would lie together and he would just hold me for hours until we fell asleep. One night, when Natalie and Nat King Cole's song, "Unforgettable," was playing on the stereo, I was able to let my defenses down, and he talked to me and touched me and brought me through the other side of my pain, and I finally understood what my mother was talking about at our kitchen table.

Amjad was in his first year of a doctorate at the University of Virginia, a two-hour drive from Washington, D.C. I was twenty-three, working full-time and going to school at night. We were married, and it was logical that we would live together. But commuting seemed out of the question, and I was terrified that if I quit my job to move in with him, I would lose all the hard-won gains I had made toward controlling my own destiny. I had met the man of my dreams too soon.

"I can move in with you in Charlottesville, get depressed and leave you, or I can stay in D.C., see you on weekends, and be happy," I informed him. He chose the latter, so we saw each other over the weekends.

The following fall I enrolled full-time at George Mason University and decided to major in women's and international studies. Here, at last, I had an opportunity to read whatever I chose and say whatever I wanted. I learned about feminism and found it odd that Western women were still struggling for some rights, like equal pay for equal work, that were guaranteed in so many of what are called "developing" countries. I learned in one of my classes what I had never heard at a family gathering: Stalin ordered Russian soldiers to rape as many German women as possible during World War II. I learned about the Holocaust, the anti-slavery movement in the United States, and the anti-apartheid movement in South Africa. My whole sense of the world was changing. Growing up as I had in a dictatorship frozen in place, I didn't comprehend the basic dynamic of a world in active flux, with justice fighting injustice, actions and reactions, political and social changes, gender equality and gender-based discrimination, good and evil fighting each other constantly. I learned that other people had undergone oppression and survived, other nations had overthrown tyrants, and it gave me hope.

Amjad gave me books he knew would help me understand the world that had been off-limits to me until now. I saw patterns in Saddam Hussein's atrocities and injustice and realized that these were common to all dictators, including Hitler and Stalin, whose work I had seen him read. I saw Saddam Hussein's Iraq in George Orwell's *1984* and felt the horror of Amo in Joseph Conrad's *Heart of Darkness*. I read Kanan Makiya's *Republic of Fear,* and learned of even more horrors Saddam Hussein had committed in Iraq and wondered if my parents knew about any of them. It was from that book that I finally came to understand that the wave of Shia deportations that nearly took away my mother was one of Amo's early ethnic cleansing operations. Makiya estimated that two hundred thousand Shia had been deported, and that didn't include thousands of families like Fakhri's that had fled on their own.

That campaign had been so ignored in the Western media, coming as it did as Saddam Hussein was fighting Iran with funding from the West, that even Amjad hadn't heard about it.

I took all this information in but spoke to no one about it except Amjad. For me, it was personal and academic. It never occurred to me to join an opposition party, which might have had dangerous consequences for my family. I also completely opposed economic sanctions, which many exiled Iraqi dissidents supported. I didn't believe in the idea of economic sanctions unless the oppressed people themselves requested it, as had been the case in South Africa. I knew that any economic blockade imposed on Iraq would only deprive average Iraqis of food and medicine while Amo got richer. Amo would never suffer, but the tortured logic behind sanctions was that Iraqis would suffer so much they would somehow rise up and overthrow him. How presumptuous this was, I thought, and how cruel, how removed from the reality of the average Iraqi family. The Amo I knew understood his people far better than those who favored imposing sanctions on him. Before I left Iraq, I already suspected he had deliberately distributed different foods to different marketplaces so people would spend all day just trying to put together a meal and have less time to make trouble. Now, I knew, he would do far worse to punish those who had risen up against him. And that, of course, is exactly what he did, making himself ever richer by selling Iraqi oil on the black market as he distributed rotten food to the Shia in the south, stole their electricity, their water, their villages, and many more of their lives.

I didn't feel safe just because I was in America. Every Iraqi knew the Mukhabarat had spies around the world. There were many stories of Iraqis in exile who were attacked in their own homes or assassinated, and in one case, a videotape that contained images of the rape of a dissident's sister was sent to him in exile as a blackmail. But my fear, like that of many Iraqis, was not based on reason alone. I feared Saddam with every part of my body and mind and soul, and that organic fear would never leave me, not even in the comfort of my marriage in Virginia. I shuddered to think how close I had been to Amo. Sometimes I envisioned fear as a part of my body, like my cells, like my blood. I'm sure my friends thought of me as odd. When I went to one friend's house and saw a bottle of Chivas Regal whiskey, I asked him to put it away. When guests came over, I instinctively turned up the stereo if anyone mentioned politics or even personal gossip. One night, I accidentally used Amo's fork as a serving utensil, and when an Egyptian friend picked it up and studied the insignia, I snatched it away and never put it out again. A careless slip. How could I ever explain how I had come by that fork? How could I explain to American authorities that my father was the one who flew Iraq's commercial airliners to Tehran for safekeeping during the Gulf War and my mother had given Saddam moisturizer when he complained his face felt dry? I never shared any of these thoughts with anyone except Amjad. If we referred to him, I always said "Amo" because I was afraid to say "Saddam Hussein" out loud, even in my own home. I never participated in classroom discussions on Iraq. I never wrote school papers about Iraq. After a while, few people asked me about it. Millions of Iraqis were embarking on a decade of pain in which they would pay the price for the tyranny of a man almost everyone wanted overthrown. Americans were on to other issues.

So was I. Amjad and I had been married for six months when I read a story in *TIME* magazine about "rape camps" in Bosnia-Herzegovina and Croatia where women were being held and raped day and night, apparently by Serbian soldiers. There was a picture of women sitting on what seemed like a hospital bed. Some were teenagers; some seemed to be their mothers. Something in those magazine pages triggered a pain so deep inside me and so sudden that I just started weeping. Amjad was in the kitchen with some friends cooking dinner, and he came running out, trying to see what had happened to me.

"We have to *do* something," I said, showing him the story as he tried to both comfort me and read the story that was the source of my pain. "I have to *do* something to help these women."

The next day, I went to the library and checked out as many books as I could find about the region. I needed to understand where it was, who its people were, what its history was, and what the fighting was about. I wasn't sure what drove me—my own rape, my understanding of what it felt like to live in a war, my outrage at the social injustice, or maybe just the possibility that I could actually do something to help—but I felt as if I were on a mission. I got out the yellow pages and called women's groups to volunteer to help support their projects in Bosnia and Croatia. To my surprise, I couldn't find any organization working with these women. "Call us in six months," one woman told me. "Maybe we will be doing something then." Six months? How could we wait six months to respond to mass rape? From my reading, I now knew that people had explained the lack of action against the Nazi Holocaust by saying they didn't know about it. No one could say that with Bosnia. Hundreds of thousands of Bosnian and Croatian civilians were being killed in a genocide that was practically being committed on television. Twenty thousand women had already been raped— *twenty thousand.* How could this be allowed to happen? What excuse did we have this time for the lack of action?

One night at a coffee shop, I told Amjad and his brother Eyad about an idea I had that was sort of like international programs in which families sponsor children, and we talked about it. A program could be set up in which one woman at a time would sponsor a rape victim, send her money each month that she could spend as she chose to help get herself going again, and write her letters of support so she would know she wasn't alone. The next day, I tried another round of calls offering to help organizations set up such a program and was able to get an appointment with the All Souls Unitarian Church. I walked into their board of directors meeting a week later with my father-in-law's briefcase, thinking it would make me look older and more serious. I had read Quranic verses asking God to release my tongue as he did Moses' when he faced the Pharaoh, and the church board of directors agreed to allow me to start such a project under their nonprofit umbrella. They would advise me as needed and do the bookkeeping for the donations raised. I had one year to turn my project into an independent nonprofit. It was perfect!

Amjad was excited and supportive. We would start this organization together. He worked on incorporation papers as I drafted brochures with the help of some church volunteers. His family's basement became our operations center where his parents volunteered to fold and collate. After two months of networking and fundraising, Amjad and I were cofounders of Women for Women International's predecessor, which we called Women for Women in Bosnia. Between the money we raised and the savings we had been keeping for a honeymoon in Spain, we had enough to go to Croatia and start work. Judy Darnell, a Philadelphia nurse with a long history of volunteer work in Croatia, helped us make Women for Women International a reality on the ground. I had called her to ask for help, and she said, "Count me in."

When we landed in Zagreb, she had meetings already set up to educate us and help us get going. Our first meeting was with Ajsa, a woman with short dark hair, a face puffy and reddened, and a polite smile. She had been recently released from a camp in a prisoner exchange—soldiers freed in exchange for imprisoned civilian women. She sat across the table from us in loose, donated clothes and started talking matter-of-factly, almost in a rote manner, after we explained to her that we were there to set up a program and needed to better understand women's needs so we could respond to them properly.

"I was imprisoned in a rape camp for nine months, and they released me when I was eight months pregnant," she said very fast, almost as if she were talking about someone else. "I had my baby two months ago, but she died because of health complications. I didn't know how to feel about that child. I loved her because she was my baby, but every time I looked at her, I remembered what the soldiers kept saying as they raped me: 'You are Muslim. You are a Turk. You deserve to be raped. This is to avenge what your ancestors have done to our people.' They never stopped with their slurs, their spitting, and their raping of me."

She didn't know which one was the father of her child. She couldn't even remember them all. I felt the blood draining from my face as she periodically stopped her recital for the interpreter, and used that time to sniff back tears before resuming. She talked about the life she used to have, a loving husband and two children and a farm with sheep.

"I had a life, and now it is all gone. Everything was taken away from me in a matter of moments. I don't know why. What did I do to them? What did my husband do? I haven't seen him or my children since the day they captured me. I don't know if I will ever see them again. If I do, will they accept me? Will they be able to love me again after they see me in this shape? Look at me. Look at me!"

Neither Amjad nor I cried when she did; we instinctively knew that would take away the dignity of her own tears. But when we got back to the hotel, we lay there and held each other and just sobbed together. We toured Croatia for a week and learned of horrors I still can barely comprehend. Eighty-year-old grandmothers and girls as young as four were raped in village squares, then discarded with their organs ruptured. Sons were ordered to rape their mothers. Fathers were ordered to rape their daughters. The most educated women were selected to be raped in front of their townspeople. Some Serbian soldiers were ordered to rape to prove their manhood and machismo. One captured soldier who refused described being ridiculed by a commander who took off his own pants, raped a woman in front of him, and told him "*This* is how it's done" as fellow soldiers laughed at him.

There was nothing random about these acts. There had been thousands of rapes and thousands of witnesses to the rapes. There are those who say that soldiers of all armies rape, but there was only one army, the Serbian army under control of Slobodan Milŏsević, that organized rape camps. These weren't informal bivouacs in the forest; the Serbian Army took over hotels and schools and public buildings for this purpose and were continuing to operate under the international public eye virtually unstopped. Then they would release their victims late into pregnancy so they could not abort their "Serbian" babies, and their families would feel shamed and abandon them. The United Nations counted sixteen rape camps organized by the Serbian Army. Rape was every bit as much a strategy of war as the ethnic cleansing fought with guns, perhaps more so because it didn't just eliminate individuals, it destroyed whole families and societies. Serbian soldiers were encouraged to hate Bosnians because the Ottoman Empire had once controlled the Balkans, and to hate Croatians because their ancestors were assumed to be Ustasha, Nazi sympathizers, during World War II. They had been told they were avenging crimes committed against their grandfathers by the grandfathers of these women.

As if women were a field of battle where two old enemies met to set scores straight.

Most of the women we met had a small bag with a few pieces of clothing and perhaps some things they thought to grab as they fled their homes, proofs of lost lives in which a high school diploma or a deed to a house mattered. Some were lucky enough to have a picture to pull out and say, Here's my son, the one they killed, or Here is my husband, have you seen him? I remember one woman talked impassively about how she escaped from her home when Serbian soldiers attacked her village. She grabbed her two sons and ran, looking back to see her house burning behind her, then running to save her boys' lives. For two days, they ran in a dark forest, a story I would hear over and over again, a running into the heart of a strange darkness you don't know, but you know you have to run and run and run and leave behind your memories and your community and sometimes the bodies of your loved ones. Except for her trembling hands, this woman might have been telling someone else's story. There was very little affect in her voice.

We went to Croatia to help rape victims, but members of women's groups in Croatia and Bosnia showed us why that instinct, while natural, would not help reintegrate them into society. Some of these women reminded me of my mother as they smoked cigarettes, whispered together, and even laughed good-naturedly at my seriousness of purpose. "Do you really want to set up lines of women who receive sponsorships every month while their neighbors point and say, Look, there go the raped women?" one of them asked me. "Isn't it enough that some of them are living in refugee camps with signs saying 'rape victims' to make it easier for the press and international workers to find them?"

That was my first lesson in professional humility. The second was that my best teachers came from women I sought to help. They had a wisdom I was hungry for. They were kind enough to share it with me, and I was grateful to have a chance to understand things that had always been forbidden to me before. I yearned to understand not only these women's suffering, but the mental state of the men who had inflicted it. How had the men's hearts been so twisted into believing they had a right to inflict such pain? How many Serbian soldiers had been forced into the army? How many had been told, here, Prove your loyalty by murdering and raping your enemy's woman? How many had resisted, and at what price? Being a victim, morally speaking, was easy in some ways. It didn't involve the same sorts of choices.

On one of our last nights in Croatia, Amjad and I talked for a long time about moral issues and personal choices.

"What kind of criminal would do these things to another human being?" he asked. He couldn't understand.

"Sometimes the price they have to pay for refusing an order is too high for some to make," I said.

"Not everybody had a gun pointed to his head."

"That is probably true for most of them. But that would make it easy. If someone pointed a gun to your head, it's easy to say I would rather die than do that. What if it's other people's lives that are being threatened, the people you love, your mother and father, your wife and children, a whole family of cousins? Tell me, Amjad, if somebody with a gun said, 'Here, kill this stranger or I'll kill your wife,' whose life would you choose, mine or the stranger's?"

He looked at me with his wonderful eyes.

"Someone has to say no," he said.

We started from different places and wound up with the same conclusion. We could not change the history that made people hate. But we pledged to each other that, no matter what the circumstances, neither of us would be party to propagate it. We gave each other permission to watch the other killed rather than to be coerced into killing another human being.

Three months later, I went to back to Croatia on my own to deliver the first sponsorship money we had raised. I spent my twenty-fourth birthday at a refugee camp in a place called Split on the Croatian coast. I met there a woman five years younger than I named Inger, who spoke very good English and who talked to me about how much she missed her father in Bosnia. She introduced me to families living in classrooms in what used to be a school. Twenty people were forced to sleep together in a small room with few blankets and very little water. I was extremely thirsty, and one woman must have understood because she said something in Serbo-Croatian, and her daughter went to a corner and brought out a hidden bottle of precious water they shared with me. I was always awed by the generosity of refugees. When I boarded a bus for the twelve-hour ride back to Zagreb, Inger stayed behind.

I couldn't sleep that night. Why was I sitting in a bus on my way to a hotel room while she had to suffer? A fluke? Luck? God's mercy? *Al hamdilalah. Al hamdilalah. Al hamdilalah.* Thank God. Thank God, that I did not have to suffer the way Inger or other refugees were suffering. As Amjad kept on telling me, if not for my horrible marriage, I would never have gone to Washington or met him or had a chance to do this work. Fighting the injustice Amjad and I had seen became the centerpiece of our lives. With the help of All Souls Unitarian Church, students holding fundraising concerts, and volunteers joining us from all over the country, we were able to raise enough money for an office and a move out of Amjad's parents' basement—but not enough money to pay me to run the organization. So Amjad set aside his lifetime dream of getting the doctorate that would lead him to become a full-time professor, and began working full-time as a temp to support our work.

American women, Canadian women—even Bangladeshi women—began signing up as sponsors who sent a monthly check along with a letter to a victim of war. I felt very strongly that this cash should go directly to the women, because it represented freedom to make a choice again in their lives, even if it was a small one. They could buy medicine for their children or fruit or cosmetics if they chose. It was their choice, not ours. Later, we began setting up a few programs to help them transition back into society, including support groups that would help replace the social networks they had lost and allow them to discuss larger issues like women's role in war, economy, politics, and society. These "invisible refugees," as I came to call them, didn't fit the stereotype of refugees starving in tatters. Basic traits and hygiene habits don't change, even if lives do. I knew that from my own experience. I never changed the way I spoke or put on lipstick or carried myself when I lost almost everything I had. Why did so many people assume that all refugees look and act alike, as if their culture and upbringing had been stolen from them along with their material possessions? Just because they wore clean dresses or spoke well didn't mean these women didn't need help. Sometimes putting on lipstick or a clean dress meant that a woman was resisting giving up that last hope that every shred of her old life was gone. I had to make hard choices when it came to something as simple as the pictures we used on our brochures; people would give more money to pictures of women in head scarves who looked hungry and oppressed. There were many such women, but for me, portraying these refugees that way was only another way of robbing them of their dignity. Eventually we would also start micro loan programs for small businesses and job training programs, including classes in nontraditional skills I had studied in junior high and high school.

Each sponsor wrote letters to her "sister," and her sister wrote back. Every day I would sit with volunteers as we processed letters and stuffed envelopes. I had originally envisioned these letters as helping war victims feel they weren't alone. But as the letters came back from women in Bosnia and Croatia, I realized the survivors of war were using these private letters to tell strangers about the pain they felt they could share with no one else. Through them, they could retain their own identity and yet remain anonymous. The letters were testaments, and the letters the women's sponsors wrote back bore witness to their suffering. They had a powerful effect on me, like a silent tide of emotions in which women talked not only about war and loss, but also about their families and their gardens. Some were poetic, some incredibly profound. "I got your letters," one Bosnian woman from Sarajevo wrote to her sponsor. "I experienced them like rays of sunlight that reach to the bottom of a dark cave. I lived through the shelling and all the other suffering, but they killed the 'I' in me."

As I began traveling back and forth between America and Central Europe, I realized why Ajsa had been selected to be the first person to talk with us. She had had time to begin to come to terms with what had happened to her. Almost all of the other women I had met spoke with dead, dry eyes. Crying, I learned later, was the first sign of healing. I wasn't a therapist, and I often just sat with women and held their hands and tried to bear witness to whatever individual grief they chose to share. If a woman talked about rape, I came to understand that she would rarely say it had happened to her. It had always happened to someone else, a neighbor perhaps, or even her whole village except for her. Were these women too embarrassed to talk about their bodies because their sexuality was tied to the honor of their families, as it was in Iraq? Was it *ayeb* for them to talk about it? I wasn't sure, but I also knew that the pain of rape transcended mere cultural issues. I hated it when people suggested Muslim women somehow felt rape differently than other women. Why on earth should they? Except for on talk shows where women got money or seconds of celebrity in exchange for exclaiming about intimate things—a bizarre trend I found desensitizing to women—women in America were reluctant to talk about rape too.

The refugees I met were so traumatized by so many things that I found many of them sitting in silence with dead eyes outside their tents for hours as small children jumped around them ignored. "I'm too helpless to be helped," one woman told me when I tried to interview her. Every story I heard made me feel more grateful at my good fortune, yet every story also fed some pain deep inside me I knew came from the same place as these women's. I was obsessed with my work, grateful to be working with women, as I had told my mother I wanted to on my fifteenth birthday. I spent days and evenings giving speeches everywhere I could, to women's rights organization, churches, synagogues and mosques, schools and universities. I wanted to rally people to rise up and stop the atrocities that were happening in front of our eyes. I lambasted the United Nations peacekeepers for standing back and observing crime instead of preventing it. I demonstrated at the White House—the Bush administration had done nothing about Bosnia, and the Clinton administration had not acted on its promises in its first couple of years. Taking the bullhorn, I led chants to stop the genocide, stop the rape. For the first time in my life, I felt the thrill of being able to speak publicly about my own opinions.

Saddam Hussein had publicly announced his support for Serbian leader Slobodan Milǒsević, and increasingly I began to see parallels between the two. From the back of my brain, I pulled out warnings from Ehab and rumors about women being raped by the Mukhabarat, and videotaped in the process, only to be told they had to become informers or the tapes would be released, subjecting some to rejection by their husbands and families and even to honor killings. The sister of Mohammed Bakr Al-Sadr, Iraq's most respected Shia cleric, had been raped—I remembered Aunt Samer telling me in the Hunting Club pool about how they had raped her at the same time they were torturing him—then released her pregnant. I knew I couldn't attack Saddam Hussein, so I attacked Slobodan Milŏsević. I couldn't fight in Iraq, so I fought in Bosnia and Croatia. Milŏsević was a criminal and I publicly demanded he be tried for war crimes. I told no one in Iraq about my work for fear that Amo would punish them for my political activism.

I did little else except go to classes, finish my homework, and go to the office. I remember walking across my college campus and seeing hundreds of students laughing, chatting, flirting, and reading around me, and wishing I had made more friends at school. But there was no time; I was always running from class to work. Nothing mattered as much as my work. I dreamed about it, breathed it, lived it. Haunted by that woman who said she was too helpless to be helped, I sometimes couldn't force myself to walk out the office door. The organization began to grow, and the demands on me and Amjad grew with it. Every penny we raised went into the program, and it still wasn't enough. We were behind on our bills, and every time the telephone rang, I was afraid it was a creditor. Bosnia was all either of us talked about, and I know some of our friends got bored with us. Even some of Amjad's family told us, "You've done good work, but you have to grow up, get real paychecks. Look what a toll this is taking on both of you." We considered letting go, but every time we did, there was the memory of Ajsa and a check from a donor that I took as a sign we were meant to keep on going.

One day, Mama called me at the home of a family with whom I was staying in Sarajevo. Amjad had to have given her my number.

"What are you doing there?" she screamed, crying, when the phone rang at the family's house. "Don't you realize how hard I fought to get you out of the wars that captured our country? Why would you put yourself right back in another war? Why are you doing this to me? Why?"

I only knew that I kept going back to war zones because I found comfort there. I was like the boy in *The Jungle Book* who kept escaping into the jungle whenever there was a problem in his own village. War zones were my jungle. I kept going back to the bullets. I kept going back to the pain of strangers. Meanwhile, I was growing more distant from my own family. Baba had immediately remarried, and I considered it a betrayal. I called my father and brothers on holidays. For the longest time, Mama kept calling me at 2 A.M. to complain about my father. Why did she have to keep calling me in the middle of the night? There was absolutely nothing I could do. I was so exhausted. I needed to sleep. The boxes I had buried away in Iraq were beginning to bob up to the surface, and sometimes I couldn't keep them down.

For the longest time after coming back from my trips to Bosnia, I stopped letting Amjad touch me. Every story I heard in Bosnia kept the pain of my own rape raw. I found myself unable to cry. I feared that I might get pregnant and have a child, and I wouldn't know how not to hurt her. Opposite things are often true at the same time, I've found, and it is true that I loved Amjad and that I feared Amjad. Poor Amjad, the more loving he was, the more I panicked. I was afraid of being confined by him or betrayed by him, yet I was the one who struggled with commitment. I remember thinking that love was its own kind of cage. The more supportive and loving he was, the more vulnerable and trapped I felt.

Sometimes I felt like an elastic band that was being stretched to the breaking point. Just when I was feeling strong, something would go snap inside me, and I could feel that elastic band bounce back into its old shape, into that child who was vulnerable. The happier I grew, the more intolerable was that awful inevitability of bouncing back with all the old feelings: the weakness, the fear, the sensation of being trapped. I was struggling hard to find peace in my heart, but it wasn't there. Life had been a torment for me since I was little, I decided. I thought of it as one torturous stage of being, and I knew that death was what came after torture. It was the reward that provided release.

One day when I returned from a trip, we got into an argument. I don't even remember what it was about. It was about 5 P.M., still light outside, when chemical explosions started going off in my mind, like blasts of light. I couldn't make sense of them. I just wanted to get out of my body. I couldn't stand myself or the cage I was living in. I had to get out of my mind and body. I didn't think twice when I went to the medicine drawer; I was on autopilot. The past and the present were coming together in my brain, the wires shorting out as the two crossed. Fear of the farmhouse walls, fear of being voiceless, fear of entrapment by Amjad's love, fear of living in my mother's cage, fear of living outside the cage. I had seen my mother doing it so many times, it was my turn to do it now. My turn to try the easy way out as she had done.

I remember thinking that what I saw there probably wouldn't be enough to kill me, mostly over-the-counter medicines, but I grabbed as many pills as I could find. I went to a corner of the apartment and poured them out onto the floor. The carpet was beige. I remember the twill. I remember they looked like the pills on Mama's bedroom floor that first night and other nights that she tried to kill herself. I swallowed some, but I was too afraid to take them all at once, so I took them in small portions, slowly and deliberately. I remember the struggle inside my brain more than what I was doing. I was a little girl imitating her mother, wanting to die to be free.

Then Amjad was there with horror on his face. He dropped down in front of me and sat next to me on the floor.

"Don't do that, Zainab," he begged me. "Please don't do that. I love you. I will do anything to make you happy. Just don't kill yourself. Please."

The scenario I was re-creating from my childhood was not reenacting itself properly. He was supposed to be sitting on the sofa numbing himself with whiskey. Instead, he was crying with his beautiful eyes, and that confused me. When I saw the hurt in his eyes, I stopped taking the pills. I recognized that hurt. I knew what it felt like, exactly. I didn't want to hurt him. I loved him.

"Oh, Amjad, I'm sorry, I'm sorry," I told him. "Please forgive me."

He tried to help me throw up the pills, but he didn't know this routine. I was the one who told him I didn't need to go to the hospital because I realized somehow that I hadn't taken enough to really kill myself. I was the one who knew about the milk. I knew because I was the one who wanted to die and the child who saved her all at once. And I remember hugging him finally, as I tried to explain thoughts in my mind that not even I could understand, about allowing myself to feel the pain I had managed to hold inside since the day I left Iraq. I had let go of the guards surrounding my castle, but I couldn't defend myself without them.

I promised Amjad I would seek help, and the next day, he helped me find a therapist. I spoke with her for an hour, but I didn't say a word about my life with Amo. I trusted no one except Amjad with the pilot's daughter and the life she had lived. I talked to her only about what was safe and personal. She diagnosed a post-traumatic stress disorder caused by my work; strangers had been giving me their pain for safekeeping, she said, and I hadn't yet learned how to deal with these stories. I had not taken any time off for myself; I had had no vacation and almost no rest since the time I arrived in the United States.

"If you expect to continue your work, you have to learn to let their pain out," the therapist said. "Breathe like a fish. Take oxygen in, then let whatever you don't need out. Take in the stories you need for your work, and breathe everything else out."

I still hadn't learned how to breathe.

What she didn't know was that I was afraid to let go of my mission even for one week because if I relaxed, more demons would pop out, and they would be my own. I was still dealing with the rape I had faced myself, but even that was hard for me to tell the therapist because that would open the door to the past I didn't want to talk about. I was afraid of even being touched. Once, when a friend grabbed my shoulder to pull me to safety from a passing car, I almost hit him.

The therapist asked about my past, and that is what opened up a whole new box I never thought I would open. When she asked about my mother, I told her about how she had tried to commit suicide when I was young, how I felt that she would go back and forth on the things that she told me, how I trusted her and then felt betrayed by that trust. I gave a few small examples, then I stopped. I sensed that the therapist was listening to me with a kind of curiosity, sort of like a reporter trying to dig out my story, and I was afraid of being fodder for some study or professional discussion. Seeing my hesitation, she finally asked me to write to my mother what I could not tell her.

"But I don't want to hurt her," I protested. "She has her own pain to deal with. I don't want to add on more pain."

"Then tear up the letters," she told me. "Burn them, throw them away. Do whatever you want to do with them. Just write them to get your own pain out of your system."

I sat in the parking lot of her office for an hour and cried before I was able to drive to school. I put on my sunglasses as I headed to class, and felt like a ghost again as I walked across the beautiful green lawn. The whole world was moving around me without seeing me, and I was trapped in my lonely brain, held back by so many memories. Would I ever be like them? Carefree? Able to just enjoy life and learning? I took school so seriously; I had never skipped a single class until that day. I found a large empty spot on the lawn with no one around me and turned my back to the students who were walking to their classes so no one could see my face. It was a beautiful April day, and I was looking out on miles of trees that surrounded the school. I picked up the pen, and without knowing where to begin, I just started writing to my parents.

Torrents of anger spilled out that I had never allowed myself to feel before. Torrents of angry questions for which I had no answers.

Why didn't you leave when Amo came into our lives? I trusted you! You are my parents. Parents are supposed to protect their children, not expose them to danger. Your choices changed not just your own lives, but mine and my brothers'. What were you thinking of? Didn't you know how bad he was? Didn't you read when you traveled abroad, didn't people tell you? What was it, denial, surrender? Why did you bury your head in the sand, why did you close your mouth, your ears, and your eyes? Didn't you know he was the Devil and that it wasn't only about your lives, it was about mine too? How could you do this to me, your own child, raise me up in a prison with you in a relationship that I hated and I know you hated? Baba, why didn't you help us fly away? You promised me once you would teach me to fly, Baba. Remember that? Instead, you abandoned me to a man you knew was a jerk? Why did you leave me all alone in a strange country with no means of support?

And Mama, oh Mama, you are the love of my life. I loved you so much. I trusted you. You gave me a beautiful childhood, and I surrendered my life to you. Then you betrayed me and my trust in such a way that you left me being the very thing you hated in women: vulnerable. How could you do that to me? Of all the men who asked for my hand, why did you choose the cruelest one? He raped me, Mama. Did you know that? I trusted you, and look what you did to me! Then you and Baba left me here all alone with no money. Why did you just throw me and my dreams and my studies away after you raised me to care about them so much? Didn't you ever stop to think that it was my life I was living, and not yours? I never asked to come to America, did I? That was your dream, not mine. Baba was right about that, you have been living vicariously through me since I was a teenager. Look how you've imprinted me. Look what I did with these pills. I almost killed myself, Mama. Just like you. I hurt someone I love very much, Mama. Just like you.

Each letter I wrote was angrier than the one before it.

Then one day I tore the letters up. The next time my mother called me at 2 A.M., I told her it was unfair to burden me with her problems, which I couldn't do anything about; I was her child, not her mother. I still called on holidays, but I divorced them in my mind. I needed to focus on myself.

A few months later, in December 1995, I got a call from the White House to let me know that ours was one of six organizations getting an award for working with women refugees. It had been over two years since that *TIME* story had come out, and we were going to receive an award for our work as part of President Clinton's effort to show that Americans cared about people in Bosnia, the day prior to the signing of the Dayton Accords in France. I was excited. The war was over. Milŏsević eventually would be put on trial for war crimes.

I had been living in black turtlenecks and jeans, and we had no money for nice clothes, so when I dressed for the White House that day, I pulled out my five-year-old wardrobe of designer clothes that we had bought on our European shopping trip with Amo's money, a Mondi suit with an Escada shirt, the Dior coat, and a pair of leather dress shoes with a hole on one toe. I had never heard of an oval-shaped office, but I loved meeting President Clinton. It was 10 A.M., and he was relaxed, charming, and chewing on ice from his glass of Coke. I crossed my ankles to hide the hole in my shoe as we honorees talked to him and Hillary Clinton about refugees in Bosnia and Croatia. When I left, it was to television lights, as well as an invitation—later cancelled because of a labor strike—to fly to Paris the next day with the president for the signing of the Dayton Accords. I was flattered by the attention until, out of the blue, came my father's voice saying, "Don't let this go to your head."

When Amjad and I left the White House that day in a media limo heading for a studio interview, we had exactly $5 between us. It made me think of Mama's old saying, "Life is like a cucumber. One day it's in your hand, the next day it's in your ass." In Baghdad, it was in my mouth financially and in my ass politically; I had everything I needed financially and no freedom. Here I had my freedom and I was broke. But I was in love and I was doing the work I was meant to do.

A week later, when finals were over, I collapsed and let myself cry for the first time since coming back from Croatia. Once I started crying, I found I didn't know how to stop. I started wailing uncontrollably. I went for so long that Amjad called an ambulance to ask someone to come over and sedate me. When the paramedics came, they started asking me questions and I sobbed through the answers.

"Is your husband abusing you?" a female paramedic asked.

"No," I sobbed. "I love him very much."

"Are you sure he hasn't hurt you?" she asked. She was ready to have Amjad taken away in a police car—where was she when I was married to Fakhri?

"Yes, I'm sure. I love him very much. He would never hurt me."

"What about work, or school?"

"I've got A pluses. I just got an award from the White House."

"I don't understand, honey. You can tell me. What's wrong?"

"Nothing is wrong," I kept saying. "Nothing is wrong. Everything is going right in my life. I just don't know how to stop crying!"

From Alia's Notebook

He never ceased to enjoy using women for his pleasure. He talked about Baghdad as if she were a woman whom he was in love with. He talked about Baghdad's palm trees, its rivers, its sands, and its women. He claimed that he loved Baghdad so much that he couldn't imagine living away from it.

He never had enough women no matter how many he had access to. He would explain this by saying that he was trying to make up for the hard days in his youth and his political activism. In one of our evenings, he told us that when he was in prison he would get excited even by seeing two birds mating. Thus, there was no limit for him on how many women he could have, starting with city women and ending with women from rural areas.

Iraq and its people were violated so many times by so many forces, but nothing compares to what Saddam has done to the country and its people. Nothing compares to his atrocities. We had to be silent witnesses to these crimes. I am left like a traumatized child at what I have seen in my life.

10

■

SETTING ME FREE

I DIDN'T SEE MY MOTHER for five years.

We spoke, but international calls were hard to place and strained by my unresolved anger. Even if I'd wanted to, how could we have had a heart-to-heart conversation when I knew there was at least one intelligence agent listening in from Iraq and possibly another in America as well? What conversations there were took on a predictable pattern in which we would edge briefly into emotional topics, then back away, often ending with Mama asking me to come home for a visit and telling me about all the parties she would have for us. The last thing I wanted was a party to prove to her friends that I had made a good marriage after all. Iraqi intelligence was done the old-fashioned way, with someone listening in, and one time our monitor spoke up and took her side. "Be a good daughter, come home for a visit," he said. Even in America Amo's secret police interrupted my phone calls. After that, I always had a perverse urge to speak to our eavesdropper directly and say, "How are you today? How are things in Iraq—everyone still terrified?"

One day in 1997, Mama called to say she wasn't feeling well and had developed a limp that doctors in Baghdad couldn't diagnose—could I help set up doctors' appointments for her in

America? Medical care in Iraq, once among the best in the Arab world, was another casualty of sanctions—another punishment for the punished. I helped arrange her visa, set up appointments, and suddenly she was back in my life, sitting in an airport wheelchair in her Nina Ricci mink. Given the limp, it didn't surprise me that they had wheeled her off the plane, but when I hugged her, her old vitality seemed missing. She was no longer the beauty I remembered. The skin around her lips sagged when she smiled, and I realized she had aged.

Amjad and I had bought a one-bedroom condo in Alexandria, Virginia, that we thought of as our "nest." We had a quiet balcony that opened up onto trees and a pool, and friends from around the world had stayed with us. Until now, it had been a refuge from my past. I was nervous as we walked in the door, full of conflicting feelings.

Mama was exhausted from the long flights and went to bed early.

"Noah's Ark?" she asked.

Noah's Ark. I felt that old flutter of love for her. That was what we used to call her king-sized bed when I was little. "Noah's Ark!" she would shout out sometimes when my father was away, especially during the war, and my little brothers and I would all run and jump in her big bed for a sleepover. I tried to sleep with her that night, in hope of bringing back some of the trust lost between us, but I found no comfort being near to her anymore, only anxiety. I lay there thinking of all the things I wanted to say to her, then slipped away when she fell asleep, and joined Amjad on the sofa bed.

"I can't even hug her," I said, crying softly into his chest. "I just can't."

Except for the limp, she seemed much better the next day. The image of the dutiful daughter, I served her breakfast in bed and told her about the appointments we had lined up and the sights we were planning to see. This was the first time we had been together in nearly seven years without a marital crisis facing us, but it was obvious from that first day that we had different needs. She wanted to bring back the loving daughter I had been, and I wanted to bring back the strong, independent mother she had been. So we politely danced and parried with each other as Amjad looked on in discomfort. We went to the Smithsonian Institution, and Mama silently made her point by lingering at a portrait of a mother and daughter. We went to the Kennedy Center to see *Phantom of the Opera*, the story of a young opera singer held captive by a hideously deformed phantom in a mask. "Those who have seen your face draw back in fear," the young singer told her tormentor. "I am the mask you wear." There it is Mother, look! I wanted to say. That's the nightmare of my life you created for me. Can't you see it? I was the mask Amo wore. I still have this nightmare that my face will disintegrate and people will see his face underneath mine. Can't you *feel* it, Mama? But all she said was how much she enjoyed the show. Except for one emotional invective against Saddam Hussein by Amjad's father, who had no idea we knew him, no one mentioned the man who had formed, or rather deformed, my life.

One night Mama invited to dinner an Iraqi couple who also happened to be visiting their children in Washington, D.C. My mother got all dressed up for the evening, and as we sat down to eat, I felt the same surge of anxiety I used to feel every time we walked into one of Aunt Sajida's palace parties together, when she would try to show me off and I would have to smile and pretend to be happy to please her. But it was different now. I was twenty-seven years old. This was my house. I had worked so hard to break out of those old habits, and I was not going to let her make me snap right back into them. I stood up politely, went to the stereo, and put on Persian music by a singer named Quoqoosh. Instantly, our dinner table conversation stopped. My mother's face flushed, and drops of sweat formed on her upper lip as they always did when she was angry or embarrassed. Mama gave me a look I would not forget for a long time. Amjad looked puzzled. He was the only non-Iraqi at the table. He didn't know our vocabulary of fear. He didn't understand what it meant to play the music of the enemy. Finally, the tension was broken when the Iraqi man said, "Ahhh, I've missed this music. It has been so long." We all laughed then, recognizing for a brief moment how silly it was to be terrified of a song thousands of miles from Baghdad, years after the war had ended. Yet, after that brief acknowledgment of common ground, we moved to safer topics about the old days in Baghdad. I cringed inside, realizing how insensitive and cruel I had been. I did not know if these visitors were Baathists. They might have been informers, and Mama would have to go back and deal with the consequences of my arrogant disregard for her safety. Instead of sharing my new freedom with her, I was rubbing her face in it and risking her life.

One of the things on my agenda was to show her what I had accomplished despite what she had done to me. I wanted to show her the new me, the women's advocate who had founded an international women's organization, the expert on women survivors of war who published papers on the subject, appeared on television, and was doing her best to make a difference in people's lives. Between doctors' appointments, I took her to our office and explained our program and what we were trying to accomplish. I taught her about the rape camps in Bosnia and the mass rape in Rwanda and showed her pictures of women I had met there. She listened to everything I said and began working as a volunteer, reading and filing letters from women in Bosnia, Croatia, and Rwanda. When I saw how she responded, I knew the mother who had taught me to care about women and their issues was still there inside her. She was the one who had inspired me to do this work, both through her example and through the feminist books she had given me. I decided to give her my own selections of feminist work, some of it about mother-daughter relationships, and I stacked them in the order I wanted her to read them: Amy Tan's *The Joy Luck Club,* Alice Walker's *The Color Purple,* Betty Friedan's *The Feminine Mystique,* and Fatima Marnissi's *The Forgotten Queens of Islam.*

After a single chapter of Amy Tan, she got it.

"Are you trying to tell me that I have not been a good mother to you?" she asked.

It was the opening I wanted, but it was a sunny afternoon, and she had taken me by surprise. For a moment I doubted my resolve.

"*La, la, la,* Mother," I answered in the traditional Iraqi way of repeating things three times. "No, no, no. You are a wonderful mother, and I love you very much."

But Mama knew my plastic smile when she saw it.

"Something is wrong, Zainab," she declared a few days later. "What is wrong? What have I done, Zainab? Why are you so angry with me?"

She was sitting in a chair that she and I had upholstered together. I was sitting on the floor next to her. I felt all the anger, rage, and disappointment rush out in a stream of bitterness and accusations.

"You destroyed everything you had helped me build, Mama!" I said. "Why did you do that to me? Yank me out of my last year of college? Take me away from my family and my friends and marry me off to a man I barely knew—a man who *hurt* me? Why did you abandon me, leave me here in a strange country all alone?"

I burst out in sobbing.

"Oh, Zanooba, you don't—"

"Understand? What is there not to understand, Mama? You used to make fun of people who married strangers! You taught me to finish college, get a career, be a strong woman, and then look what you did to your own daughter! I *believed* in you, Mama, and you sent me halfway around the world into the arms of a man who had no respect at all for anything you brought me up to care about. I trusted you with my life, Mama! You were the one who kept preaching to me that I should never let myself be abused by any man, and then what did you do? You married me to a cold, horrible man who didn't think twice about raping me!"

I don't know how to describe the look she gave me. It was a look of devastation, of irredeemable failure. I think I saw her fall apart. Her shoulders collapsed. She leaned over, looking down at her hands, and began crying too.

"I had to get you out, *habibiti*!" she finally said. "I had to! He *wanted* you, Zainab. I didn't see any other way."

"*He?* Who was *he*?"

I had been in America too long. There was only one *he* in Iraq. *He* was Amo.

So Mama hadn't sent me off to America to live her dream? She had married me off to Fakhri because she was afraid Amo was going to rape me? Me? The enormity of this revelation wouldn't sink in.

"But, Mama, I was only nineteen," I said, realizing how naïve that sounded.

"In his eyes, you were a woman, Zainab," she said. "You had been engaged to be married. Then you broke off your engagement. You were a woman."

She beseeched me to understand and went back through times I had spent with Amo that I had tried to put out of my mind, hoping to make me see them as she had.

"Do you remember that night when you were standing out on the balcony by the lake and he and I were watching you? The wind was catching your hair in the moonlight, and he just stood still staring at you, as if he was breathing you in. I was standing next to him, *habibiti*. I knew that look. He didn't even turn around when he said to me, 'Your daughter is so beautiful.' I knew that night I had to keep him away from you until I could get you out."

"But, Mama," I stammered, trying to understand the one crime it had never occurred to me he was capable of. "We were like his family, he couldn't—he wouldn't have hurt *me*, would he?"

"Oh, honey, I hoped never to have to tell you all this! But I could see his infatuation with you. He started using his smile on you, you know the one, his charming smile. I knew that damned smile. Trust me, Zainab. You don't know how he can be."

And I remembered the first night I saw him after I had broken off my engagement, how he had gazed into my eyes for a long time with what I read as sympathy. That was the same night he gave me that shining-eye look for playing the *Blue Danube,* and I had assumed he was punishing Sarah. Had there been more to it than that? Yes, I suddenly knew, there had.

I looked at Mama's beautiful eyes, so red and wrenched in pain from how unfairly I had treated her. I felt such an outpouring of trust and love that I fell into her arms, and we sobbed together at what he had done to both of us and at the years we had lost. I felt her pain and her ragged releasing of it. That was one of the most powerful moments of my life. It was the time I became her daughter again, and the moment she regained her ability to comfort me. I asked for her forgiveness and she asked for mine. How could she possibly have known that to save me from rape, she was sending me into the arms of a rapist?

After we both calmed down, she told me she and the other parents had started to worry about their daughters that day Amo took us off in his sports car without telling them.

"How worried we were for you girls! When you got back, he saw the look on our faces and sent you off. Then he took us aside and lectured us and said, 'How *dare* you think I'd do anything to your daughters!' "

I heard his voice in hers. I knew the intonation, and it chilled me to the bone.

No wonder they were scared, watching Saddam Hussein drive up with their daughters, all in the bloom of young womanhood. They were totally impotent. He could have done anything to us he pleased, and there was nothing they could have done about it. I was totally unaware of any danger. There were only two times I could remember that I had actually enjoyed his company, and that afternoon was one of them. After all these years and all my education, I realized, I had never reconciled the Saddam Hussein who committed genocide with the Amo who drove us around that day in his red sports car. Intellectually, I understood, but emotionally I didn't. The wall between the two was still there in my brain, sturdy as fear.

Later, someone who never lived under Saddam Hussein posed

questions to me that I found hard to answer. Wasn't there another way out for me besides an arranged marriage? Couldn't Mama have simply told me the truth, especially after I had left Fakhri? I knew that part of the answers to such questions lay in logistics, such as restrictions on travel and money transfers and even university credits, but the questions themselves showed a fundamental lack of understanding of what we all knew we needed to do to survive. We simply never had the freedom to think that way in Iraq. Terror had carved out the narrowest of safe passageways in our brains, and those were the ones we took. If Mama had told me why she had married me off to Fakhri, she would have destroyed any hope for what had seemed to her a good marriage. Instead, she preserved the illusion, gave me a chance, and limited the likelihood that Amo would sense her motives and punish her and my family. Whatever other theoretical escape routes there might have been, this was the only one many Iraqi mothers perceived that could spare their daughters from rape by Uday and, apparently, Amo himself. How many others like me were there? I wondered. How many of us had been married off to pictures or to voices at the other end of the telephone?

Mama had done what desperate mothers had done down through the centuries. Like Moses' mother putting her son in a basket of rushes and trusting him to the currents of the Nile, like Vietnamese mothers desperately flinging their babies to departing American soldiers at the end of the Vietnam war, like women I had met in refugee camps who pleaded with me to take away their daughters, she had cast me off.

And I had punished her for loving me so much.

Mama was diagnosed with clinical depression, a conclusion hard to argue with except for her obvious symptoms of a more physical problem. Though they could not pinpoint the cause, doctors felt the limp was a separate issue that could be later addressed in Iraq. I tried to convince her to stay with us, but she felt she had to return to my little brother, who was still in school in Baghdad. This time, it was with deep misgivings and pain that I finally put her on the plane, along with a supply of Prozac.

She did not get better. Instead, over the next few months, she underwent more tests and procedures that culminated seven months later in near-fatal and probably unnecessary surgery in Amman. By the time I managed to clear the immigration hurdles to bring her back home with me, there was no doubt she was gravely ill, though no one knew why. She spent months off and on in American hospitals and more months in what was euphemistically called "rehab" before she was finally handed one of the most terrifying diagnoses imaginable: amyotrophic lateral sclerosis—Lou Gehrig's disease. ALS is a progressive neurological nightmare that is often described as a "living prison" because the body deteriorates steadily around the brain until it finally shuts down altogether. Mama's muscles, already so weak she could barely move, would become completely flaccid. But her mind would remain perfectly intact and aware of every moment until her death. Though there was no way to know if there was a connection in her case, ALS had recently been tied to the "Gulf War Syndrome" afflicting British and U.S. soldiers who had served in the Middle East.

She was fifty-one years old. The disease was incurable. She had perhaps two years, or if she was lucky—or, some would say, unlucky—ten. The fear of losing her that I had lived with all my life was coming true.

"I want to die at home," she told me. "That is my only wish."

Amjad and I moved into a two-bedroom apartment, bright and homey and handicap-accessible. Mama wanted to sleep in a regular bed, sit in a regular chair, and live as normal a life as it is possible to live if you cannot move your own body without assistance. I re-covered an antique chair she had bought me with burgundy fabric from Pakistan and surrounded it with plants. I furnished her bedroom in her favorite colors of burgundy and green and hung paintings on the walls of old Baghdad that used to hang in our living room. By the time she came to live with us—to die with us—she could not walk or even turn her head unless someone did it for her. Her beautiful smile was gone. The muscles in her body and lovely face were slack, and her skin hung over her face like a curtain over a closed window. Her face, once so expressive I worried for her, was dead except for her huge brown eyes, made even more huge by illness. I couldn't even hug her for fear of disrupting her breathing; we kept a respirator in her room. She could not talk, but oddly, fortuitously, she could still move her hands, so if we put a pen into her hand, she could communicate with us through notes she jotted down in a drugstore spiral notebook.

At first we took her on trips around the city in a wheelchair, but everywhere we went, people just stopped what they were doing and stared. We had visitors at the beginning too, but they found it hard to even look at her without breaking down and crying. The last thing she wanted was pity, so the final few months of her life came down to her family, her correspondence, and a Tanzanian caregiver named Fatima who took care of her when Amjad and I were out. Amjad was in his last year of law school and came home to put on Beanie Baby puppet shows for her. He bought her an aquarium that he filled with goldfish she could watch during the day, and if one would die, he would replace it before she could see. It became a kind of nightly tradition for me to read her Rumi poems. Haider, the brother I had remembered as an annoying computer nerd, had recently gotten a visa to work in Detroit and came to see her whenever he could, bathing her, brushing her hair, and revealing an amazing depth of kindness and love. Mama had not seen my little brother Hassan for nearly a year by this time, and she worried about him. No matter how much we begged U.S. officials to allow him to visit, we couldn't get him a visa. When we managed to reach him on the telephone, I would hold the receiver to Mama's ear, and she would listen to him speak and I would lower the receiver and she would use a finger to tap on the mouthpiece—*tig, tig, tig*—to let him know she had heard.

This was not a fate any of us ever could have wished for her. Yet she wrote to me that these were the happiest days of her life. How sad, I thought, and yet I understood. There was no struggle to wage, nothing we could do, and that brought its own kind of peace. We had time to plan, and we set up a signal that would tell me she was thinking of me after she died—the feeling of a gentle brush of the back of her fingers against my cheek. We were on the seventh floor and had a view of Virginia that stretched to the horizon. Mama had become more religious, as had many Iraqis in the 1990s, and it was odd at first for me to see her holding prayer beads, praying without moving her lips or making a sound. Yet there was a kind of beauty in these days. The fear she had lived with for twenty-five years was gone, and it felt like a blessing for me just to witness the humility and dignity with which she went about wrapping up her life. She marked the *Surah,* the passages from the Quran she wanted me to read after her death, and began writing notes to old friends in Iraq, telling them how much she loved them, and asking forgiveness and forgiving others for any differences that had arisen in their lives. When I came home from work, there would always be something new for me to see, a vibrantly colored watercolor of the face of an aunt that she had painted from memory, a letter for me to mail to an old friend, an Iraqi dish she had somehow managed to instruct her caregiver to cook for me.

In Baghdad, Mama used to complain that her hands were too chubby. Now they were oddly elegant—tools of grace bestowed on her by a belatedly compassionate God. She knit two blankets, a yellow one for me and a white one for the baby I had pledged never to have—"in case you change your mind," she said on paper. With every knot she prayed for God to forgive her: "Forgive me God, forgive me God, forgive me God," she prayed. She became a different sort of role model to me now. The beauty she used to have on the outside had been replaced by a column of beauty and strength inside. She was an example to me in this, and I tried after that to clear up any misunderstandings in my own life in case death took me by surprise.

After so many years of trying to erase my past, I finally realized how much I needed to understand it. How much had she kept from me when I was growing up? I was afraid, selfishly, that she would lose control of her hands before she talked with her only daughter, so one night I asked her to write to me too, and she agreed.

It was only then, when she could no longer speak, that she began to open her life to me.

She started with the night she and Baba had first met Amo. I was three. She had told me about Pig's Island when I was young, but it had sounded like a fantasy story to me then. Now, though her notes reflected a certain devil-may-care quality, I began to see it as darkly portentous of what was to come, a guerrilla operation planned by a ruthless strategist who chose his weapons well: guns and champagne. I tried to imagine Mama as she was then, five years younger than I was now, a beautiful young socialite a few years out of college, dancing with a debonaire young husband to a live band on a party boat alongside younger versions of Aunt Layla and Uncle Mazen, Aunt Nada and Uncle Kais. I felt the engines turn against the current of the Tigris and slide onto Pig's Island, discharging them directly into the welcoming, outstretched arms of a handsome young man dressed all in white like an actor on a moonlit stage. As they stepped down, wondering at this surprise their host apparently had planned for them, this figure in white snapped his fingers, and boats appeared from out of the darkness, surrounding them. Soldiers came forward bearing trays of champagne. Who was this man? friends asked each other. But even after he was introduced, they didn't recognize the name. Everyone knew the president, but who knew his cousin Saddam Hussein, who was merely the vice president? Certainly not my parents. It was Mama who had asked, no doubt more carelessly than she would ever refer to him again, "And who is Saddam Hussein?"

As I read, I saw Amo's white shoes muddied in the silty sand of Pig's Island. I had played in that sand, and with a child's sense of transgression, I regretted that it was that place that he had chosen to invade our lives. I remembered Baba water-skiing around Pig's Island, trim and elegant, a perfect arc of spray flying out behind him, making funny faces and sticking one leg out now and then just to be silly and show off to me and my cousins. What would my parents have been like today, I wondered, if Saddam Hussein had just left them be? When was the last time my father had done anything silly? Would my mother still be here now, locked in her body even as she went about freeing her soul?

Amo pursued my parents with the cunning of the hunter I knew he was. For two years, he had sent them invitations, and they made excuses to avoid him. By 1974, his patience had waned, so he devised a trap: he asked Mahmood, the mutual friend who had arranged the initial meeting at Pig's Island, to throw a party and not tell my parents he was coming. When they rang the bell, Mahmood answered it, and warned them Saddam Hussein was inside. Standing on the front porch, they pondered their options and saw only one. To leave would have been a dangerous act of *ayeb*.

"So we stayed," Mama wrote, "and that changed our lives."

They chose survival, cloaked in courtesy, and it became our prison. I tried to imagine myself standing there on that doorstep in my mother's heels, nervously fingering the old coin at my throat, exchanging glances with my husband and hurriedly weighing the consequences that might befall us and our child if we were rude. And, I knew, I would have stepped inside too. That was the first step they took in their deal with the Devil. Mama herself had called him the Devil once. What would the Devil be but just another fallen angel, without his charm and power to damn the living little by little, until he took away what you thought you were at your core?

"At first, we thought we could manage the relationship if we were careful," she wrote to me. I wanted to scream, Impossible, Mama! Look at the consequences we'll all pay!

Yet I recognized in her words the unwittingly arrogant undertaking of the innocent. They had stayed in Baghdad, naïvely unaware of what lay ahead. Mahmood, who apparently knew better, fled the country. I had never met their friend Mahmood, but as I read her writing, I imagined him a smart risk-taker who was bold enough to venture into the unknown while my parents stayed behind. They had been afraid to take that step and naïvely assumed they could somehow stay safe and protect our home. Why hadn't they been bold enough to leave like Mahmood? Why did some people leave and others stay? It was hard to look at Mama and not see how battered and bruised she was from all her attempts to escape, and yet when I was reading her journal, I felt I could still see a little of that innocent young mother in her eyes.

Each night, I came home from work and read what she had written, like a series. Sometimes there were just a few sentences, sometimes more. She showed me Saddam Hussein as a young despot on the rise, before he attracted much international attention. In cinematic validation of my own fears, her memories helped me conjure scenes of Amo as a night owl predator prowling the streets, rousting my parents and others out of their beds to party or just to listen to him for hours on end. Familiar moments came to mind framed in disturbing new contexts: Mama hurriedly searching the cupboard for pistachios to set out for him on our rosewood table; Amo with his charm smile on striding into our front hallway with his box of Chivas Regal; Baba drinking it on our blue sofa, resentful of this "unequal friendship" as he and Mama called it, yet drinking more; and Mama judiciously turning down the volume on the stereo so as not to wake her young children who were upstairs asleep, Haider and me; the corrupt mixture of whiskey and cologne.

It was both riveting and painful to read what she wrote, like watching a disaster movie in which everyone but the heroes can see the coming disaster. I hadn't seen Aunt Nahla in years. She had been one of Mama's best friends. Now, through Mama's writings, I saw her slow dancing with Amo after Amo had given her husband so much whiskey he was sick and needed help, and yet he kept Aunt Nahla dancing with him, slow dance after slow dance. I imagined the expression on her face over Amo's shoulder, a portrait of quiet fear, as she kept on dancing, unable to stop to help her own husband. She was an artist who got together with Mama for Turkish coffee in the afternoons, and I remembered the sound of the little cups being flipped over onto the saucers so they could study the *finjan* and try to foretell the future. Then Mama came crying one day, and when I asked her what had happened, she told me Aunt Nahla had gossiped about her in front of Amo. She never told me what Aunt Nahla had said, but I saw it had hurt her deeply. There had been many disappointments like this, I knew, and I had seen her grow bitter as, one by one, so many of my aunts disappeared from our lives during the farmhouse period. Now, some fifteen years later, she handed me a letter to mail to Aunt Nahla telling her she loved her, forgiving her and asking her for forgiveness. For what, I didn't know and didn't ask. I had seen erasures sometimes on the notes she left me at night. I knew how hard it must have been for her to manage the strength to erase.

Women for Women International was growing at this time. We had four offices now, and war was starting in Kosovo that had all the earmarks of another human disaster. I was reading letters from women in war zones, then going home and reading Mama's journals, and there was much about them that was similar. The same fact-based recitation, the same stoic bearing of witness to wrongs, the same curious juxtaposition of mundane details and horrors. I thought of the hundreds or thousands of faces of women I had met who had been traumatized by war or rape or both. Except for Ajsa, their faces had been numb, but none was as numb as my mother's.

She rarely wrote about her own feelings. Often, she started stories she didn't finish. She mixed trivia with historic events, and her

250 SETTING ME FREE

observations about Amo's dress and his palaces and his childhood received almost as much attention as his confessions of murder. Much of what she wrote I either knew or had supposed. Some of her stories I had heard from Amo myself, or had even been taught in school. But, as I read on, I realized that Mama and Baba had understood his capacity for murder almost from the beginning. He had made no secret of his public execution of political opponents, so there was no reason for me to be surprised by the fact that he had bragged about killing friends in private. But what hit at some soft spot inside me, whatever was left of the little girl in me, was that Mama had heard his boastful confessions one night, then driven me to school in the morning. Just a few days after she had told me to make the thought of "Amo" fly like an arrow out of my brain, she had had to listen to him boast that he had just killed a friend with his own hands and murdered an old fortune-teller as well. He had murdered a woman he loved as she slept with her mother and three-year-old daughter, who would first scream that he killed her mother and then reportedly stop speaking altogether. "We had to be silent witnesses to his crimes," she wrote. "We were among the victims for no one can survive his atrocities. And we kept on being imprisoned by our own fear, afraid of saying no to him or even of showing our horror at his acts."

I had barely learned how to deal with the stories of the women I was working with in war zones. I didn't know how to deal with the stories my mother was telling me about what she had witnessed in Iraq. Breathe like a fish, I told myself. Remember to breathe.

"Why did you stay, Mama?" I finally asked. That was the question that may have mattered to me more than any other, and I tried to ask it without blame. In response, she only looked at me with round, open eyes. She laughed with her eyes and cried with her eyes, though there were no more tears. Don't tell me you don't understand, that you have forgotten the arguments your father and I used to have, she said with her eyes. Have you been gone so long you have forgotten what it was like, Zanooba?

As I read her journal, I realized Amo's appetite for sex was as strong as for violence.

I don't think my mother ever would have told me about this aspect of him if she hadn't seen my work. He had told my parents about Hana'a, the mistress he had loved, then murdered with his own hands. Then there was Amel, whose husband resisted being "friends" with Amo and wound up dead on the airport road, and her sister Samira, the mistress-wife whose snub by my father had caused Amo to scream at my mother that night. What struck me as I read my mother's notes was how tawdry it all was, as Amo, over whiskey, justified his need for women by claiming he had missed out on sex during a stay in prison, when he had gotten excited just watching birds touching out a window. I remembered the slow dithering of Samira's fingertips on Amo's thigh that night in Mosul. No wonder Baba wouldn't let her into our home.

Mama looked at me with her big eyes full of questions and curiosity, and I knew she wondered what I was thinking. Calling on every lesson I had learned in refugee camps, I offered only sympathy and understanding. I kissed her or held her hands and told her I loved her. Nothing else. I did my best to show no judgment at all. Be strong so she won't worry you can't handle this, or she will stop explaining, I told myself. Be there for her, don't make her have to be there for you. What she did not know was that when I had a moment for myself, I would go into our walk-in closet, close the door, and cry into the clothes.

One night she wrote about how much Amo enjoyed "People's Day," a day in which citizens would go to him seeking help for their problems. People's Days were highly publicized when I was a teenager. Amo would travel around Iraq in his trailer wearing a white doctor's coat like a therapist and hold private audiences with citizens, then make a public show of waiving a law, giving someone money, or granting a woman a divorce from a reluctant husband to show his generosity. Mama wrote that he would invite women in and try to charm the most beautiful ones into sex. If his charm failed, he would simply rape them. When they were released, often with some small favor granted, they would be expected to express their gratitude. *"Shokrun jazeelan sayyed al ra'aees,"* they would say, sometimes before television cameras. Thank you very much, Mr. President. His favorite place for People's Days, Mama wrote, was a village in Samarra, near Ehab's home, that was known for its beautiful women.

Mama had the other half of my memories, the half that made mine make sense. Her writing jolted a memory in my mind of a time Mama and I went to a potluck dinner at one of my aunts' houses. I was probably nine or ten. I was sitting around with the adults in the living room. Aunt Lamya'a was talking. She was a beautiful widow, and she was telling the other women about how she had gone to see the president about a problem she had had—financial, I think. She had to wait with several other women in an outer office, and when the president came out, they went around in a circle, and each named her problem. When Aunt Lamya'a named hers, Amo told her it was "complicated"—*muaqada*—I remember this word because it seemed so laden with meaning. He asked her to join him in his private office to discuss it further. Mama and her friends all leaned in very close to Aunt Lamya'a, and she began to whisper. Minutes before the room had been filled with laughter and noise, then there was near silence and I remember sitting there feeling alone and left out, wondering whether I should stay or go into the other room as the women all wrapped their arms around Aunt Lamya'a the way they sometimes did with other aunts in our garden when they went outside to say things they didn't want me to hear. And I could hear her crying inside this circle of arms. When the women finally pulled back, Aunt Lamya'a was wiping tears away. All the women, including Mama, looked very sad.

"Is Aunt Lamya'a all right?" I asked her on the way home.

"She will be all right," Mama said, adding, "Zainab, honey, please leave this subject alone."

I couldn't leave it alone. It had become my life's work.

I knew that most rapes are committed by family members and friends, yet in Iraq and much of the Arab world, women are still seen as innocent in rape only if they are assaulted by armed strangers. I had heard rumors in high school that the Mukhabarat subjected women to rape and made videotapes in order to blackmail them into becoming informers. If they admitted to rape, they opened themselves up to abandonment by their husbands and separation from their children because women carried the family's honor, or *aar*. In conservative Arab cultures and in other parts of the world as well, I knew that a family's honor is *judged* by the behavior of women, but it is effectively *owned* by men: her husband or father or brothers, or even her sons. To protect a man's honor, then, it is his right to marry an unmarried woman off to her rapist or even to kill her. If the rapist is a family member, it is overlooked or buried. If the rapist is a criminal, the woman is judged unmarriageable. But when the rapist is the government itself, the woman is victimized and the man is emasculated because there is nothing at all he can do. It was said that husbands had committed suicide over these rapes or abandoned their wives and children—all in the name of saving their family honor.

Saddam Hussein had institutionalized rape just as he had institutionalized the hatred of Persians and Shia—I was sure of it. He was using the same tactics as Milošević, and Stalin before him, using women to send political messages to men to consolidate his own power. The more I thought about it, the more I felt the evil, the horror, of the man I had been trained to call Amo, and the more certain I was that he had used sex to glue together his network of fear, insinuating himself into every human relationship he touched, including marriage. Except for Kuwait and part of Iran, Amo had simply taken everything he ever wanted, from gold to pomegranates. Why not women?

"Mama, what did you mean when you told me I didn't know

how Amo could be?" I asked her one day. She looked at me with her huge open eyes and I knew what she was asking: are you sure you want to hear this, Zainab?

Yes.

She talked about the gypsy women and women bused in for parties from villages. Sometimes women were simply stopped on the street and pulled over by secret police because Amo or his brothers or sons, apparently, had seen them and wanted them. There was a woman who would call up women and invite them to her apartment for "tea," who was apparently his madam. One woman my mother knew who got an invitation for tea was afraid to reject her invitation. So she dressed in very tight jeans and a big belt and extra clothing in hopes that if Amo did arrive, the clothes might deter him. Instead, he only treated her more roughly and forced himself on her.

"She was raped," I stated with horror.

"You can call it rape or you can call it really bad sex," she wrote, and I thought that was the saddest thing I had ever heard from a woman who had once described sex to her daughter as beautiful.

That night, when I went to bed, I lay there, unable to sleep. I started questioning my own judgment of Fakhri's violation of me. Was that rape, or was it just "bad sex"? Had I been wrong in my judgment? I hated it when I doubted myself. I remembered the bed, the flowered pillowcase I still kept in my closet even now as a reminder. I remembered how I felt, violated in every way. Not one part of my body, not one ounce of my soul, was a participant in that act. He might as well have been raping a piece of wood. It was forced. It caused pain. I hated it. I fought it. It wasn't bad sex. It was rape, and that was why I left him.

When I got home from the bus stop after work and opened the door, Mama looked proud and happy in her armchair. It was amazing, really, how much emotion she could convey through her eyes. She was all alone. Amjad was preparing for his bar exam. Her caregiver had gone.

"Where is Fatima, mother?" I asked, chiding her as I gave her a light embrace, drinking in the smell of her and allowing her, I think, to drink in mine.

"I let her go," she wrote, clearly proud of herself. "We cooked *bamya* for you. Serve yourself and come sit with me." *Bamya* was my favorite dish, okra cooked with garlic, tomato sauce and tamarind, lemony in the Iraqi style. I got my dinner and sat down with her to watch *Xena: Warrior Princess,* our nightly routine. Xena was a kind of female Hercules inspired by Greek mythology, a latter-day version of the Women's Village fantasy my aunts used to talk about. Xena had a dedicated following among women prisoners, lesbians, teenaged girls, and one Iraqi mother living for the time being in Alexandria, Virginia.

"The hardest part of this disease is not being able to laugh," she wrote.

We played backgammon for a while, the familiar sound of dice clicking away our limited time together. I was alone in my own home with my own mother. There was no one to scare us. No listening walls. No man at all at that moment in our Women's Village. I knew that the opportunity had finally come, after so many years, to ask the questions I couldn't as a child. It wasn't Zainab Salbi who worked with women war victims, it was me, her daughter. I needed to know the price we had paid for his friendship.

"Remember when you called me in Sarajevo and you were crying over the phone asking me why would I bring myself to a war when you risked everything to take me out of Iraq? I have thought a lot about that, Mama. Here's what think. I think I have been going from one war to another asking other women questions to find answers to questions that only you know, Mama, and you are sitting in front of me now. I have this pain inside me that won't go away, Mama. You have had this pain inside you. And I wonder if it's the same. I have to ask you, Mama, why were you so tormented all the time? Did he hurt *you,* Mama?"

She had her notebook in her lap and her knitting at her side. She tried to write, but her hands began shaking. She struggled for breath, and drops of sweat appeared on her face. Her face turned a deep red. I was afraid I was going to lose her. I ran to her bedroom to get her ventilator and oxygen to save her life, if only for a few more weeks or days. I cared about nothing else but keeping my mother alive in that moment. If I have to make choices, I choose you, Mama. And I never asked her again.

It was May 1999, and refugees were fleeing war in Kosovo in massive numbers, to Albania and Macedonia, most of them women and children. Mama, remote control in hand, kept watching this news. Women were being found half-naked and dazed in the middle of the street after being raped and released, and we talked about how vulnerable women were to rape in the midst of the chaos of war. If not for my mother, I would have gone to Kosovo in a heartbeat to start a new program there, but I couldn't leave. Mama was the most important thing in my life.

"You need to go to Kosovo, Zainab," she said. "Help those women, *habibiti.*"

"No, Mama. I need to stay with you. You are the most important person to me."

"You need to go, Zainab—don't worry about me," she said. "I will wait for you."

"But I want to be with you before you leave me, Mama," I said. "I don't want to risk being away."

"I will not die before you come back, Zainab," she said. "I promise."

I came back a week later, exhausted from travel and work and sharing the pain of shattered strangers. Mama had kept her promise, and she looked through the photographs of the women I had met, asking me about them and staring at some of the pictures for so long I felt she was trying to learn the life story behind each face. She had painted a series of watercolors while I was gone, of determined young women, in colors so vivid no one would imagine they had been applied by a dying woman. She had painted them on cards, like greeting cards. The last one she made was for me.

Shortly after I returned, Mama's caregiver told me she was going on vacation. I couldn't trust Mama with a replacement when I knew she was so close to death, so I began caring for her almost around the clock. By the time the hospice nurse came for her weekly visit five days later, I was an emotional and physical wreck, surviving on coffee and exhausted by the physical and emotional demands of keeping Mama alive. The nurse suggested Mama go into the hospice for a few days, to allow me to rest so I could resume her care, and Mama reluctantly agreed.

Haider came and stayed with her in the hospice. But two days later, when Amjad and I went to bring her home, it was too late. I saw her try to pick up a pencil, but her hand faltered and I couldn't read what she wrote. Haider and I each held one of her hands as Amjad read the Quran for her. I saw her try to catch just one more breath, and she was gone. I couldn't believe it. She couldn't be dead. I had to bring her home to die. I had promised her she would die at home. That was the one thing she had asked of me. I kept on telling the doctor over and over again to check her pulse because she had come so close to death before.

"Your mother is dead," he told me finally, softly, a kind man. "But she will always be with you, and there will be times in which you will feel her touch. I know about this. My mother died ten years ago and there are still times in which I would be driving or something and there would be her touch on my hands. She will always be there for you."

I washed her body with the help of local Muslim women, feeling not only grief as tears streamed down my face into the white shroud we wrapped around her body, but an overwhelming guilt as well. As I read the Surah she had selected, I kept thinking that in the one thing she had asked of me, to die at home, I had failed. I had failed her.

She had asked to be buried next to Bibi in Najaf, but it took me almost a week to arrange the paperwork to take her back to Iraq. Because of sanctions, there were still no direct flights, so after twelve hours of flying to Jordan, we had another twelve-hour drive to Baghdad. My father met me at the airport and had hired a driver to take us to Baghdad. I hadn't seen my father for nine years. He looked much older and carried prayer beads in his hand like so many other Iraqis who'd been encouraged by Amo to turn to God for relief from the hardship of sanctions. I had been running nonstop for a week trying to make the arrangements, and I was exhausted and grieving and just wanted to fall into his arms and have him comfort me and tell me he would take care of everything from then on. Instead, he was the one who collapsed in my arms, sobbing. "I loved your mother very much, Zainab," he kept saying. He expected me to be there for him to pick up the pieces, and I felt once again like the adult, the parent, rather than the child. It felt unfair to me after all I'd been through. Baba slept through the night on that long desert road, and it was during that long night that I bid my farewell to Mama and felt her soul leave me.

"Don't you recognize our neighborhood?" Baba asked as we drove toward our house.

I didn't. I had been away nine years. During that time, nearly a decade of sanctions had taken its toll. Iraqis had paid the price of Saddam's tyranny. Everything had aged and been drained of color. The streets were painted with resignation. Our cul-de-sac was filled with family members waiting for me in front of our home, all in black. I looked for my baby brother, Hassan, who was eleven years old when I last saw him, and found myself hugging a twenty-year-old man in a full beard of mourning. There were people crowding around me, cousins I was trying to recognize, everyone kissing me and crying. In the middle of it all, a stranger introduced himself as the head of our tribe. What tribe? I thought, distractedly, as we prepared to take my mother's body immediately to Najaf for the long-delayed burial. Aunt Samer sat with me in the car as she directed me to read the passages of the Quran to bless my mother in the final leg of her journey.

For centuries, Shia families have sent their dead to be buried in that holy place in the middle of the vast yellow sand desert of southern Iraq, until it has become one of the largest cemeteries in the world. When we had gone for Bibi's funeral, I remembered walking for perhaps fifteen minutes through the eerie city of the dead, past young men reciting the Quran and women sprinkling rose water on the graves of their loved ones, until we finally arrived at the mausoleum of my mother's family. The cemetery was so jammed with war dead then that it was difficult to walk without bumping into small white stones in front of the tombs. Now we drove straight up to the mausoleum. The cemetery seemed half the size it used to be, yet surely more people had been buried here in nine years. Where were the rest of the graves? When I was little, I had been afraid of this place the way children are afraid of vampires and zombies. Now I felt a different fear, as if even the dead were too scared to talk.

"What happened here?" I asked Aunt Samer. She looked around, the familiar look of worry and fear on her face.

"Saddam ordered that the cemetery be paved over to punish the Shia for rising up against him back in 1991," she told me quietly. "But, as the bulldozer came, a guard ran up and said, 'Stop, that mausoleum belongs to friends of the president's.' And that is how our dead were spared."

Saddam Hussein had spared our dead, but not our living.

Hot and exhausted, feeling someone had twisted my heart out of my chest, I watched my mother's body being lowered into the yellow sand next to Bibi: the hardest thing I had ever done. My mother's life was finally over. You never were afraid of death, Mama, were you? I asked her. Was it rest you were seeking, Mama? Is it rest you have now? Are you at peace now, Mama?

Throughout the three-day mourning period, our home was filled with people. Women gathered separately from men, and our house was filled with women wearing black, reading the Quran for my mother and crying. Some brought hired "mourners" as offerings, whose job it is to recite religious stories and eulogize the dead, inducing everyone to cry to purge their sorrow. We emptied all the furniture from the main part of our house and filled it with cushions so there would be enough space for the visitors, setting only a few chairs aside for VIPs, like Amo's sisters, who came to give their condolences.

No one expected me to be polite to anyone. "Cry as much as you can, honey," my aunts told me. And for three days I did. All the women seemed so bereft, I remember wondering if they were crying for Mama or for themselves. It was as if the entire country were in mourning for what had been lost.

It is traditional for the family of the person who has died to provide a feast for mourners on the third evening. Hundreds of women came that night, many of them aunts I hadn't seen since Mama's potluck dinners and my school years. They had organized the feast for us, and when I was asked to lead the women into our garden, I found it full of lights and my mother's favorite foods—stuffed lamb, *fesenjoon, tourshana,* dolma. The garden was decorated so beautifully it felt like a wedding, and the moment I stepped outside and saw what the women had done, I stopped crying. I felt the beauty of the Iraqi night and a gentle desert breeze on my face, like the back of Mama's fingers against my cheek.

"Your mother's soul is so clearly here, Zainab," Aunt Samer said, kissing me. "She is all around us. This is a blessed night. I can feel it."

Amo sent a driver to our house during the mourning period. He asked for my father, but he wasn't there, so the driver handed me Amo's condolences along with an envelope containing the equivalent of $500 to cover burial costs. I stiffened, and without thinking, my old fear returned, unsummoned and utterly intact. I smiled my plastic smile, thanked him, and left Iraq a few days later with no plans to return.

The wait was long at the Jordanian border. Throngs of people were trying to leave the country, and there were full body inspections. It turned out that it was forbidden to leave Iraq with any art or more than fifty dollars. Everything of any value was confiscated, including a small sketch my mother had done. It was there, at the Iraqi-Jordanian border, that my mother made her last gold donation: a small box of necklaces she had entrusted to my aunt to give to me in case of her death. Inside was a small sapphire pendant that had been given to her by Saddam Hussein.

Alia's Last Letter

To the light of my eyes, Zanooba,

    The day you were born was the happiest of my life. You were the most beautiful child and I loved you every second of my life. You were my friend since you were three years old. I planted in you strength because I hate women's weakness. And now, I can see my beloved Zainab with her strong personality, nice manners, and her success in her humanitarian work. If you only knew how proud I feel. You have accomplished all my dreams for you. I am grateful for God bringing you into my life. I am happy to see you happy and successful and I will always pray for God to protect you from any evil and from human evil and pain. May you always be happy with Amjad and may you always be blessed.

    Your mother who loves you.

11

❖

THE MIDDLE FISH

I PUT MAMA'S NOTEBOOK into the white carry-on bag I used to sit on in crowded airports and I put the bag away. I took time to mourn her and to spend time with Amjad. I realized after her death that Amjad and I needed to take care of ourselves, and we went on vacations together as she had made us promise we would. I began to heed the advice she had been giving me ever since I was small: to enjoy life, to sing, to dance, to live in the moment and to see the beauty around me. In time, I began to think of myself as the "free spirit" she had always wanted me to be. "Who is this woman?" Amjad asked me one night as we were dancing. "Where had you hidden her before?" It was almost as if Mama had passed on to me the spirit of her youth and the gift of laughter that had been locked inside her for years. A year after her death, I decided to work on my master's degree. I may not have accomplished my dream of a doctorate, but I got my master's degree from the London School of Economics while Amjad went to the Middle East to begin work involving the Palestinian–Israeli peace talks. When we moved back to Washington, D.C., after a year of living abroad, I was looking at the future, not the past.

Women for Women International was growing rapidly amid

what sometimes felt to me like a global epidemic of violence and genocide. Everywhere I went to assess the need for our services—Nigeria, Rwanda, and the Democratic Republic of Congo and other violence-ravaged countries where we set up offices—I heard women speaking in different languages about the same stories of sexual violence. So often when brutal armies invaded, it didn't matter whether they called themselves rebels or soldiers, they claimed women along with disputed territories. It wasn't a matter of politics, but of patriarchy. Yes, it had been happening since the beginning of time, but it outraged me that this violence against women was still somehow expected. Rape was practiced even at times by armies representing the United Nations. It was as if mankind had conditioned itself to expect such violence. Instead of recognizing violence against women as a reflection of the society in which it occurred, and often as an early indicator of genocide, the world seemed to respond with indifference and passivity.

Amjad and I were on our long-delayed honeymoon in Spain on September 11, 2001, the day the World Trade Center in New York was attacked. Thousands of Afghan refugees streamed over the border into Pakistan in anticipation of U.S. retaliation against the Taliban for its role in supporting the terrorists. I was meeting with a group of Afghan women leaders of non-governmental organizations that were working with refugees when word came to us that the Taliban had been overthrown. The Taliban had been one of the most oppressive regimes for women in modern history, and I was thrilled for the Afghan women. I imagined them helping write a new constitution, free to work again, educate their daughters, and throw off the shroud-like burqas the Taliban had required them to wear.

"Isn't this exciting?" I said. "It is all yours now that the Taliban are no longer ruling!"

Of course they were excited about the Taliban's overthrow. But they also had reservations about what would replace it. "We are Muslims and that is the most important part of our identity," one woman told me. "No one should confuse our hatred of Taliban with Islam." The women I was meeting with that day said they wanted Islamic law, Sharia, to regulate their society and planned to continue to cover their hair, although not with burqas. I understood and respected their identity as Muslims, but it took me a moment to recognize my own disappointment. I had wanted them to reach out for secular laws that I thought would help free them. Instead, I was reminded that my own political burka, like that of the West, was as blinding in its way as the robes these women had been compelled to wear. My job was to help them achieve their own goals, not impose mine. Living in a culture in which women and men talk about intimate parts of their lives on television, I had to remind myself not to become desensitized to the struggle of Afghan women and all women who have lived under different forms of despotism their entire lives. For them, freedom isn't the next step after tyranny, it is often a long and arduous personal journey.

Every trip I took to a refugee camp proved a humbling experience that deepened my own empathy for the women I met. Everywhere I went I saw men made public heroes for enduring torture while women were forgotten or even abandoned for surviving it, leading to a horrific silence on both a societal and personal level. Filled with rising anger and frustration over seeing the same patterns of oppression and violence repeat themselves around the world, I encouraged the women I met to speak out about the violence they had seen in their lives and in their societies. In private, on television, and at international conferences, I told women that if we didn't take ownership of our voices, change would never come. We would never be able to pressure government and societal leaders to address the particular needs of women war victims, let alone halt new violence or prosecute the criminals responsible.

It never occurred to me that I was asking other women to do what I was unable to do myself. I had interviewed hundreds of women who had been raped, yet I had never told anyone except Amjad and my mother what had happened to me. I would never think of comparing my experience to the trauma of the women I met around the world; even in rape I was the lucky one. I encouraged women to speak out about the injustice in their lives, yet I was too afraid to say Saddam Hussein's name even in my own home. As long as Saddam still ruled Iraq I knew I could never talk about Amo. My fear was so much a part of me it virtually circulated in my bloodstream. I still hung up the telephone twice no matter where I was, just to make sure no one was listening.

I still do.

For the longest time, I thought I was fighting my fear through my work, but I was only willing to talk about that injustice that was not related to me. I was willing to talk about Milŏsević but not Saddam, about injustice in Rwanda but not Iraq, about the plight of Afghan women but never Iraqi women. I might have gone on that way for years had the United States not claimed that Saddam Hussein possessed weapons of mass destruction that posed an imminent global threat. I had intensely mixed feelings as the world debated the U.S.-proposed invasion of Iraq. I desperately wanted Saddam out of power, but I knew that the Iraqi people, including my own family, would be the ones to suffer. In December 2002, when war seemed imminent, I decided I had to fly back to Iraq. I wanted to find out for myself what Iraqis and Iraqi women in particular were thinking about the possibility of the war. I also wanted to help get my little brother, Hassan, out of Iraq in case of an Iraqi draft in preparation of war.

Except for my mother's funeral, when grief blinded me to almost everything else, I had not been back to Iraq since I had left to marry Fakhri thirteen years before. As I drove from the airport to my family's house, I felt as if I were going back into history, both personally and as an Iraqi. Amo's eyes looked down on me from posters and monuments on almost every street corner. The very streets my mother and I used to drive looked as if they had surrendered to him. What was forbidden before was allowed, and what was allowed, forbidden. Alcohol was banned, and prostitutes were executed in public, their heads dropped off at their parents' doors. I heard people speaking Farsi on street corners; Iranians were now our "friendly enemy" and Americans were the enemies about to attack us.

When I walked up to my old house, I had the oddest sensation. I felt actual cold hanging over the front porch like invisible trellis of fear. Inside the house, almost nothing had changed. Hassan, a handsome but lonely college student, was living there alone, in a country where children typically remain with their families until marriage. The upholstery was almost threadbare. The tables were topped with old photographs and knickknacks in exactly the same spots my mother had once placed them. My father was living in another house with his new wife but visited Hassan every day. It was painful to see the two of them trying to hang onto some vestige of what our family used to be. My first night there, Hassan shyly asked if I would lie with him until he fell asleep as I used to when he was small. As I lay next to him, this all-grown-up boy fell asleep and I stayed awake. I felt haunted by the stories this house had witnessed. Nothing felt the same without my mother in it.

A confusion of feelings rushed painfully back when I saw my father. Though barely sixty, he seemed in ill health and looked little like the father I remembered cutting a fresh gardenia for me before I went to school in the morning. Amo had cast him out and blessedly left him alone after Mama betrayed the motherland for Jordan, and international restrictions on Iraqi aviation had made the former captain of an Iraqi Airlines 747 superfluous. He had opened a small business that provided a modest income and long since given up drinking. "These," he told me, fingering his prayer beads, "give me more comfort than whiskey ever did." Aunt Samer, the beautiful former activist I remembered dancing so elegantly, prayed day and night in a house that was barely standing. She had abandoned the world around her and retreated to her prayer rug and prayers beads. She was too afraid to say Saddam Hussein's name, even to me.

Everyone was waiting for the fateful inevitability of yet one more war. My cousin Dawood met me with tears and grief. "My son was the first casuality of this war, Zainab," he said. He had driven his family out of Iraq only to lose his son in an accident in Jordan. Dawood and his Kurdish wife had decided to come back to Baghdad to bury their son, and live or die near their families. To live or die together. I remembered those same words, that same debate, during the war with Iran. Why did that always seem to be our choice?

Economic sanctions had taken every last bit of energy or hope people once had. There was an eerie timidity in every sentence I heard. If Saddam's name was mentioned, anyone in hearing distance would say, "The sire! The leader! The president Saddam Hussein! May God protect his life!" That last phrase I was accustomed to hearing only when it referred to historical religious figures like the prophet Mohammed or Jesus or Moses. It seemed obvious to me that Amo had simply entered a new phase and invoked traditional Iraqi notions of fate or kismet, shuffling responsibility for his people's suffering off on to God.

I didn't recognize the broken hearts of the Iraqi people. Through my friends and family, I was able to escape government censorship and meet families from marginalized communities, where I was introduced as a social worker. Poverty had overtaken most people's lives as they struggled under the burden of economic sanctions imposed on them in the name of setting them free. For the first time in my life, I met literate mothers with illiterate daughters. There was no money for books or bribes the teachers required because their salaries were so low they couldn't survive otherwise. I asked a young woman about her dreams for the future: "Dreams for the future are things of the past. We no longer have them," she answered. I noticed ten-year-old platform shoes on her feet; she had once dreamed of being a fashion model. "One more bomb does not make a difference," said another woman. "Maybe it will finish us off and relieve us from this life."

In one of the houses I visited, there were twenty-three women. They all wore black. Their husbands and sons had died in one of the previous wars. A grandmother had gone blind for lack of medicine, and the whole household lived off the labor of a single seventeen-year-old boy. There was no furniture because it had all been sold.

When I turned to go, a woman about my age spoke up.

"I remember you," she said. "I remember your clothes. I remember your car. I remember you."

I flinched. She remembered me? She told me we had gone to high school together, but I didn't remember her. I lowered my eyes and felt embarrassed and helpless over the differences in our lives. The look on her face stayed with me long after I left. I knew that the only person she had seen standing in front of her was that privileged teenager she knew as a friend of Saddam.

On New Year's Eve, 2003, I spent the evening with my brother and his friends as they passed forbidden champagne under the table. Before leaving with Hassan for Jordan, I helped my father take our family pictures down from the living room walls and gather up family albums for safekeeping in case of looting. Baba seemed curious about my work with refugees, and I told him how important those papers and photographs were to every refugee I had ever met. I wanted to ask him about the past, but I knew it wouldn't work. Instead, as we sorted through the pictures, I tried just to talk to him.

"Are you afraid, Baba?" I asked.

He thought about that.

"I am fatigued, *habibiti*," he said. "As long as you and your brothers are safe and happy, I want nothing more out of life."

When I left after that trip, I pledged never again to return to Saddam Hussein's Iraq. I decided that Baghdad was no longer my home. The concept of home had confused me for the longest time. Where was my home, anyway? In Iraq where I was born? In the United States where I now lived with my husband? In any of the countries I worked in and had also come to love? I reflected on the meaning of home for a long time on my flight back to Washington, D.C. I wasn't sure I had a home. I didn't feel as if I belonged in any one place. I was as much at home in the air, flying from one country to another for my work, as in any country I knew.

In March 2003, I watched on television as the United States went to war against Iraq once again. The war I saw on TV looked nothing like the wars I had witnessed. There was no sound of anti-aircraft missiles or bombs or bullets or shattering glass. There was nothing to convey what it felt like to have your whole house shake when a missile explodes nearby. To this day, when I hear a sudden noise I jump and sometimes tears come to my eyes. War is dirty and cruel and hurtful, but during the invasion there were no dead bodies or blue feet hanging out of caskets for Westerners to see on American television news. There were no cameras I remember that looked out from the point of view of women and men who had learned to fear, as I had, anyone in a uniform. There were no cries of mothers losing their children that didn't transition into a famil-iar announcer's voiceover. Instead, there were computer-generated graphics of missiles flying over nice clean maps of Baghdad with clear blue skies in the background.

I hate all wars because all I see of them is the impact they have on people's lives. Still, I think the day I learned Saddam Hussein had been removed from power was the happiest day of my life. I was anxious to go back and help the Iraqi people as I had once told my mother I would. I wanted to help rebuild and set up an office in Baghdad to share with Iraqi women what I had learned from work-ing with women in other countries. When I left for Iraq three weeks after war ended, I didn't realize how scary and wonderful that would be. I returned just three weeks after the initial attack on Baghdad. There were no more than eight passengers, all of them from nongovernmental organizations, on that flight. When our small plane landed at the airport my father used to run, I felt deeply conflicting emotions at seeing American soldiers with their planes on our runways surrounded by burned-out Iraqi planes and tanks.

"Who's with Women for Women International?" asked a cap-tain processing the landing papers in the VIP lounge I had last seen when I waited to fly to America to be married to Fakhri.

"Me," I said nervously. I had never stopped being afraid of men in military uniforms.

"Welcome to Iraq!" said a Capt. Chasteen, shaking my hand. "We need you and your organization here."

I was speechless as he shook my hand. A soldier supporting my efforts? It turned out that he had seen me on *The Oprah Winfrey Show* and that he and his wife had been supporters of the organization for two years. He told me he felt that the United States needed to focus more on supporting organizations like ours rather than on military efforts in order to help win the hearts and minds of the Iraqi people; I took our meeting as a sign I was on the right path. As I drove out of the vast empty airport toward the city, we passed the entry to the farmhouse. I looked away, toward the skyline of Baghdad with its charred palms and looted, still-smoking ruins. My emotions swung back and forth wildly. Tears flowed down my cheeks. My city was free; my city was in ruins. The Mukhabarat were gone; ten-year-old boys pointed Kalishnikovs at people on the street. The violence under Saddam, which had been controlled vertically by the government, had now spread horizontally out across the neighborhoods, enabling anyone with a gun or criminal intentions or revenge on their mind to rape, steal, and pillage.

Tears were streaming down everyone's faces. My father hugged me harder than I had ever felt him hug me before. He told me that during the bombing he had thought he would never see his children again. He and other family members had built their own bunker and he had had a stroke as shrapnel fell on them. Five of the ten people in it had been injured, and it took them three days to reach a doctor.

Saddam Hussein was still in hiding somewhere, but for the first time in my life I saw a crack in the wall of fear he had created. I set about pounding at that wall as hard as I could, talking to women gathered at mosques and prisons who were looking for the disappeared, gathering their stories and doing whatever I could to avoid letting women's voices be silenced once again. Every woman's story was different, every one compelling. When I drove over to see Uncle Adel, I saw a handwritten message on the house of the Shia factory owner who had been deported to Iran years before. "This house is now restored to its original owners," it said. I spent several hours listening to the woman who lived there, recording her tale of forced marches and imprisonment. When she and her family returned after twenty years in exile in Iran, they found stacks of documents and a table with electrical equipment in a bedroom. Their home had been used by secret police for torture. One victim had left a will that his torturers had never bothered to deliver to his family.

As I set about assessing how to establish our program in Baghdad, the pain from my childhood that I had successfully hidden began to surface. Lines blurred. I went to meetings with U.S. officials occupying Amo's old palaces with their ghosts and familiar gold faucets. When my driver found out about my work, I learned that his fiancée had been raped by Uday. A bodyguard of one of Saddam's brothers confessed to me he used to rape teenage girls. I met one woman who told me Uday had cut off the nipple on one of her friends' breasts and another woman whose sister was killed by a brother of Saddam after she threatened to reveal he had raped her. A security guard talked to me about women being raped as they were being tortured, and a doctor friend of my mother's revealed that she had managed to quietly treat women rape victims of "Iranian origin" who had been put in prison with their children instead of being deported. How many stories were there like his? How many women had been raped? Baghdad didn't have rape camps like Bosnia or mass rapes like Rwanda and Congo. It was more insidious here and harder for me to work. I knew how to do my job in other countries and do it well. But I wasn't prepared for what it meant to work in my own country, with my own people, in my own language, sharing with them a pain that was so much a part of who I am.

With Amo out of power, yet still unaccounted for, I wanted justice for Iraqi women. I wanted justice for the gypsy women he kept for his amusement after he sent their husbands away to war and for the village women I knew Saddam had raped on the pretense of helping them. At the end of the day, I wanted to know what had happened to just one woman: my own mother. What had she tried to tell me when she started gasping for breath?

I decided to visit my mother's friends and talk to each one to find out the truth as she knew it. I prepared talking points in my head. You can confide in me the way you confided in my mother, I would say. Mama told me a lot already, but you know how ill she was, she couldn't speak at the end. Tell me, what happened to her? I'm her daughter. I'm grown up now. I need to know what you were whispering about in our garden years ago. What happened with you? You can trust me, not only because I am the daughter of your friend but also because I work with women victims of war from around the world and over the years I have become a witness to horror stories of what women face in wartime.

I started with Aunt Nahla, the woman at the potluck dinner I remembered talking about going to People's Consultation Day with Amo.

"Zanoooooooooooooooba!" she screamed when she saw me and hugged me. "He is gone! Oh, I wish your mother was here with me to celebrate!"

She invited me in and I found myself surrounded by her husband and daughters and grandchildren. We laughed and drank Turkish coffee and ate *gliche* and baklava. It was a happy visit. It took a while before I could find a way to be alone with her.

"Aunt Nahla," I said, "I wanted to ask you about some things about Mama."

"Oh, honey, your mother and I went through so much! I am glad I can forget it all now. I miss your mother so much. There were days when Saddam was still ruling that made me wish I could join her in her death."

She talked about all kinds of crimes committed during Saddam's time, but she didn't mention women. I pushed her gently about helping me fill in the gaps of Mama's life.

"We can sit down one day and talk about the past," she said, setting a tray down in front of me. "But now, let's have some fruit and celebrate your visit!"

Don't bring that past back her eyes begged me as she looked at her family gathered around her.

When I went to visit Aunt Nada, Luma was there too. I was astonished to find they were still living in denial.

"I don't understand why everyone is celebrating Amo's removal, Zainab," Aunt Nada said. "He never hurt us."

What about other people? I asked myself but didn't say. Doesn't it matter that other people got hurt and the whole population suffered?

"He did nothing wrong!" Luma declared in the same self-righteous tone of voice I remembered. "They're even blaming him for bombing the Kurds!"

Being with them felt like our kitchen talks at the farmhouse. Sitting across a tray of coffee cups from Amo's close friends, I could still feel the fear. After weighing the odds of learning anything helpful, I decided I didn't feel comfortable talking to them.

"How is Sarah?" I asked.

"Oh, that crazy sister of mine!" Luma said. "I don't know what happened to her once she got to England!"

We talked politely for a while and then I left. It turned out that Sarah had married for love. I later looked her up on one of my visits to the U.K., and we timidly tested each other out. She told me then that she had discovered what Amo was really like only after she went to live abroad. Her anger at her parents was so profound that she didn't know how to deal with them for several years. They had reconciled, but she told me she still couldn't penetrate their denial. She had found peace with her husband and children, she said, but she didn't want to dig up the past. We haven't tried to meet again. We are a reminder to each other that the nightmare was real.

Every "aunt" I visited treated me like my mother, serving me cigarettes, though I didn't smoke, and Turkish coffee as Mama liked it, with no sugar. But, they didn't talk to me as they talked to her.

"You look so much like your mother!" Aunt Layla told me. "I miss her so much!"

She was the most open of all my mother's friends. I remembered a time we had been on an escalator once in a mall outside the country and she had said, "Let's talk about Amo!" But by that time, Amo had robbed Mama of her trust in her own friends, and I remember her looking away.

I asked her something I had always been curious about. "Aunt Layla," I said, "Do you know what happened to Mama's Abbasid coin?"

That was an easy question, given other subjects I wanted to broach, and she told me she had been there the night Mama had given it to him.

"Amo walked off and forgot it after he opened the package," she said. "Your mother had to go after him and remind him to take it with him."

"Aunt Layla, I want to talk with you about some things that you and my mother and the other aunts lived through," I said. "Can you help me?"

"I just want to live in peace, honey," was what she said.

I persisted. I needed her to talk with me.

She warned me to be careful of Raghad and Rana. What would they do if they heard we had been talking about Amo?

"I'm still afraid of them," she said. "Why bring all this up now, Zainab? They're still out there. Maybe later we can talk."

"How much later, Aunt Layla?" I asked. "When his daughters die or when his grandchildren die or when his whole clan dies? How long are we supposed to let ourselves be held prisoners by our fear?"

I was disappointed and frustrated when I left Aunt Layla's house. It seemed to me that my aunts had grown comfortable with their fear the way people grew comfortable with bad jobs and bad marriages. I understood that talking about private family matters, especially anything involving a woman's sexuality, was hard; I knew that that could bring on gossip or even dishonor. But, I had also grown up thinking of my aunts as liberated, independent women. I knew them. We spoke the same language. Most of the women I worked with in other countries were socially and economically marginalized, and as I thought about it more, I realized that some of my aunts' hesitation was related to class. They were worried about the name of their family, their honor, and social prestige. Social prestige was not a concern of women who had lost everything, including husbands, children, family, homes, and sometimes entire communities.

There was a part of me that wanted to bow down in awe at the courage of the women I had met around the world. I thought of Nabito, a displaced woman from a small village in the Democratic Republic of Congo. Four million people had died there in an ongoing war, and tens of thousands of women were raped. Even among courageous women, Nabito had a special sense of dignity. A white-haired mother of twelve, she had seen the most brutal side of humanity. She had been gang-raped by men who cut her legs and arms and belly with knives and machetes as they raped her, and broke her arm so badly her forearm is permanently bent. They ordered one of her sons to rape her and when he refused, they shot him. All the while, she could hear the screams of her daughter being raped nearby. I was shaking inside as she told me what had happened.

"What should I do, Nabito, when I hear stories like yours?" I had asked her. "Should we tell the world about the injustice you faced so we might help bring a stop to what is happening to other women, or should we keep our secrets to ourselves? What should we do?"

Nabito had looked me in the eyes and said, "If I could tell the whole world about what happened to me to bring justice to the men who did this to me or to prevent other women from being hurt, then I would. But I can't. You go ahead and tell the world my story, but just don't tell the neighbors."

I kept traveling to other countries as Iraq's destiny lay open, and on my next visit to Congo I sought out Nabito. I did something that day I had never done before. I put my head into the lap of a woman I was trying to help and I cried. Nabito let me draw strength from her without ever asking me why. She somehow helped me realize that in Iraq, I was the neighbor. I had been trying to force "the truth" out of my aunts and whatever their own truths were, they belonged to them, not to me. How arrogant I had been to demand they tell me their stories in order to find my own peace and satisfy my curiosity! What right did I have to persist in my quest to find the answer to a question my mother could not tell me when she was alive? And these thoughts led me to another: I had the right to only one story, and that was my own. What had happened to me with Fakhri was nothing compared to what other women I met had experienced, yet I was afraid of telling anyone about it, in part because it made me feel weak and I wanted to seen as strong. Maybe because others had said so, I had come to think of myself as a courageous woman who was willing to tell the truth. But I realized I had gone around the world talking about other women's courage. Had I, too, grown comfortable in my fear?

There was an afternoon when I sat outside my uncle's house and watched the sky over the Tigris turn a deep coral with an approaching dust storm at sunset. Thousands of river gulls flew in and out of the gathering cloud, appearing, vanishing, and reappearing. What was courage about? I had been helping other women talk and then telling their stories to the rest of the world so others could understand what they were going through. But never once had I opened up to the women I worked with the way they had to me. I head preached to them about breaking their silence, yet I was afraid to break my own. I preached against fear, yet I was afraid. I preached rising up against injustice, yet I had never acted upon the injustice in my own country for my own people.

Courage wasn't about facing other people's injustice, but about revealing our own deepest secrets and risking hurting the ones we love. I didn't want to be like my mother and my grandmother who died silent and took their stories with them to their deaths. I didn't want to be like generations of women who died in silence because they didn't want to hurt their family honor or their men's feelings. But, did I have the courage to taint the image I had worked so hard to create for myself of a strong, independent woman who advocates women's rights? To reveal that I was vulnerable and had been an abused wife in an arranged marriage? Did I have the courage to speak out if it caused a single tear in my father's eye?

My thoughts kept returning to a poem written by Rumi, the medieval Sufi poet Amjad and I often read aloud to each other. The poem is about three fish in a lake that watched fishermen as they approached with their nets. The first fish was the intelligent fish. When it saw the fishermen it said, "I'm leaving" and decided against consulting the other two. "They will only weaken my resolve because they love this place so," the intelligent fish said. "They call it home. Their ignorance will keep them here." And the first fish set out immediately on the long difficult voyage to the safety of the sea. The second fish was the semi-intelligent fish. "My guide has gone," it thought. "I ought to have gone with it, but I didn't, and now I've lost my chance to escape." So it played dead and floated belly up to avoid being eaten. A fisherman pulled it out by the tail, spat on it, and tossed it on land. Quietly, it rolled over back into the lake and survived. The third fish, the dumb one, jumped about trying to show how clever it was as the net closed around it. As it lay in the pan, it thought, "If I get out of this, I'll never live again in the limits of a lake. Next time, the ocean! I'll make the infinite my home."

Ever since I first read that poem, I had thought of my parents as the middle fish. Was I the middle fish as well?

Fate has its own way of dealing with each and every person. Fate turned up for me a DVD containing footage from looted videos found in Saddam's palaces.

"Zainab, we saw you in one of the DVDs they're selling on street corners," Dawood's wife told me at Uncle Adel's one day; one of the best things about Baghdad was seeing my cousins and their children. "My nine-year-old recognized you."

"What?"

She handed me a disc with cheaply copied pictures of Amo and his daughters on the cover. In the rubble of one of Amo's palaces, someone had found a videotape of a palace party, copied it on disk and was selling it as the inside story of palace life. I couldn't bear to look at it until everyone else in my uncle's house went to sleep that night. I sat close to the television and put it on. The video jumped about erratically, attesting to the speed with which the looters had mass-produced the DVDs. It started out in black and white, then shot into color as women I hadn't seen in years danced to traditional music in the outlandishly overdone sequined dresses of the 1980s. I saw them whirl by with all my old prejudices intact. There was Sajida, disdainful under her heavy makeup and her youngest daughter, Hala, whose bodyguard tossed Hassan around like a soccer ball. I saw Raghad and Rana and tried to muster sympathy for them, knowing that their father would one day have both their husbands killed, but I still couldn't manage.

Which party was it? I had no idea. It was in a large carpeted room somewhere in Baghdad, a palace maybe, though it was hard to tell where. Except for the singer, all I could hear was the background chatter of women talking to each other in the slightly elevated voices used everywhere at parties. Sometimes the soundtrack went out altogether and the women danced on in silence, arms and wrists crossing each other high in the air. Then, abruptly, I found myself face to face with the girl I had been hiding from, the pilot's daughter, a girl of maybe seventeen, exactly half my age now. My hair was still long and curly. I was wearing a gray dress and was seated on one of a dozen sofas against a wall at a party. The photographer must have set up his tripod across the room from me because I was in the background, which was where I always tried to be. I clapped inattentively, slightly out of synch with the women around me, until that girl who had been me shyly stood up, put on her plastic smile, and joined the crowd as it danced to a patriotic song.

All the old anxieties I associated with those parties came back. I had put all this away, not unlike the way my aunts had put away their old lives, but someone had invaded this hated past and made my "artificial" life real again. I had chosen to be in Iraq at that moment as president of an international women's organization—not as a child who had been called a "beloved one" by the despot who had caused the chaos in which we were all living. Would anyone recognize me?

I spent a nearly sleepless night in the same room where I had once held my mother because I was afraid of losing her after her attempted suicide. I was afraid. But I was even more afraid of the fear. I couldn't live my life in pieces anymore. I couldn't ignore the person I was, and I wasn't willing to sacrifice the person I had become. I was that girl. I am this woman. I am both.

I was in a conference in Jordan when we heard the news that Saddam Hussein was captured. I watched the television screen as Amo crawled up out of what American soldiers called a "spider hole." There was no air-conditioned bunker. There were no closets of canned goods or stashes of whiskey or even a bodyguard or a bar of soap. He was living in the Tikriti dirt in a pit of his own making. As he crawled up out of that hole, looking dirty and disheveled in a way I could never have fathomed, I think the man I called Amo and the dictator I called Saddam Hussein finally came together for me. I was shocked to find myself shed tears of pity. My tears were more for me than for him; I didn't want to enjoy another person's humiliation even if he was my enemy. One Iraqi woman at the conference looked around as we were all watching his capture on television and said, "This is revenge for my father!" I learned that day that her father had been killed the same day as Basma's father. "This is to avenge my brother!" an Iraqi man said. "For my mother," I murmured quietly to myself. I could no longer justify being afraid. I wasn't a government so I couldn't charge Amo with crimes, but I could carry out my own personal truth and reconciliation commission.

I wanted to talk with my father. I had tried, but he seemed caught between past and present, a lost soul searching for his own peace who spent evenings with his new wife and hours every morning walking in our old neighborhood or working in our garden. During the years I was gone, he had patiently clipped our hedges and trees into towering topiary sculptures. He was no longer able to fly, but when he stood in the middle of our backyard in the Airlines Neighborhood, he was surrounded with enormous leafy birds rooted in the soil and stretching their wings as if to take flight.

Of all people, Baba, why didn't you just fly us away to safety?

Out of loyalty to Mama after their bitter divorce, I had never met his new wife. But, one day, I decided I wanted peace in our family, and I went to his new house to meet her for the first time. Baba embraced me with tears in his eyes as he welcomed me to his new home and introduced me to her. She was generous enough to give Baba and me time alone. He and I sat together in their garden drinking tea, eating fresh almonds and pistachios and smoking mint-flavored *sheesha* tobacco in my grandfather's water pipe. It was a beautiful evening. I felt more relaxed around him than I had in a long time, and I could see the tension in his face beginning to loosen.

It was with new humility that I was able to ask him questions about the past.

"I want to talk with you about Amo, Baba," I said. "Mama told me many things. I finally have my peace with her with all that happened in the past, my marriage, my being left in America, all of that."

"You know I didn't want you to leave, Zainab," he said.

"Yes, Baba, I know, and I always appreciated your position," I said. "But now, I want the chance to learn from you about our relationship with Amo. Now that he is gone, I would like to talk with you about all the things we never could talk about before. More than anything else Baba, I want to know this: Why didn't you leave?"

He thought about that. I didn't know if he would answer.

"You know, Zanooba, I never wanted that relationship, nor did your mother," he said. "We were not interested in politics or politicians ever and we kept telling ourselves he would never come that close. By the time he took over our lives, it was too late for us to leave and too dangerous for the family members we would leave behind."

My father was acknowledging his fear of Amo to me for the first time in his life. It made me wonder what he was processing in his daily walks.

"Besides, Iraq is my home, Zainab. This is my country. I had three children. I was responsible for your education and well-being. How could I have provided for you if I had taken you out of the country? I couldn't have given you the life you had if we had left, Zainab. And when an opportunity came, it came at a price I was not willing to pay."

"You had a chance to leave and you didn't?"

He told me a story I vaguely remembered hearing years before, though I couldn't have pinpointed when, about a Boeing executive eager to sell airplanes to Saddam Hussein. Once, when Baba was in his office, the executive had signed a blank check and pushed it across the table to him. "A million? More? Write what you like!" the executive had said.

"I pushed the check back across the desk," Baba said. "To take it would have meant losing everything I had: my ethics, my principles, my self-respect. I couldn't do that, Zainab. I don't regret it. I never did. Staying in Iraq came at a price but it was better than the price of losing who I was in my own eyes."

I was reminded of the same stubborn man who wouldn't let Samira in our house on principle. For the first time in many years, I felt sympathy and enormous respect for my father. His integrity had come at a price, but at least I understood why he felt he had to pay it. What did courage mean in his case? Was it not compromising his own ethics? Despite the price our family had paid, I realized as he spoke that I would rather be the daughter of a man who made such a choice than the daughter of a man who took a bribe and sold out his country. Who said courage was defined only one way? That the only smart fish was the first fish? Oh God, I thought as I sat with my father, who gave me the right to judge my parents at all? Each of us had to find our own way. I saw that now, and I needed Baba to see it, too.

"You named me after a figure that was known for her courage

and for her speaking about injustice," I said. "I used to think about myself as such a person until it came down to the question of me speaking out on behalf of me and our own family."

And I began talking to my father about the most intimate parts of my life. I told him about Fakhri and how I had gone back and forth debating whether to speak out about what he had done to me. I told him I felt I had lived two lives and that to bring the two back in focus, I couldn't keep silent anymore. I didn't believe that a family's honor should be borne by women when the price of that honor is their silence about things that hurt them and their families. I was worried that raising my voice about family concerns, not just those related to sex, could cause some to consider me to be dishonoring my loved ones. But if there was anything a woman owned, wasn't it her voice? And if I wanted to raise mine to tell my own story, how could I possibly separate it from the stories of the ones I love?

"You made your choices to be true to your values, Baba," I said. "Today it is my turn to do the same, and I need your support. I need to take control of my own voice, and that entails breaking our family vow of not talking about our relationship with Amo. Our family has always been lost between two worlds, Baba. People inside the palace considered us outsiders and people outside considered us friends of Saddam. If we remain silent, people will think our silence was agreement. I can't remain silent anymore. If we don't write our truth, history will write it for us."

He had remained quiet as I spoke. The furrow between his eyebrows deepened.

"This is your decision, Zainab," he said finally. "I just want you to know that I always tried to be a good father to you."

I could ask no more of him than that.

"I know, Baba," I told him. "I love you."

And we reached over and held onto each other trying to understand each other's paths and the price each of us paid for taking them.

When I was little, my father showed me what it meant to fly. Later, my mother pushed me out of the cage. I didn't take the flight path either laid out for me, but between them they gave me wings.

We opened our office of Women for Women International in my grandfather's house. Mama had always told me that the house she had grown up in was a house of charity, and I went back to look for it after I arrived in Baghdad. The neighborhood was impoverished and wary of outsiders. The streets were filled with uncollected trash and sewage—part of Saddam's institutionalized ghettoization of predominantly Shia neighborhoods in Baghdad and elsewhere. As I walked up Mama's old street and tried to identify which house had been hers, I felt myself being watched from windows.

"What are you looking for?" a man asked me warily.

"I am the granddaughter of Hajji Mohammed," I said, using my grandfather's name. "I am his granddaughter."

His expression completely changed. He opened his arms.

"Of course!" the man said.

Suddenly I was surrounded by a flock of children and I felt myself being swept along by strangers and into the old house. A homeless family had been living there watching the house for our family and they gave me tea. Pigeons were nesting everywhere and the windows were shattered. But, we rebuilt Mama's childhood home into a place where women could meet and learn new job skills and organize. We filled rooms with cushions on the floor where they could talk about their social, economic, and political roles in society, as well as just share laughter and tears. I remember in particular the day we held an event to celebrate a small but critical victory: a neighborhood organizing campaign in which women had overcome a cultural proscription against women cleaning public streets. Hundreds of women in black *abayas* filled the courtyard. I couldn't help myself; tears started dropping from my eyes. The house looked as I had imagined it from my mother's stories about Ashura and other times when my grandparents used to open their home. We brought out that day the same pots my grandparents had used, only instead of *fasenjoon tourshana* and rice, they were filled with kebab sandwiches, pizza, and cans of Pepsi.

"I am back, Mama," I told her. "I wish you were here with me."

I went upstairs to her old room, an office now, and walked out onto her balcony. I looked over the river that was rising once again and breathed in air that was free of Saddam. I followed the shadows of the gulls scatter-flying the clay-colored water and reminded myself that our choices were not easy ones. Amo had commanded fish to swim in his lakes. He had reduced the Tigris to a trickle and drained the ancient marshes that led to the sea. When did our choosing times come? I heard the call to prayer from a mosque near the ancient shrine of the prophet Khedir, also known as Elijah. I looked across the river to the spot where the boatmen could moor once again and saw one of the world's oldest universities. Beyond, in a troubled afternoon sky, I could see a cloud of black smoke rising. How many cities on earth were so desperate to survive they nearly tore themselves apart trying? How many were so old and yet unborn? The damp fresh smell of the Tigris took me back to my childhood. I remembered my mother's eyes rimmed with kohl as she had stood on this balcony years before. Terrible things are happening, Mama, but Amo is gone. Between the world of right-doing and the world of wrong-doing there is a meeting ground. There is a garden where women no longer need to whisper, I know it. Your real country is where you're heading, Mohammed said, not where you are.

AFTERWORD

AFTER I FINISHED GIVING a speech about the journey of women refugees at a gathering of women journalists in the fall of 2002, many of the audience members came to the stage with questions and comments. One of the women standing around the podium looked familiar, but I couldn't remember where I had met her until she introduced herself as Laurie Becklund, a journalist from Los Angeles. I immediately interrupted her as she started to ask a question. "I have a newspaper story written about me during the first Gulf War in the *Los Angeles Times*. It was by a reporter named Laurie . . ." She took a step back and looked at me. "You're not that same Zainab, are you?" she asked, incredulous, with a surprised look on her face. "Yes, I am. I look different now. I am different now," I responded as chills spread all over my body.

Laurie covered Iraqi Americans during the first Gulf War and had met me at a press conference held by the Iraqi-American community in Los Angeles. She noticed a young woman who was constantly crying on the sidelines. She wrote a story about how I had been stranded in America while I didn't know whether my family was dead or alive in Iraq. That was the first of several stories in the *Los Angeles Times,* and led to a series of interviews I did on U.S. and international television networks about life in Iraq through my eyes, about how Iraqis had normal families and professional lives, and even about a letter my mother had sent me during the war describing the hardship they were going through as they tried to survive. While many Iraqi-Americans were being harassed because of their national heritage, I saw the most kind and generous side of Americans, mainly due to her coverage. People would stop me in the mall where I worked, asking if I needed anything, giving me hugs and sharing their prayers for my family's safety.

When I saw her again at that journalists' gathering, the United States was on the verge of another war with Iraq. I knew there was a reason for that meeting as I hugged her and fought my tears at the coincidence of meeting the woman whose coverage helped sustain me during that time.

Days and months passed, and another war with Iraq was launched. Saddam was overthrown this time, and I decided to write a book about women in Iraq, as I felt very little was known about Iraqi women. I called Laurie and asked her to write the book with me. I didn't think twice about it. I knew that was the reason why I met her two years earlier.

This book did not start out as a memoir. I did not want to write a memoir. Who was I to write a memoir? I thought to myself. I definitely did not suffer as so many Iraqi women had. I grew up in a privileged household and, if anything, I was isolated from the rest of the country. I wanted to write about what Iraqi women had suffered under Saddam Hussein's regime. When I was asked to focus the book more on my own story, I resisted vehemently. I cried, I screamed, I kicked, I wanted to do anything but write my own story. I was afraid that my story had no legitimacy. I did not want to be yet another privileged person able to share my perspective with the world. I saw myself as a mere messenger, telling the stories of other women, in my work with Women for Women International. I did not want my voice or my story to take precedence over theirs just because I had access to the international media and they didn't. And yet, in the end there was a point at which I felt that I had to take ownership of my voice, my truth, and my story. I felt I had lived through other women's stories and through their courage in breaking their truths. Perhaps, it was my turn to take that jump and to speak up. So, here I am, taking ownership of my story by telling it.

The experience proved a humbling one for me. It was my personal decision to write this book and I could not write it without talking about my family and friends. To protect their identities and privacy, I changed the names of my family members and friends. My mother's journal entries are taken from a series of notes she wrote to me over a period of months during her illness that I translated from the original Arabic into English and edited here for purposes of chronology and clarity.

It is difficult for anyone to retrieve memories from childhood and from life's painful moments. One memory prompts another, then another. I have done my best to recall them accurately. I have tried to give Western readers a glimpse of Iraqi culture and religion, but these come only through a very personal filter. The last thing I would claim is to represent all Iraqi women, let alone all Arab women or all Iraqis. I am a mix of the cultures and times in which I have had the privilege to live.

I must have filled an ocean with tears in the process of writing this book, but at the end of it all I feel grateful for this experience. I came out of it with a better understanding and respect for my parents. I now have a better appreciation of my fortune and even my misfortune. And for the first time in my life, I am true to myself and the women I work with.

I couldn't have gone through this process without the love and support of many people around me. I am incredibly grateful to Laurie for helping me through the process, for pushing me to dig deeper and deeper into my past and into my pain as I searched for answers, and for being patient and kind in the process. Special thanks to our agent Sandy Dijkstra and our friend Liz Bianco for their help, patience, and belief in this book and for the feedback and the support they gave me and Laurie. I couldn't be more thankful for the staff and board members of Women for Women International for their understanding and support of the process I needed for writing this book.

On a personal level, I am grateful for the friends who were the first people—besides my husband—to whom I revealed part of the story told in this book. This process started with a group of strangers I met in the wilderness of Canada during a leadership retreat led by my friend David Baum. I learned from them that there are points in life where we need to take that jump off the cliff. It was at that retreat that I first heard the poem by the thirteenth century Sufi poet Rumi that inspired the title of this book: *Out beyond ideas of wrongdoing and rightdoing, there is a field, I will meet you there*.

I am also thankful for the warm hugs and response I got when I first told my story to my close friends Hoda, Rene, Niraj, Amerjit, Narayan, Faith, and Farah. They helped me recognize that my past does not erase my present and that Saddam's face does erase mine when I tell my story. Special thanks to my very dear friend Emad Fraitekh, who helped me so much in the process of writing this book by reading and rereading versions of manuscripts, giving me his feedback, helping me in some research, and, well, just being a wonderful friend in this process. Thank you.

Special loving thanks to my father and my brothers for understanding the need for writing this book. I love you so very much. Finally, I am incredibly grateful to my loving husband, Amjad Atallah, whose love and care helped give me the support I needed to become the person I am today. I am grateful for his patience, support, and belief in me, as well as his willingness to trust my instincts in the process of writing this book. Thank you, honey, for the beauty you brought into my life.

COLLABORATOR'S NOTE

THE VERY FIRST TIME I met her, Zainab Salbi stood out in a crowd, though she was just twenty-one. She had a presence even then that she has translated into an international organization that simultaneously brings to light the suffering of women in wartime and helps improve thousands of lives. Many women have trusted Zainab with their most intimate stories, and I feel honored that she trusted me to help her write hers. She has afforded me the privilege of watching another human being grapple with some of life's most profound questions. I have learned so much along the way.

While this book was being written, Zainab was running a major organization, grappling with many other priorities, and somehow finding time to rethink her life and write reams of amazing insights on inconvenient deadlines. At one point after I asked her the same question over and over again, perversely trying to revive her pain, she turned to me and said, "Do you know that this is a certified method of torture in many countries?" Thank you, Zainab, for your patience and your insights, and for sharing your own journey with me. Your reservoir of strength is an inspiration to me, and no matter what you say in these pages, you are the first fish. That is apparent to anyone who meets you, including me.

I also am the lucky one. Thank you to perceptive and generous friends who offered significant suggestions for this book: Sandy Lowe, Phyllis Peacock, Kathryn Harris, Victoria Riskin, and especially Anne Roark, a friend and fellow writer who went beyond the call of duty in helping me sort through the myriad choices facing anyone trying to do justice to Zainab's life. I also wish to thank, each for different reasons, Carty Spencer, Rocky Dixon, Julianne and Nicki Spencer, Bud Larsen, Steve Lowe and Marilyn Levin, Jeff and Susan Brand, Amanda Parsons, Hilary Terrell, Ted and LeeAnn Lyman, Greg Krikorian, and Ann Hailey. Dan McIntosh and Doug Mirell stepped forward at critical moments. Liz Bianco and Marc Green gave critical encouragement early on. Zainab's family and her husband, Amjad Atallah, provided warm hospitality in Baghdad and Washington. Without JAWS, the Journalism and Women Seminar that brought Zainab and me together again, this project would not have happened.

I appreciate enormously the skills and personal thoughtfulness of our agent Sandy Dijsktra and her staff, including Elisabeth James, Elise Capron, Taryn Fagerness, and Jill Marsal. Thanks, Sandy, for your guidance. We are both grateful to our publisher, Bill Shinker of Gotham, as well as to our editor, Lauren Marino, for their support and vision and for recognizing that Zainab's story is only incidentally about a famous tyrant.

Finally, I thank my family. My sister Julie Strasser Dixon, who helped teach me to write, co-authored my last book and made spot-on suggestions to this one. My sister Nancy Spencer, an insightful reader and observer of people, helped me understand that paragraphs market honest emotions. During the year I have been thinking about Zainab and her mother, I have had less time to spend with my own mother, the indomitable Elizabeth Larsen. It is to her that I dedicate my own effort in this book; it is she who has defined for me what being a mother means.

I have had at my disposal the two best editors of all, my husband, Henry Weinstein of the *Los Angeles Times,* and our daughter, Elizabeth Weinstein. Henry brings not only his wisdom but his heart to every professional challenge he takes on, including mine; he has never once given me a single piece of bad advice. Elizabeth is not just a peer editor, but a peer whose sophistication as a young writer amazes me and whose very existence buoys every day of my life.